TEKSTURA

TEKSTURA

Edited and Translated by

Alla Efimova and **Lev Manovich**

Foreword by **Stephen Bann**

THE UNIVERSITY OF CHICAGO PRESS   Chicago + London

Alla Efimova was born in St. Petersburg and is a doctoral candidate in visual and cultural studies at the University of Rochester. Lev Manovich was born in Moscow and teaches in the Department of Visual Art at the University of Maryland, Baltimore County. Stephen Bann is chairman of the Board of Studies in the History of Art and professor of modern cultural studies at the University of Kent at Canterbury.

The University of Chicago Press, Chicago 60637
The University of Chicago Press, Ltd., London

03 02 01 00 99 98 97 96 95 94 93   1 2 3 4 5

ISBN: 0-226-95123-5 (cloth)
      0-226-95124-3 (paper)

Library of Congress Cataloging-in-Publication Data

Tekstura : Russian essays on visual culture / edited and translated by
    Alla Efimova and Lev Manovich ; foreword by Stephen Bann.
        p.   cm.
    Collection of essays, most are previously unpublished translations
from the Russian.
    Includes bibliographical references and index.
    1. Arts, Russian.   2. Arts, Modern—20th century—Russia
(Federation)   3. Socialist realism in art—Russia (Federation)
I. Efimova, Alla.   II. Manovich, Lev.
NX556.A1T453   1993
700'.947—dc20   93-7803
                                                      CIP

CONTENTS

Foreword

For the past thirty years, at least, the Western engagement with Russian visual culture has been characterized at one and the same time by a rapidly accelerating interest and by a radical selectivity. The West has seen, on the whole, what it wanted to see. And this was above all the spectacle of a brilliant and innovatory avant-garde, which received its legitimation with the October Revolution but did not outlive the Stalinist terror of the 1930s. This efflorescence of hardly more than two decades made all the rest seem dull and doom-laden by comparison.

It would be inappropriate, in this context, to do more than summarize the history of this passionate engagement with the Russian avant-garde. But a few general points may be touched upon. In particular, it was the practical interest of Western critics, artists, and museum directors that fueled the phenomenon. The culture of the Russian revolution offered a number of tools that could be put to work in a wholly new situation.

Hence the critical writings of the Russian formalists, which had been magisterially evaluated in 1955 by Victor Erlich, acquired a much more immediate relevance when Tzvetan Todorov published his anthology of classic Formalist texts in 1965. By the latter date, literary criticism itself was entering the hegemony of structuralist method, and it was possible to see the Formalist pioneers as virtual contemporaries in their search for the "theory" of literature.[1]

By the same token, the art of the Russian avant-garde exerted a special fascination in the decade or so preceding 1968, when the formal and geometric art of the Modern Movement appeared to revive under the new colors of op art and kinetics. In 1962, Camilla Gray was the first to map out the contours of the "Great Experiment" in

Russian art up to 1922. By 1968, however, Tatlin had become perhaps the first modern artist to have a major retrospective exhibition composed overwhelmingly of poor photographic reproductions and newly made models. The important show held at the Moderna Museet in Stockholm gave a conceptual twist worthy of Duchamp to this most craftsmanlike of artists, when his most exciting work was barred from export by the Soviet Ministry of Culture.[2]

By the late 1970s, this fascinated preoccupation with the Utopian message of the Russian avant-garde had, of course, yielded to a more historical estimate. The mythic objects of the earlier period had begun to figure in the sober calculations of the art market. George Costakis left the Soviet Union in 1977, having been authorized by the state to take with him a large proportion of his unequaled private collection of the Russian avant-garde: it was to be magnificently cataloged and exhibited throughout the West in the early 1980s.[3] By 1979, however, the Soviet authorities had relented sufficiently of their previous obstructive attitude to permit the organization at the Centre Pompidou of the vast "Paris-Moscow" exhibition. Here, at least, in the rich display of French and Russian art from the period 1900 to 1930, there was a place for one of those Tatlin "counterreliefs" which were being "systematized" and "restored" ten years earlier.[4]

My point in making these brief allusions is to stress that Western engagement with the Russian avant-garde has traversed several stages since the 1960s. But it is also true that increased knowledge of its history, and increased access to the objects, has not by any means liquidated our investment in the myth of the avant-garde. Even a remarkably scholarly and extensive exhibition like the one organized at the University of Washington at Seattle in 1990 betokens by its very title, "Art into Life," the high expectations still placed upon the energizing power of this historic phenomenon. We still need that notion of metamorphosis, no doubt, to set against the dubious social utility of the art which the West has produced over the past century.[5]

Yet what has this to do with the analysis of visual culture as it is practiced by present-day Russian scholars and critics? What has it to do with the development of a continuing tradition of reflection upon cultural phenomena which draws strength from the precedents of formalism and constructivism, but by no means remains fixated on them? The answer is that the Western perceptions of the brilliant mirage of the avant-garde is a real obstacle to seeing such a continuing tradition

with clarity. We need to put out of our minds, to some extent, the
decade following the 1917 revolution, and appreciate that the Russian
cultural commentators have had an altogether more extensive, and
more chequered, history to come to terms with. This anthology of
essays collected by Alla Efimova and Lev Manovich enables us to do
just that. If the message of the Russian avant-garde resonates in these
texts, it is present as the remembered inside of a glove that has been
turned inside out. We no longer feel the cosiness of the sequestered
period. But we can begin to explore the seams and structurings of
social life through the unique evidence of visual phenomena noted
over a wide variety of genres and periods.

To some extent, the essays in this volume can be read as an illumi-
nating (and subversive) commentary on the brief history of the Western
reception of the Russian avant-garde which I have summarized here.
For example, the artist Francisco Infante might be said to epitomize
the Western notion of the 1960s, that a reborn art of the Modern
Movement was spreading throughout the East as well as the West
and bringing with it a revival of the internationalist, rationally based
ideology of the former period. He is commemorated in reference
works on kinetic art as a new artist-engineer, utilizing motors, colored
light, loudspeakers, and temporal programming to produce multi-
media spectacles.[6]

Yet when Infante appears in Mikhail Epshtein's essay of 1988, it is
as the designer of a "lyrical museum" which will facilitate the private
"encounter with Things." If, in the 1960s, Infante was associated with
Lev Nusberg in the "Movement" ("Dvizhenie") group and planned
spectacular public displays to mark the fiftieth anniversary of the
USSR, he has become twenty years later the author of a visual scenario
which systematically evacuates the public character of the exhibition
space, and abandons the object to an intense and individual meditation.

The same stark contrast can be noted when we pick up the name of
"the underground millionaire Costakis" in Zinovy Zinik's effervescent
article on "Sots-Art." It must indeed be the celebrated collector of the
Russian avant-garde who is described as visiting the two "Famous
Artists of the 1970s," alias Komar and Melamid. Yet Costakis is
portrayed as being thoroughly disconcerted by what he sees of the
work of these defiantly contemporary artists. "He, Costakis, works
for eternity." It is an ironic juxtaposition to place the collector who

heroically salvaged a whole stratum of historic Russian art for posterity (in the West as well as in the East) against the two artists who will have nothing to do with such a conservationist attitude. "He does not understand that our *Paradise* is like his collection: it exists only in Russia; because it can't be taken abroad, and because it can't be taken out, it is worthless."

Of course, Komar and Melamid are here speaking in the period before 1977 when the Costakis collection was indeed barred from leaving the Soviet Union. Since 1977, not only works of the historic avant-garde but also works by Komar and Melamid themselves have circulated freely in the West. But this simply transfers to another, more refined level the irony implicit in this confrontation. For, just at the stage when Costakis's achievement was giving "eternal" (i.e., museo-logical) status to the fragile objects of the Russian avant-garde, their successors were devoting themselves to the production of elaborate and often rebarbative works which would conquer the West in spite of (or perhaps because of) their parodic relation to the accepted view of Russian art: works such as the *Ropes* of Ilya Kabakov, described here in Alexander Rappaport's essay, or indeed the neoclassical paintings based on Stalinist and social realist themes devised by Komar and Melamid.

So this anthology of essays reveals the contemporary state of a culture which will not acquiesce in the oversimplified views taken of it by the West, as far as the visual arts are concerned. The authors are too much immersed in the difficult business of stitching their own history together, for any exceptions to be made in the interests of a Utopian dream. That is why Boris Groys's treatment of "Stalinism as Aesthetic Phenomenon" is specially significant in the collection. For a great deal has been invested, over the years, in the view that the Stalinist period was indeed the blank negation of any form of culturally significant activity: in Groys's own words, " . . . the history of the 1930s–40s usually is perceived only as the history of the persecution of 'real' art, as a monotonous and frightening martyrology." We do not have to turn history on its head, or deny the horrifying character of Stalin's personal rule, to see that lines of continuity and development do indeed exist between the practice of the avant-garde and the period which ensued. For artists like Malevich and Rodchenko stressed the "projective character" of their work and derided the notion of artistic autonomy. The response of the totalitarian leader to the challenge of the avant-garde was, therefore, logical: the avant-garde artist would not be given political power, but, on the other hand, the political leader would acquire aesthetic power. So Groys concludes: " . . . Stalin was the only artist of the Stalin era; . . . he was a successor of Malevich or Tatlin to a much greater degree than the later museum stylizations of the avant-garde."

The boldness and cogency of Groys's argument demonstrate in an exemplary way how this collection succeeds in exploding some of the tenacious myths about Soviet culture. As has been the case with the recent historiography of Italian fascism, the problem is one of dispensing with the convenient pretext that a rupture took place—a kind of cultural lacuna from which we can avert our eyes. In this sense, the work of cultural commentary becomes an effort to reconstitute the very broad lines of historical development rather than privileging particular moments which have the nostalgic charm of a "Golden Age." A recent article by Alexander Jakimovich in fact singles out two of our contributors—Groys and Epshtein—as leading voices in the "archaeology of culture" which is developing in "Late Soviet Civilisation." For Jakimovich, the decisive feature is that these writers reject the age-old view of "Neo-Romantic conflict between the isolated group of West-oriented elite and the rest of Soviet society." Instead, such critics as Groys and Epshtein:

> . . . do not set apart the "true" art of the non-conformists from the rest of Soviet society. Instead they approach Homo Sovieticus from a broader perspective, embracing mentality, and social and national identity, in order to redefine art and formulate meanings through which they can relate to Soviet reality.[7]

It should be added that, in Jakimovich's acute reading, the type of cultural analysis represented by the recent contributions to this volume is as beneficial to the Western viewpoint as it is necessary for the Russian critics themselves. It is all too easy for the West to subscribe to the "neo-Romantic" myth which recognizes only the plight of the persecuted avant-garde. It is much more productive to be informed of the "broader perspective," which incorporates the history of the avant-garde within a development whose ironies cannot obscure the distinctive and salient continuities.

What we have here, therefore, is a collection of essays which relates to a coherent and contemporary point of view. The editors have been careful to choose essays which, in spite of the apparent heterogeneity of their subject matter, all contribute to a more integral knowledge of the long-term development of Russian visual culture, conceived in its own terms but also as engaged in a fruitful and dynamic interchange with the West. They have rightly chosen not to go over the ground that has been covered already. Consequently, there are none of the "classic" texts from the postrevolutionary period which have been translated and anthologized already to an adequate degree. The era of the revolutionary avant-garde, so often the object of fascination which obscures all else with its dazzling lure, appears here in a series of oblique reflections and diffractions: as a result, the sense of a broader and more various history is effectively maintained.

This strategy can be perceived first of all in the writings which are chosen from a few undoubted "stars" of the postrevolutionary period. It would have been a pity to exclude altogether the rich ferment of ideas and techniques which were generated during these years. Two texts are, therefore, chosen from the work of the highly influential critic Mikhail Bakhtin, who also published as a linguist under the pseudonym of V. N. Voloshinov. As early as 1970, when Julia Kristeva wrote her enlightening preface to Bakhtin's *Dostoevsky*, it became evident that Bakhtin's writings formed a bridge between Russian Formalism in its initial phase, and the preoccupations of structuralist and psychoanalytic critics in the last twenty-five years.[8] Certainly no Russian theorist has been more influential, over that period, in generating new approaches to the form of the novel. It is useful to see him here, in an early text, considering the "world" of the fictional hero from the visual criterion of spatiality as it is mediated in the written form. It is also particularly valuable to have the first chapter of Voloshinov's fundamental investigation of philosophy of language, which unequivocally places the study of the sign at the center of any ideological investigation. This could be seen as a theoretical underpinning for the whole range of texts represented here.

It would have been difficult to bar from this anthology the work of the most brilliant and easily the most famous Russian analyst and practitioner of visual culture, Sergei Eisenstein, whose range of references to the art and literature of Russia, Europe, and the wider world was truly prodigious. The little known text on "Yermolova" which is included here is especially revealing in its treatment of the continuity of visual culture between the nineteenth century and the period of the avant-garde. Eisenstein formulates the general principle that an established art form—in this case, academic salon painting—"contains, as part and parcel of the artist's *method,* elements of what in the next phase of development will become the *principles* and *methods* of a new stage in the forward progress of that art." The "new stage" to which Eisenstein refers is, of course, the art of cinema, with its characteristic method of montage. It is remarkable how much can be gleaned, with this later stage in mind, from the study of the visual system at work in the portrait of the actress Yermolova by the painter Valentin Serov. Eisenstein never seems to be enforcing a retrospective reading, but, on the contrary, he shows how the dynamic superimposition of phases implicit in Serov's composition establishes the work's effectiveness compared with the failure of Repin's *Tolstoy Renouncing Earthly Life.* In the first case, Serov portrays the great actress through sacrificing everything theatrical; in the second, Repin falsifies the other-worldly dedication of the novelist by an intrusive and ridiculous theatricality.

Common to Bakhtin and to Eisenstein (as indeed to all the pioneers of Russian Formalism) is the enviable ability to observe the interrelations of the verbal and the visual, and to detect the complex intermeshing of different genres over a long historical development. It is indeed the main dividend of the semiotic approach that it provides the basic categories for an analysis of this kind. Second to none in his importance as a Formalist critic of the second generation, maintaining an academic forum for the continuance of the work of the earlier group, is Yury Lotman. His lively and provocative commentary on the "intermediate position of theater between the moving, continuous, real world and the still, discrete world of visual arts" is a model of innovatory genre analysis. Through a range of striking examples, which extends from Van Eyck to the role of Talma at the Napoleonic court, he displays the reciprocal influences of theater on painting and painting on theater. As with so many of the other essays included here, this is an argument used to stimulate further work rather than to exhaust the subject matter; Lotman's lightness of touch should not, in any sense, be equated with superficiality of approach.

Several of the younger contributors pursue the strategy outlined above with regard to the postrevolutionary period. They do not plunge into the middle of the maelstrom but rather regard it carefully from a distance, noting how its prevalent features in the domain of visual culture were anticipated, or echoed, in other historical circumstances. In this way, Gennady Rezvin builds upon the important architectural research into the avant-garde undertaken by scholars like Khan-Magomedov, and he draws attention to the significant parallels between the Russian architectural projects of the 1920s and the so-called Utopian architecture of the French eighteenth century. But he has no desire to endorse the questionable historical argument that an architect like Leonidov knowingly referred to the projects of Boullée in his design for the Lenin Institute. It is enough for him to show that the French and the Russian revolutionaries both faced similar demands for "objective" and "rational" architecture. Hence their visionary projects took similar forms: "Iconography becomes the expression of objective signification."

Paralleling the historical scope of this architectural study is Mikhail Yampolsky's excellent essay on "Transparency Painting," which analyzes the different stages whereby new approaches to the physics of light progressively aided the transformation of painting into a form of theatrical spectacle. There has recently been a growing interest among Western art historians in the forms of public visual display, such as panoramas and dioramas, which attracted a large and growing public in the century leading up to the rise of the cinema. Yampolsky skillfully traces the links between the emergence of a scientific and visionary theme in the visual culture of the eighteenth century and its culmination in cinema as a "cathedral of light."

Rezvin refers in passing, in his discussion of Utopian architecture, to the great project of Tatlin for a "Monument to the Third International" (usually known as "Tatlin's Tower"). Yampolsky could easily have referred, though he does not do so, to the interest in transparency shown by such avant-garde Russian artists of the revolutionary period as Naum Gabo and El Lissitsky. Such references, whether explicit or implicit, may be taken for granted in these texts, which do not (as I have stressed before) merely aim to consolidate our attachment to the icons of the avant-garde. Two of the most detailed and innovatory historical enquiries included here, however, approach at a tangent the all-important question of how far the Russian masses were visually educated enough to accommodate the shifts in pictorial style which were taking place well before the avant-garde made its bid to be the pacesetter in visual culture. Grigory Sternin looks very carefully at the relationship of "Public and Artist in Russia at the Turn of the Twentieth Century" and finds numerous indications of the deepening gulf between "genuine art" and the mass public, although he is reluctant to see this process as entirely negative when interpreted alongside the "objective historical process." Alexander Zakharov chooses the exciting theme of "Mass Celebrations" in the Stalin era and shows that, as early as 1927, these were carefully stage-managed so as to "nip in the bud" any attempt at expressing the individual at the expense of the collective. A sharp sidelight is provided here on Bakhtin's notion of the *carnivalesque,* which was then being developed in relation to the work of authors like Rabelais. For "satirical carnival laughter" was precisely what the official mass celebration could not tolerate: it preferred and required a "flaccid humor uncapable of either denying or asserting anything."

All of the previous four contributions are concerned with establishing the overall continuities within which the Russian experience of the twentieth century—so dramatic in its apparent cultural ruptures—can be made intelligible. They reinforce the message of Boris Groys's previously mentioned and intentionally transgressive essay on "Stalinism as Aesthetic Phenomenon." A final group of contributors, however, takes its stance more directly in the present period. Here we can begin to take the pulse of a cultural life that is creative, responsive, and still related in significant ways with the special tradition of the visual arts in Russia. When Epshtein writes eloquently on the project of a "lyrical museum," it is obvious that he relies upon the particular significance and etymology of the Russian word for "thing": *vesch.* Students of the Russian avant-garde will recall that the most accomplished propagandist of revolutionary art, El Lissitsky, chose to entitle his trilingual magazine *Vesch,* ending his first editorial with the slogan: "Make 'Objects.'"[9] Epshtein's essay shows in a highly persuasive way how Lissitsky's reaction against the traditional genres of painting and sculpture could be integrated into a development toward what he terms "thought through singularities." The lyrical museum builds upon a significant history in which poetry gives value to the "magic moment" or epiphany, and presents even the "scanty candy wrapper" as a treasure house of intimate meanings waiting to be teased out in individual contemplation. It offers, one feels, the very opposite experience to the "mass celebration."

Although ostensibly concerned with a museum project, Epshtein is, of course, proposing an aesthetic of singularity which harmonizes well with the recent, and remarkable, developments in the visual arts in Russia. We can, in fact, detect two phases of this contemporary development in the texts included in this collection, which themselves parallel the critical review of earlier phases of Russian art production. Zinovy Zinik's article on "Sots-Art" (the work of Komar and Melamid), originally dated Moscow 1974, shows a stage in which Russian art polemically contests the incorporation of the revolutionary avant-garde into the market economy, and chooses to work upon the critical transformation of the Socialist Realism of the Stalinist period, which remains unrecuperated by the market. Dated more than ten years later, the article by Alexander Rappaport on the *Ropes* by Ilya Kabakov is a profound meditation on the continuing relevance of an avant-garde which rejects the blandishments of kitsch and folk art as well as the specious rules of academicism. It is extraordinary to follow such a passionate defense of a "conceptual installation" as being both profoundly rooted in the history of modernist art, and self-justifying as an ontological form representing contemporary life. The continuing success of Kabakov's disquieting and powerful work in international exhibitions—such as the 1992 Kassel Documenta—is a tribute both to the fact that his approach is indeed rooted in Russian and European tradition, and to the fact that critical response of this high quality within the Russian cultural milieu must have sustained Kabakov's work well in advance of his international celebrity.

It is not possible to draw a line at the end of this collection, or to sum up in final terms the diverse strands of a history that is still in a process of ferment. Russia continues to swing between nationalist and internationalist inclinations, between acceptance and rejection of the successive phases that have constituted her chequered history in the modern period. As Vladimir Paperny indicates, the movement between "Culture One" and "Culture Two"—between the ideal of mobility and bodily liberation championed by the Constructivists and that of a controlled and normalized existence untouched by the avant-garde—has become a recurrent feature of the Russian cultural debate. Such a debate is not going to be settled quickly. But its very intensity augurs well for the vitality of a visual culture which these essays epitomize in its rich diversity.

STEPHEN BANN

1. See Tzvetan Todorov, *Théorie de la littérature: Textes des Formalistes russes* (Paris: Seuil, 1965); and Victor Erlich, *Russian Formalism* (The Hague: Mouton, 1955).

2. See Camilla Gray, *The Great Experiment: Russian Art 1863–1922* (London: Thames & Hudson; New York: Abrams, 1962); and *Vladimir Tatlin* catalog (Stockholm: Moderna Museet, July–September 1968).

3. See Angelica Zander Rudenstine, ed., *Russian Avant-Garde Art: The George Costakis Collection* (London: Thames & Hudson, 1981).

4. See *Paris-Moscou 1900–1930* catalog (Paris: Centre Georges Pompidou, 1979).

5. See *Art into Life: Russian Constructivism 1914–1932* catalog (Seattle: Henry Art Gallery, University of Washington/Rizzoli, 1990).

6. See Frank Popper, *Naissance de l'art cinétique* (Paris: Gauthier-Villars, 1967), 179–80.

7. Alexander Jakimovich, "The Late Soviet Civilisation," *Kunst & Museumjournaal* 3, no. 6 (1992): 18.

8. See Julia Kristeva, "The Ruin of a Poetics," trans. Vivienne Mylne, ed. S. Bann and J. E. Bowlt, in *Russian Formalism* (Edinburgh: Scottish Academic Press; New York: Van Nostrand Reinhold, 1973), 102–19.

9. See Stephen Bann, ed., *The Tradition of Constructivism* (New York: Viking; London: Thames & Hudson, 1974; new ed., New York: Da Capo, 1990), 53–57.

We would like to thank the following people for their help in preparing this book. Norman Bryson inspired us to look far and wide for new ways to think about the visual. Susan Buck-Morss encouraged us to translate not only between languages but also between cultural experiences. Michael Ann Holly and Keith Moxey provided crucial help in turning an idea into this book. Hal Foster's suggestions were invaluable in organizing, presenting, and re-thinking the material. Mieke Bal and Janet Wolff allowed us the time and resources needed to complete the translations. The careful reading of translations by Vladislav Todorov helped us avoid many mistakes. Viktor Kukharsky ably assisted in translating the essay by Grigory Sternin. Karen Wilson, our editor at the University of Chicago Press, guided us through the three-year-long publishing process and believed in the project. Finally, we would like to thank our parents to whose lives and visions this book is dedicated.

ALLA EFIMOVA AND LEV MANOVICH

Object, Space, Culture: Introduction

This anthology brings together for the first time in English recent writings in art history and cultural theory from Russian language writers. While the tradition of Russian literary theory has been influential for many decades, Russian writings on visual culture have remained unknown. Although this work does not fall within a coherent school or tradition, it introduces equally innovative concepts and offers new directions for the study of visual culture.

These essays are not limited to a single discipline or a theoretical approach. They range from art history to literary studies, from architectural theory to film theory, from semiotics to social history. They focus on subjects as diverse as modern architecture and candy wrappers, mass celebrations and urban refuse.

What then justifies bringing these essays together under the heading "Russian" other than the common language? Many of the authors are not ethnically Russian, and some no longer reside in Russia. Thus "Russian" refers not to a geographic location or ethnic background, but to a number of shared historical references and theoretical concerns the authors bring to their interpretations of visual culture. The essays often deal with material from Soviet and Russian cultural history; and they rely on philosophical concepts and categories specific to the Russian tradition.

Reinterpreting Soviet Visual Heritage

Among the selections, the reader will find innovative interpretations of Russian prerevolutionary art (Sternin, Eisenstein) as well as radical reappraisals of the Soviet visual heritage (Paperny, Zakharov, Groys, Rappaport, Zinik). The latter go beyond issues which typically surround discussions of Soviet culture, such as censorship in the arts or the opposition of avant-garde and Socialist Realism. For example, in his analysis of the relationship between Soviet architecture and political life, Vladimir Paperny shows how political forces were themselves manifestations of cultural forces, reversing the conventional logic of causality according to which Soviet culture was molded by politics. Another writer, Aleksander Zakharov, considers various aspects of mass celebrations throughout Soviet history—their aesthetics, institutional organization, psychology, and the changing sociological structure. These aspects may appear to be unique to Stalinism or twentieth-century totalitarianism, but Zakharov treats them in relation to the modern tradition of ideological channeling of spontaneous mass gatherings and suggests that the Soviet celebrations need to be reconsidered in a comparative historical framework.

Such a comparative approach also structures the essays by Boris Groys and Gennady Revzin who reevaluate the historical role of the early twentieth century avant-garde in relation to international totalitarian phenomena, a theme central for many contemporary Russian and East European writers and artists. Boris Groys proposes that by explicitly merging the aesthetic and the political in its project, the avant-garde opened the way to totalitarianism in the Soviet Union, Germany, and Italy. The manifestos of the artistic avant-garde calling for a radical aesthetic transformation of society were taken up by the dictators, who themselves assumed the role of avant-garde artists: "In Stalinist Russia (just as in Nazi Germany) the project of the avant-garde was realized in its final phase: political power refused the services of the avant-garde artists and itself set about to transform the world artistically following its own notions."[1]

Revzin analyzes the similarity in the architectural language of the avant-garde of two revolutionary epochs—the French Revolution of 1789 and the Russian Revolution of 1917. He shows that behind the iconographic resemblance lies the shared desire to refuse meanings of architectural forms based on tradition and convention and, instead, to make these meanings "objective" and prescriptive. As Revzin points out, it is this belief that meanings can be transformed at will that gave the avant-garde the confidence in the possibility of radical transformation of society.

The Russian writers' work to reconsider the project of the avant-garde, to interpret the role of visual culture in Soviet ideological and social regime, is closely connected to the work of the Russian conceptual artists of the 1970s and 1980s. In fact, it was such artists as Vitaly Komar, Aleksander Melamid, Eric Bulatov, and Ilya Kabakov who, in the early 1970s, were the first to explore the language of Soviet propaganda, the iconography of Socialist Realism, and the visual forms of the everyday environment, thus opening these subjects for subsequent critical analysis. The essays by Zinovy Zinik and Alexander Rappaport provide insightful interpretations of this body of work. The subject of Rappaport's text is a 1985 installation by Ilya Kabakov. Zinik's essay is based on conversations with Komar and Melamid. Combining astute satire and lyricism, he reconstructs from the artists' early works an image of an ideologically monolith environment in which everything and everybody is implicated, no one walks away innocent, and artistic imagination pales in contrast to the absurdity of life itself.

Although a number of selections contribute to the growing interest in the reinterpretation of Soviet cultural history and its visual heritage, the anthology is not limited to this topic. Rather, it aims to reveal the distinct theoretical approaches to the study of visual culture developed by Russian writers, the usefulness of which is not specific to Soviet material. From this perspective, the texts are conceptually organized around three core categories important to the Russian intellectual tradition and semantically distinct from the categories of Western discourse on visual culture: *vesch* (thing, object, *res*), *prostranstvo* (space, world), and *khudozhestvennaya kul'tura* (artistic culture). Before discussing these categories, it would be useful to examine the notion of visual culture in some detail.

What Is Visual Culture?

Bruno Latour, a social historian of science, concisely defines visual culture in this way: "A new visual culture redefines both what it is to see, and what there is to see."[2] In other words, we must pay attention to what it means "to see" as well to what is considered to be worth seeing in each period or each culture. Indeed, recently historians have turned to investigating such sites and objects of vision as penal architecture, medical and scientific practices, visual metaphors in philosophy, and optical apparatuses.[3] Their investigations demonstrate that ways of seeing are responsible for structuring an extremely wide range of cultural phenomena.

To unpack what it means "to see" is to expose the relationship between the philosophical (in a broad sense, including scientific and theological) ideas about vision and their embodiment in actual material forms—painting, architecture, maps, illustrations, etc. For instance, Michael Baxandall in *Painting and Experience in Fifteenth Century Italy* relates the development of perspectival drawing to the contemporary theological discourses on vision.[4] Baxandall suggests it may be possible to interpret perspective as a type of visual metaphor which "is open to interpretation first as an analogical emblem of moral certainty and then as an eschatological glimpse of beatitude."[5] Perspectival drawing was a way for the mortals to approximate the divine vision which is capable of penetrating through all obstructions and covers.

Just as the definitions of seeing are particular to a culture, so are the phenomena deemed to be worth looking at. As an example drawn from contemporary visual culture, consider the special value attached to the visualization of objects situated below and above the threshold of human vision. On the one hand, we visualize and represent the workings of the living organisms—cells, neurons, microbes—the infinitesimal entities invisible to the eye. On the other hand, our perception of Earth is now fundamentally changed since its photographs taken from space became commonplace. The objects too small and too large to be grasped by sight are leveled and brought to a scale where they can be conveniently manipulated and studied.

Although the concept of visual culture originated within the study of art, today its relevance is not limited to art history but extends to political theory, history of science and technology, and any other discipline that deals with cultural and social history. Given that visual culture forms a layer stretching over the multitude of cultural phenomena, how is it to be studied? What categories can we use to describe it, what are the worthwhile directions of investigation, which sites would reveal its general features more readily?

In practice, the investigative strategies are limited by the available conceptual categories. One example is the category of *gaze*, which today permeates so much discussion in the humanities and leads to a particular strategy—to analyze the dialectic of looks possible between the subject and the object. This strategy, in turn, points to particular sites where this dialectic is encountered—representational painting, fiction films, or the architecture of surveillance, where the relationship between the viewer and the viewed is explicit.

This anthology aims to introduce the Western reader to the categories that structure discussions of visual culture in recent Russian writings.[6] Being distinct from the categories that currently enjoy popularity in Western humanities, they point to new directions for the study of visual culture, to sites and objects previously overlooked.

What are the reasons for this difference? First of all, it can be related to the prevalence of particular philosophical traditions. To stay with the same example, the category *gaze* can be traced back to the discussion of the master-slave dialectics in Hegel's *Phenomenology of the Mind*. Through Alexander Kojève's Paris lectures on Hegel during the 1930s, the concept was introduced into French philosophy. Because of this heritage *gaze* attained its specific contemporary connotations.

Second, the difference in categories is also related to different semantic associations that words possess in one language but not in another. For instance, consider the emergence of the term *constructivism* in the 1920s. In Russian, *konstruktor* (the one who constructs) is a synonym for engineer. This allowed a group of Soviet avant-garde artists to refer to themselves as *konstruktors* and their movement as constructivism. The term conveniently emphasized that, like engineers, they would construct utilitarian objects on the basis of scientific principles, in contrast to traditional artists who were said to rely on inspiration. In English translation, the word *constructivism* loses its close association with engineering, leading to a somewhat different interpretation of the entire movement. In this way whole theories grow around the semantics of certain words.[7]

Third, the difference in the directions of research is due to the fact that only certain aspects of visual culture are considered significant in a given cultural system. In the Soviet Union the pathos of creating a proletarian society in the 1920s manifested itself in the erosion of boundaries between high, applied, and popular arts. Moreover, all cultural objects were thought of as equally capable of carrying ideological values and, therefore, as suitable for propaganda. Subsequently, the experience of living in an environment thoroughly saturated with ideological signification has led Russian intellectuals and artists of the 1970s and 1980s to treat all manifestations of Soviet visual culture with equal attention—from cinema to design, from painting to propaganda banners. This general tendency to see the reciprocity of different cultural spheres is also evident in the paradigm of the "semiotics of culture" advanced in the 1960s by Yury Lotman and his colleagues from the Moscow-Tartu semiotics school. In contrast, cultural studies in the United States has to consciously struggle to overcome the divide between "high" and "low," between art and mass culture, between the Museum of Modern Art and Madison Avenue. The attention given to this problematic in the American humanities shows that this conceptual gap is fundamentally unresolved in theoretical discourse.

We will next discuss the three categories important to the essays in this anthology: *vesch, prostranstvo,* and *khudozhestvennaya kul'tura.*

Vesch

The Russian word *vesch* is not easily translated into English. Its meaning crucially depends on its opposition to the word *predmet* (object). Although in modern dictionaries *vesch* is defined interchangeably with "object" as a material, inanimate entity, its use in speech and its etymology point to a different meaning. If *predmet* refers to strictly inanimate and functional entities, *vesch* is an entity endowed with human spirit. For example, this is how the word is used in Russian literature: "For such people talent is an unnecessary *vesch*" (Belinsky), or "But the sky is a different matter. The sky is not a trifle. The sky is a *vesch*" (Paustovsky).[8] Etymologically the word *vesch* originated from the Latin *vox* (word, speech), and it is also related to the verb *veschat'* (to prophesy, to bring news).[9] The use of the word "thing" in the English expression "it's the real *thing*" would perhaps most adequately convey the meaning of *vesch.*

The conceptual juxtaposition between *vesch* and *predmet* (object) makes possible the particular directions for the interpretation of material culture and its representations, illustrated by the essays of Epshtein, Rappaport, and Voloshinov.

Mikhail Epshtein's essay "Things and Words: Toward a Lyrical Museum" was written in the context of the conference "Vesch in Art" held in Moscow in 1984. The conference and Epshtein's essay inspired a year-long discussion in the journal *Decorativnoe iskusstvo* (Decorative arts).

V. N. Voloshinov's opening chapter from *Marxism and the Philosophy of Language* (1929) is the classic, and perhaps the original, formulation of the semiology of material culture. Starting from the materialist Marxist position, Voloshinov insists that ideology must be located not in consciousness but in the concrete forms of material reality—consumer goods, images, and speech. He develops a "general philosophy of ideological signification" that treats all material forms as signs. This theme is further developed by Roland Barthes (*Mythologies* and *Elements of Semiology*) and Jean Baudrillard (*Le système des objets*) who treat all objects as a part of a system of signification, acting to naturalize bourgeois norms (Barthes), or to classify society according to the logic of consumption (Baudrillard).

The goal of Epshtein's essay is to go beyond semiotics, which, via Voloshinov, Barthes, and Baudrillard, became the dominant paradigm for the interpretations of objects of everyday life. Working against the semiotic negation of the object itself, always treated as a sign, Epshtein wants to emphasize the individuality of objects, the individuality attained through the history of an object's life in the human world. He proposes a hypothetical "lyrical museum"—a memorial dedicated to the objects we live with, the insignificant fragments of reality that are endowed with meaning. Throughout the essay the word *vesch* is translated as "Thing" in order to keep a clear distinction from *predmet*. In fact, in the essay Epshtein suggests his own English neologism—"verbject."

Rappaport indicates yet another way out of the semiotic and ideological impasse in the essay devoted to the installation *The Ropes* by Ilya Kabakov. Kabakov is well known for his representations of the world of domestic and everyday life as a microcosm of Soviet society. *The Ropes* is a collection of rubbish, both verbal and material—cigarette butts, bottle corks, scraps of paper with inscribed obscenities and chance phrases, methodically arranged and hung on threads from sixteen stretched ropes. In Rappaport's interpretation the systematic composition of the installation only emphasizes the insignificance of content: the objects, rather than being treated as ideological signs, are refused meaning altogether, turned into semiotic refuse. They are neither *vesch* nor signs.

Prostranstvo

Unlike *vesch*, the word *prostranstvo* is not semantically unique. *Prostranstvo*, accurately translated as "space," is another important category of Russian writings on visual culture, used in a number of contexts not typical for Anglo-American humanities. Two meanings should be mentioned here as they are encountered in several essays in the anthology: space as an environment surrounding the subject and space as a metacategory of cultural analysis.

The first meaning of space can be understood best in opposition to the concept of space characterized by its vectorial and geometric qualities. This is the space of Renaissance perspective described by Erwin Panofsky as "systematic," that is, ontologically primal in relation to bodies, homogeneous and isotropic.[10] A similar meaning is evoked when we talk about the organization of architectural and urban spaces, for instance, the linear or grid-like spaces of modern cities as opposed to the concentric or more chaotic spaces of medieval cities. This space is objective, empty, independent of the bodies that occupy it. In contrast to this meaning, the notion frequently evoked by Russian writers is *prostranstvennaya sreda*—the space-environment or space-medium, from which the geometric connotations are absent. It is a subjective, dense, filled-in space. The space-medium is used by Russian writers interchangeably with the object-world (*predmetnaya sreda*) and even the space-object-world (*predmetno-prostranstvennaya sreda*). "The space-medium is objects mapped onto space . . . We have seen the inseparability of Things and space, and the impossibility of representing Things and space by themselves."[11] The author of these statements is Father Pavel Florensky, the scientist, theologian, philosopher, and art historian. The above statements are quoted from the notes of a course on "Spatial Analysis of Art" he developed in VKhUTEMAS while teaching there from 1921 to 1924.[12]

The concept of space-medium is encountered in the essays by Rappaport and Epshtein as well as Bakhtin. Rappaport uses it as a category to classify the different types of visual representations; Bakhtin employs it in his philosophical analysis of subjectivity and its construction in literary texts; Epshtein uses it to emphasize the continuity between the subject and the everyday environment.

Rappaport discusses the status of the ground (or the field) in such visual artifacts as painting, printed page, tables, window displays, and drawings. The understanding of space as a medium, as a substantial rather than empty entity, allows him to group these types of images according to the different qualities of the "empty" fields in between marks, lines, or objects.[13] In this respect Rappaport singles out painting as the only type of representation where the ground is as meaningful as the objects it envelops and serves to foreground.

Bakhtin also evokes the notion of space-medium in the *Author and Hero in Aesthetic Activity,* an excerpt from which is included in this anthology. Written in the early 1920s, the work develops many theoretical positions that form the basis for Bakhtin's later literary studies. The excerpt deals with the problem of construction of a character in literary texts. Bakhtin considers the problem in spatial terms as an interaction of two partial viewpoints—the author's and the character's. Neither the character's nor the author's positions can be represented directly; they can only be evoked through the descriptions of the object-world seen respectively by each. Thus, for Bakhtin, the space-medium plays two crucial roles: it represents what lies in the character's field of vision, on the one hand, and what the author chooses to evoke about the character, on the other hand. According to Bakhtin this condition is not limited to literature but plays an important role in visual representations as well.

Along with its meaning as space-medium, the notion of space has another important meaning as a metacategory of cultural analysis. Again, Florensky presented it most succinctly: "All culture can be interpreted as an activity of organization of space."[14] Subsequent writers have used spatial categories to analyze the organization of texts, cultures, and social phenomena. Thus, in the 1937–38 work *The Forms of Time and Chronotope in the Novel,* Bakhtin developed the concept of "chronotope" to describe the unique relationship of space and time in literary texts. Recent writers have extended this concept to talk about not only texts but entire historical periods.[15] Yury Lotman also repeatedly relied on spatial, particularly topological, categories in his semiotic studies of literature and culture.[16]

The selection "Motion—Immobility" from Vladimir Paperny's book *Kultura "Dva"* is a good example of the use of spatial categories in cultural analysis. Although the immediate object of Paperny's analysis is the history of Soviet architecture from the 1920s to the 1950s, architecture turns out to be just one realm of Soviet society which on every level was organized along the same spatial and topological tropes, such as horizontality versus verticality or uniformity versus hierarchy. The selected excerpt considers one of these tropes, showing the images of motion and immobility to be at work in such diverse spheres as architectural and artistic practices, government policies and social norms, and the organization of everyday life.

Khudozhestvennaya Kul'tura

Another category, central for Russian writings on visual culture, is *khudozhestvennaya kul'tura*. Literally, it can be translated as "artistic culture." It means much more, however, than the study of fine arts. Thus, the leading art historical annual *Sovetskoe iskusstvoznanie* (Soviet art history) runs a regular section entitled "Problemy Khudozhestvennoi Kultury," which is set apart from the sections dealing with the interpretations of particular works of art, historiography, or connoisseurship. However, the notion *khudozhestvennaya kul'tura* is narrower than the notion of visual culture in its broad meaning, that is, all visual objects and practices of a culture, its ideas about vision, and the particular modes of seeing and representing.

Khudozhestvennaya kul'tura encompasses the study of all visual representational practices, including art, in their intellectual and social context. One example of the use of this category is provided by Grigory Sternin's essay "Public and Artist in Russia at the Turn of the Twentieth Century." Sternin takes the organization of an 1896 Russian industrial exhibition as a starting point for the discussion of a complex sociocultural network in which artistic production was only a part. He investigates the social pressures that lead to the democratization of art, the changing role of criticism, and the evolution of aesthetic conceptions. The essay uniquely combines institutional, economic, and discursive analysis in the discussion of a crucial moment in modern history—the emergence of mass visual culture with its emphasis on the concerns of a mass viewer.

What makes Sternin's approach unique is the direction of his investigation. His ultimate goal is not to explain particular art objects by placing them in a social context but rather to illuminate the changes in cultural and intellectual life through the analysis of the artistic processes. This approach is shared by Mikhail Yampolsky, whose essay "Transparency Painting: From Myth to Theater" also considers visual artifacts not for their own sake but in order to highlight the shifts in the functioning of the concept of light in modern European culture. Yampolsky discusses the history and mythology of light in a variety of eighteenth- and nineteenth-century European discourses—from Newton's physics to Romantic literature to theological doctrines. His analysis of the moral-religious nature of the concept becomes the foundation for the reinterpretation of such elements of the nineteenth-century visual culture as theatrical decorations, dioramas, and photography.

The concept of *khudozhestvennaya kul'tura* points to an approach to visual culture that emphasizes the affinity of different mediums of representation. Indeed, Russian writers have done considerable work in the area which may be called comparative poetics—the analysis of codes common to literature, theater, film, painting, graphic arts, etc. While this approach can be discerned in a number of selected texts, it comes to the foreground in the essays by Sergei Eisenstein and Yury Lotman.

Although Eisenstein is primarily recognized as a filmmaker and film theoretician, his writings, many still untranslated, reveal the breadth of his theoretical concerns and a recurring interest in comparative poetics. The selected text is a fragment from an unfinished book on montage on which Eisenstein worked in the 1930s. Eisenstein defines montage as a juxtaposition of different points of view, a definition that allows him to compare cinematic montage with the construction of other visual representations, such as realist painting.

If Eisenstein demonstrates how the same device is common to different arts regardless of their medium, Yury Lotman is concerned with the transfer, the traveling of codes among distinct cultural realms. In the essay included here, Lotman theorizes the exchange of semiotic codes between theater, painting, and everyday behavior. Significantly for the theme of comparative poetics, the essay was presented at the 1978 conference on "Theatrical Spaces" held at the Pushkin Museum of Art in Moscow, where the participants discussed the concept of performance space in theater, painting, popular entertainment, and other cultural sites.

In editing the following selections we have generally tried to preserve the full original texts. However, a number of passages which are highly technical or specific to the Russian context have been omitted in cases where their pertinence to the texts was not crucial.

In conclusion, we would like to remark on the dual project of the anthology—to offer theoretical approaches to the problems of visual culture as well as a reappraisal of the Soviet visual heritage. We believe that these projects are inseparable and that concrete studies of Soviet visual heritage are invaluable for the broader theoretical search for new ways to understand modern visual culture.

First, the specificity of the organization of Soviet cultural practices exposes the limitation of standard categories of cultural analysis. For instance, the practices of Socialist Realism cannot be adequately explained through such categories as "style" and "authorship."

Second, general theoretical paradigms are usually derived from the studies of particular cultural sites. A case in point is Critical Theory of the Frankfurt School, which is inseparable from the German interwar mass culture, and the British cultural studies that have relied on ethnographic and sociological analyses of British subcultures. Similarly, we feel that Soviet visual culture provides unique material for theorizing the functions of the visual in modernity and the relations between visual forms and social structures.

NOTES

1. Boris Groys, "Stalinizm kak esteticheskii fenomen," *Sintaxis* (Paris) 17 (1987): 105.

2. Bruno Latour, "Visualization and Cognition: Thinking with Eyes and Hands," *Knowledge and Society* 6 (1986): 10.

3. As, for instance, in the works by Svetlana Alpers, Bruno Latour, Michel Foucault, Jonathan Crary, and Martin Jay.

4. Michael Baxandall, *Painting and Experience in Fifteenth Century Italy* (Oxford: Oxford University Press, 1972).

5. Ibid., 108.

6. The majority of selections are untranslated writings from the last two decades, either from recent collections and journals published in the former Soviet Union or from Russian language publications in the West. We have also included three earlier essays by authors well known in the West and already available in English (Mikhail Bakhtin, V. N. Voloshinov, and Sergei Eisenstein). The essays are arranged chronologically to reveal a sense of continuity as the later texts make references to the earlier ones. For instance, Groys's essay was written in response to Paperny's book, while Paperny is indebted to Lotman's cultural semiotics.

7. Other examples would include the French verb "serveiller" which became the focal point of Foucault's theory of modern regimes of power developed in *Serveiller et punir* (translated as *Discipline and Punish*).

8. Quoted in Margarita Izotova, "Vesch v prostranstve," *Dekorativnoe Iskusstvo*, no. 2 (1985): 30–31.

9. Although *veschat'* was formed from a different Indo-European root (*veid*), this relationship is well grounded. The root *vek* that gave rise to the Russian *vesch* produces similar meanings in other languages: voice and speech in Latin, epos in Greek, and word in Sanskrit. Moreover, the Slovenian *rec* and Polish *rzecz*, while sounding like the Russian rech' (speech), have a meaning corresponding to that of *vesch*. The connection is not limited to

Indo-European languages; in ancient Hebrew the single word *dabar* means object, word, and action.

10. Erwin Panofsky, trans., *Perspective as a Symbolic Form* (New York: Zone, 1991).

11. P. A. Florensky, "Analiz prostranstvennosti v khudozhestvenno-izobrazitel'nykh proizvedeniyakh," in *Sobranie Sochinenii,* vol. 1 (Paris: YMCA Press, 1985), 334.

12. VKhUTEMAS was the leading school of art and design in the USSR in the 1920s and the center of avant-garde artistic culture.

13. This understanding of space is not unrelated to Heidegger's *Being and Time* and Sartre's *Being and Nothingness,* which theorize the substantiality of emptiness and nothingness.

14. Florensky 1985, 317.

15. For instance, in Sergei Kavtaradze, "'Khronotop' Kul'tury Stalinizma," *Arkhitektura i Stroitel'stvo Moskvy,* no. 12 (1990).

16. Yury Lotman, *The Structure of Artistic Text,* trans. Gail Lenhoff and Ronald Vroon (Ann Arbor: University of Michigan, 1977), 217–31.

The Study of Ideologies
and Philosophy of Language

The problem of the ideological sign. The ideological sign and
consciousness. The word as an ideological sign par excellence.
The ideological neutrality of the word. The capacity of the word
to be an inner sign.

Problems of the philosophy of language have in recent times acquired
exceptional pertinence and importance for Marxism. Over a wide
range of the most vital sectors in its scientific advance, the Marxist
method bears directly upon these problems and cannot continue to
move ahead productively without special provision for their investigation and solution.

First and foremost, the very foundations of a Marxist theory of ideologies—the bases for the studies of scientific knowledge, literature,
religion, ethics, and so forth—are closely bound up with problems of
the philosophy of language.

Any ideological product is not only itself a part of a reality (natural
or social), just as is any physical body, any instrument of production,
or any product for consumption, it also, in contradistinction to these
other phenomena, reflects and refracts another reality outside itself.
Everything ideological possesses *meaning:* it represents, depicts, or
stands for something lying outside itself. In other words, it is a *sign.*
Without signs, there is no ideology. A physical body equals itself, so

V. N. Voloshinov, "The Study of Ideologies and the Philosophy of Language," in *Marxism and the Philosophy of Language* (New York: Seminar
Press, 1973 [1929]), 9–15. Copyright © 1973 by Seminar Press, Inc.

to speak; it does not signify anything but wholly coincides with its particular, given nature. In this case there is no question of ideology.

However, any physical body may be perceived as an image; for instance, the image of natural inertia and necessity embodied in that particular thing. Any such artistic-symbolic image to which a particular physical object gives rise is already an ideological product. The physical object is converted into a sign. Without ceasing to be a part of material reality, such an object, to some degree, reflects and refracts another reality.

The same is true of any instrument of production. A tool by itself is devoid of any special meaning; it commands only some designated function—to serve this or that purpose in production. The tool serves that purpose as the particular, given thing that it is, without reflecting or standing for anything else. However, a tool also may be converted into an ideological sign. Such, for instance, is the hammer and sickle insignia of the Soviet Union. In this case, hammer and sickle possess a purely ideological meaning. Additionally, any instrument of production may be ideologically decorated. Tools used by prehistoric man are covered with pictures or designs—that is, with signs. So treated, a tool still does not, of course, itself become a sign.

It is further possible to enhance a tool artistically, and in such a way that its artistic shapeliness harmonizes with the purpose it is meant to serve in production. In this case, something like maximal approximation, almost a coalescence, of sign and tool comes about. But even here we still detect a distinct conceptual dividing line: the tool, as such, does not become a sign; the sign, as such, does not become an instrument of production.

Any consumer good can likewise be made an ideological sign. For instance, bread and wine become religious symbols in the Christian sacrament of communion. But the consumer good, as such, is not at all a sign. Consumer goods, just as tools, may be combined with ideological signs, but the distinct conceptual dividing line between them is not erased by the combination. Bread is made in some particular shape; this shape is not warranted solely by the bread's function as a consumer good; it also has a certain, if primitive, value as an ideological sign (e.g., bread in the shape of a figure eight [*krendel*] or a rosette).

Thus, side by side with the natural phenomena, with the equipment of technology, and with articles for consumption, there exists a special world—the *world of signs.*

Signs also are particular, material things; and, as we have seen, any item of nature, technology, or consumption can become a sign, acquiring in the process a meaning that goes beyond its given particularity. A sign does not simply exist as a part of a reality—it reflects and refracts another reality. Therefore, it may distort that reality or be true to it, or may perceive it from a special point of view, and so forth. Every sign is subject to the criteria of ideological evaluation (i.e., whether it is true, false, correct, fair, good, etc.). The domain of ideology coincides with the domain of signs. They equate with one another. Wherever a sign is present, ideology is present, too. *Everything ideological possesses semiotic value.*

Within the domain of signs—i.e., within the ideological sphere— profound differences exist: it is, after all, the domain of the artistic image, the religious symbol, the scientific formula, and the judicial ruling, etc. Each field of ideological creativity has its own kind of orientation toward reality and each refracts reality in its own way. Each field commands its own special function within the unity of social life. *But it is their semiotic character that places all ideological phenomena under the same general definition.*

Every ideological sign is not only a reflection, a shadow, of reality, but is also itself a material segment of that very reality. Every phenomenon functioning as an ideological sign has some kind of material embodiment, whether in sound, physical mass, color, movements of the body, or the like. In this sense, the reality of the sign is fully objective and lends itself to a unitary, monistic, objective method of study. A sign is a phenomenon of the external world. Both the sign itself and all the effects it produces (all those actions, reactions, and new signs it elicits in the surrounding social milieu) occur in outer experience.

This is a point of extreme importance. Yet, elementary and self-evident as it may seem, the study of ideologies has still not drawn all the conclusions that follow from it.

The idealistic philosophy of culture and psychologistic cultural studies locate ideology in the consciousness.[1] Ideology, they assert, is a fact of consciousness; the external body of the sign is merely a coating, merely a technical means for the realization of the inner effect, which is understanding.

Idealism and psychologism alike overlook the fact that understanding itself can come about only within some kind of semiotic material (e.g., inner speech), that sign bears upon sign, that *consciousness itself can arise and become a viable fact only in the material embodiment of signs*. The understanding of a sign is, after all, an act of reference between the sign apprehended and other, already known signs; in other words, understanding is a response to a sign with signs. And this chain of ideological creativity and understanding, moving from sign to sign and then to a new sign, is perfectly consistent and continuous: from one link of a semiotic nature (hence, also of a material nature) we proceed uninterruptedly to another link of exactly the same nature. And nowhere is there a break in the chain, nowhere does the chain plunge into inner being, nonmaterial in nature and unembodied in signs.

This ideological chain stretches from individual consciousness to individual consciousness, connecting them together. Signs emerge, after all, only in the process of interaction between one individual consciousness and another. And the individual consciousness itself is filled with signs. Consciousness becomes consciousness only once it has been filled with ideological (semiotic) content, consequently, only in the process of social interaction.

Despite the deep methodological differences between them, the idealistic philosophy of culture and psychologistic cultural studies both commit the same fundamental error. By localizing ideology in the consciousness, they transform the study of ideologies into a study of consciousness and its laws; it makes no difference whether this is done in transcendental or in empirical-psychological terms. This error is responsible not only for methodological confusion regarding the interrelation of disparate fields of knowledge, but for a radical distortion of the very reality under study as well. Ideological creativity—a material and social fact—is forced into the framework of the individual consciousness. The individual consciousness, for its part, is deprived of any support in reality. It becomes either all or nothing.

For idealism it has become all: its locus is somewhere above existence and it determines the latter. In actual fact, however, this sovereign of the universe is merely the hypostatization in idealism of an abstract bond among the most general forms and categories of ideological creativity.

For psychological positivism, on the contrary, consciousness

amounts to nothing: It is just a conglomeration of fortuitous, psycho-
physiological reactions which, by some miracle, results in meaningful
and unified ideological creativity.

The objective social regulatedness of ideological creativity, once
misconstrued as a conformity with laws of the individual consciousness, must inevitably forfeit its real place in existence and depart either
up into the superexistential empyrean of transcendentalism or down
into the presocial recesses of the psychophysical, biological organism.

However, the ideological, as such, cannot possibly be explained in
terms of either of these superhuman or subhuman, animalian, roots.
Its real place in existence is in the special, social material of signs
created by man. Its specificity consists precisely in its being located
between organized individuals, in its being the medium of their communication.

Signs can arise only on *interindividual territory*. It is territory that
cannot be called "natural" in the direct sense of the word:[2] signs do
not arise between any two members of the species *Homo sapiens*. It
is essential that the two individuals be *organized socially,* that they
compose a group (a social unit); only then can the medium of signs
take shape between them. The individual consciousness not only cannot be used to explain anything, but, on the contrary, is itself in need of
explanation from the vantage point of the social, ideological medium.

The individual consciousness is a social-ideological fact. Not until
this point is recognized with due provision for all the consequences
that follow from it will it be possible to construct either an objective
psychology or an objective study of ideologies.

It is precisely the problem of consciousness that has created the
major difficulties and generated the formidable confusion encountered
in all issues associated with psychology and the study of ideologies
alike. By and large, consciousness has become the *asylum ignorantiae*
for all philosophical constructs. It has been made the place where all
unresolved problems, all objectively irreducible residues are stored
away. Instead of trying to find an objective definition of consciousness,
thinkers have begun using it as a means for rendering all hard and fast
objective definitions subjective and fluid.

The only possible objective definition of consciousness is a sociological one. Consciousness cannot be derived directly from nature, as
has been and still is being attempted by naive mechanistic materialism
and contemporary objective psychology (of the biological, behavioris-

tic, and reflexological varieties). Ideology cannot be derived from consciousness, as is the practice of idealism and psychologistic positivism. Consciousness takes shape and being in the material of signs created by an organized group in the process of its social intercourse. The individual consciousness is nurtured on signs; it derives its growth from them; it reflects their logic and laws. The logic of consciousness is the logic of ideological communication, of the semiotic interaction of a social group. If we deprive consciousness of its semiotic, ideological content, it would have absolutely nothing left. Consciousness can harbor only in the image, the word, the meaningful gesture, and so forth. Outside such material there remains the sheer physiological act unilluminated by consciousness, i.e., without having light shed on it, without having meaning given to it, by signs.

All that has been said above leads to the following methodological conclusion: *the study of ideologies does not depend on psychology to any extent and need not be grounded in it.* As we shall see in greater detail in a later chapter, it is rather the reverse: *objective psychology must be grounded in the study of ideologies.* The reality of ideological phenomena is the objective reality of social signs. The laws of this reality are the laws of semiotic communication and are directly determined by the total aggregate of social and economic laws. Ideological reality is the immediate superstructure over the economic basis. Individual consciousness is not the architect of the ideological superstructure, but only a tenant lodging in the social edifice of ideological signs.

With our preliminary argument, disengaging ideological phenomena and their regulatedness from individual consciousness, we tie them in all the more firmly with conditions and forms of social communication. The reality of the sign is wholly a matter determined by that communication. After all, the existence of the sign is nothing but the materialization of that communication. Such is the nature of all ideological signs.

But nowhere does this semiotic quality and the continuous, comprehensive role of social communication as conditioning factor appear so clearly and fully expressed as in language. *The word is the ideological phenomenon par excellence.*

The entire reality of the word is wholly absorbed in its function of being a sign. A word contains nothing that is indifferent to this function, nothing that would not have been engendered by it. A word is the purest and most sensitive medium of social intercourse.

This indicatory, representative power of the word as an ideological phenomenon and the exceptional distinctiveness of its semiotic structure would already furnish reason enough for advancing the word to a prime position in the study of ideologies. It is precisely in the material of the word that the basic, general-ideological forms of semiotic communication could best be revealed.

But that is by no means all. The word is not only the purest, most indicatory sign but is, in addition, *a neutral sign*. Every other kind of semiotic material is specialized for some particular field of ideological creativity. Each field possesses its own ideological material and formulates signs and symbols specific to itself and not applicable in other fields. In these instances, a sign is created by some specific ideological function and remains inseparable from it. A word, in contrast, is neutral with respect to any specific ideological function. It can carry out ideological functions of *any* kind—scientific, aesthetic, ethical, religious.

Moreover, there is that immense area of ideological communication that cannot be pinned down to any one ideological sphere: the area of *communication in human life, human behavior*. This kind of communication is extraordinarily rich and important. On one side, it links up directly with the processes of production; on the other, it is tangent to the spheres of the various specialized and fully fledged ideologies. In this chapter, we shall take note of the fact that the material of behavioral communication is preeminently the *word*. The locale of so-called conversational language and its forms is precisely here, in the area of behavioral ideology.

One other property belongs to the word that is of the highest order of importance and is what makes the word the primary medium of the individual consciousness. Although the reality of the word, as is true of any sign, resides between individuals, a word, at the same time, is produced by the individual organism's own means without recourse to any equipment or any other kind of extracorporeal material. This has determined the role of word as *the semiotic material of inner life—of consciousness* (inner speech). Indeed, the consciousness could have developed only by having at its disposal material that was pliable and expressible by bodily means. And the word was exactly that kind of material. The word is available as the sign for, so to speak, inner employment: it can function as a sign in a state short of outward expression. For this reason, the problem of individual consciousness as the *inner word* (as an *inner sign* in general) becomes one of the most vital problems in philosophy of language.

It is clear, from the very start, that this problem cannot be properly approached by resorting to the usual concept of word and language as worked out in nonsociological linguistics and philosophy of language. What is needed is profound and acute analysis of the word as social sign before its function as the medium of consciousness can be understood.

It is owing to this exclusive role of the word as the medium of consciousness that *the word functions as an essential ingredient accompanying all ideological creativity whatsoever.* The word accompanies and comments on each and every ideological act. The processes of understanding any ideological phenomenon at all (be it a picture, a piece of music, a ritual, or an act of human conduct) cannot operate without the participation of inner speech. All manifestations of ideological creativity—all other nonverbal signs—are bathed by, suspended in, and cannot be entirely segregated or divorced from the element of speech.

This does not mean, of course, that the word may supplant any other ideological sign. None of the fundamental, specific ideological signs is replaceable wholly by words. It is ultimately impossible to convey a musical composition or pictorial image adequately in words. Words cannot wholly substitute for a religious ritual; nor is there any really adequate verbal substitute for even the simplest gesture in human behavior. To deny this would lead to the most banal rationalism and simplisticism. Nonetheless, at the very same time, every single one of these ideological signs, though not supplantable by words, has support in and is accompanied by words, just as is the case with singing and its musical accompaniment.

No cultural sign, once taken in and given meaning, remains in isolation: it becomes part of the *unity of the verbally constituted consciousness.* It is in the capacity of the consciousness to find verbal access to it. Thus, as it were, spreading ripples of verbal responses and resonances form around each and every ideological sign. Every *ideological refraction of existence in process of generation,* no matter what the nature of its significant material, *is accompanied by ideologi-*

cal refraction in word as an obligatory concomitant phenomenon. Word is present in each and every act of understanding and in each and every act of interpretation.

All of the properties of word we have examined—*its semiotic purity, its ideological neutrality, its involvement in behavioral communication, its ability to become an inner word and, finally, its obligatory presence, as an accompanying phenomenon, in any conscious act—* all these properties make the word the fundamental object of the study of ideologies. The laws of the ideological refraction of existence in signs and in consciousness, its forms and mechanics, must be studied in the material of the word, first of all. The only possible way of bringing the Marxist sociological method to bear on all the profundities and subtleties of "immanent" ideological structures is to operate from the basis of the philosophy of language as the *philosophy of the ideological sign.* And that basis must be devised and elaborated by Marxism itself.

NOTES

1. It should be noted that a change of outlook in this regard can be detected in modern neo-Kantianism. We have in mind the latest book by Ernst Cassirer, *Philosophie der symbolischen Formen,* vol. 1, 1923. While remaining on the grounds of consciousness, Cassirer considers its dominant trait to be representation. Each element of consciousness represents something, bears a symbolic function. The whole exists in its parts, but a part is comprehensible only in the whole. According to Cassirer, an idea is just as sensory as matter; the sensoriness involved, however, is that of the symbolic sign; it is representative sensoriness.

2. Society, of course, is also a *part of nature,* but a part that is qualitatively separate and distinct and possesses its own *specific* systems of laws.

Yermolova

The subject for discussion is Valentin Serov's portrait of Yermolova in the Tretyakov Gallery.[1]

Many were those who experienced the quite special feeling of *exaltation* and *inspiration* that gripped the spectator when watching the original of this portrait.

The portrait shows an extremely sparing use of color. It is almost chilling in the severity of its pose; it is almost crude in its disposition of masses; it is devoid of background and "stage props." A single vertical black figure stands against the gray background of a wall and a mirror. This cuts the figure at the waist and reflects a piece of the opposite wall and ceiling of the empty room in which the actress has been painted.

Yet, in contemplating this canvas, one is seized by something of the same emotion which the personality of the great actress must have evoked on the stage.

There have been, of course, malicious tongues which denied there was anything in any way remarkable about this portrait.

One such, for instance, was the late Ivan A. Aksionov, who grumbled about it: "Nothing special. She always used to act with her stomach stuck out. And in Serov's portrait she is standing with her stomach thrust forward."[2] Here, no doubt, Aksionov's odd "non-acceptance" of the actress herself (whom he disliked) has become fused with his

S. Eisenstein, "Montage" (fragments), in *S. M. Eisenstein: Selected Works,* vol. 2, trans. Michael Glenny, ed. Richard Taylor (London: British Film Institute, 1991 [1937–38]).

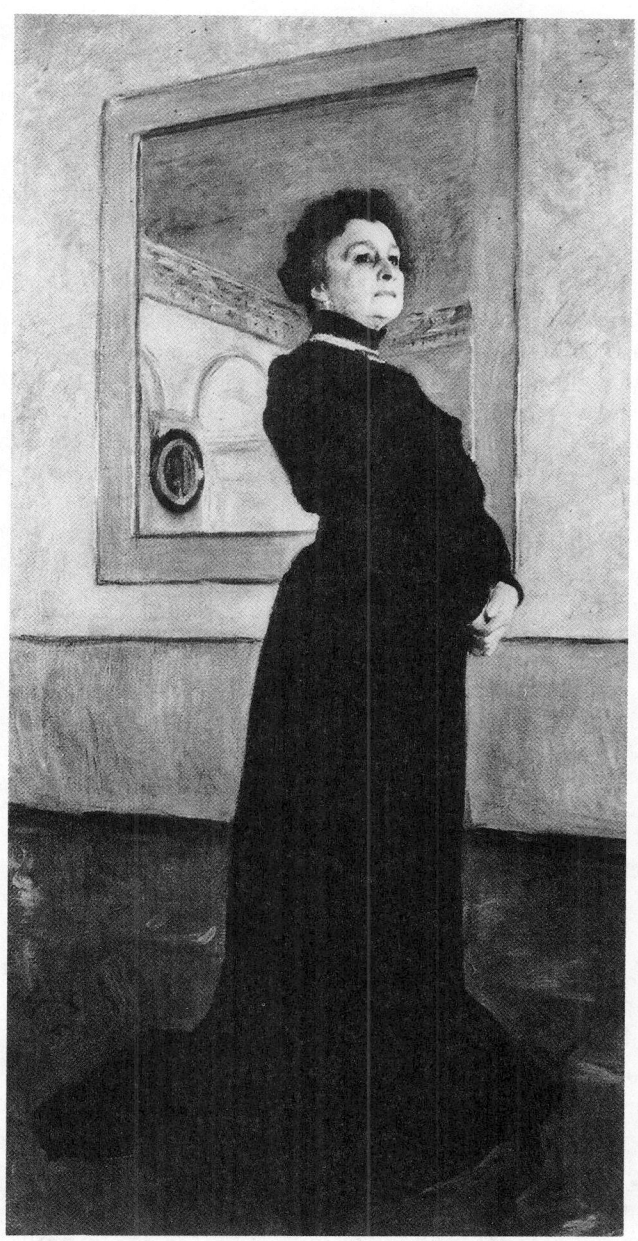

Valentin Serov, *Portrait of Maria Yermolova* (1905). Oil on canvas.
The Tretyakov Gallery, Moscow.

attitude towards the way Serov recreated her image with such exactitude.

I never saw Yermolova on stage, and I only know about her acting from the descriptions and very detailed accounts of those who saw her, but my impressions of Yermolova, gained from the "data" of the Serov portrait, are similar to the enthusiasm with which Stanislavsky wrote about her:

> Maria Nikolayevna Yermolova represents a whole epoch of the Russian theatre, and for our generation she was a symbol of womanliness, beauty, strength, emotional power, genuine simplicity and modesty. Her gifts were unique. She had a power of insight amounting to genius, an inspired temperament, great nervous sensitivity, inexhaustible spiritual depths. . . . To every part that she played, Yermolova always gave a particular image that was unlike the preceding one and unlike that of any other actor.
>
> The roles which Yermolova created live on in the memory with an independent existence, despite the fact that they were all compounded of the same organic material, of her single spiritual personality.
>
> . . . All her movements, her words, her actions, even if they were misjudged or mistaken, were suffused with fire from within, with an emotion that could be warm and gentle or fiery and thrilling. . . . Wise in the ways of the female heart, more than anyone else she had the ability to reveal and display *das ewig Weibliche*.[3]

Something resembling this feeling overcame me when I stood in front of this portrait at the exhibition of Serov's work at the Tretyakov Gallery in 1935. For a long time I reflected on how, with an almost total absence of a painter's usual external effects—and Serov possessed a considerable arsenal of effects—he had achieved such a remarkable inner power of *inspired exaltation* in painting the figure.

I think I have solved this mystery. This *unusual* effect has been achieved through the application of truly unusual means of compositional expression. Furthermore, the means used here are such that in essence they have already outdistanced that stage of painting to which the picture itself still belongs.

To my mind, every truly great work of art is *always* distinguished by this characteristic: it contains, as part and parcel of the artist's *method*, elements of what in the next phase of development of that particular art form will become the *principles* and *methods* of a new stage in the forward progress of that art.

In the given instance this is especially interesting, because these *unusual* compositional factors not only lie beyond the limits of the methods of painting used in Serov's era, but *altogether beyond the limits of painting as it is narrowly understood,* at least from the viewpoint of those who do not regard the pictorial medium of cinema—its dynamic use of light and montage to make pictures—as a contemporary form of painting. There actually are such eccentrics who obstinately refuse to understand this and are totally unable to accept cinema—that miracle of pictorial potential—as part of the mainstream of the development and history of painting. This seems to me profoundly unjust: the difference of "technology" is irrelevant. After all, the hospitable edifice of the history of painting embraces such technically diverse media as, say, etching and . . . the mosaics of Ravenna!

As for the fundamental and decisive factor, that is to say *artistic thinking,* then the "gap" between Picasso and the cinematographer is significantly narrower than that between Paul Signac and the Wanderers [*Peredvizhniki*].[4] And as for the classification of photography as a "mechanical" art, allegedly devoid of the direct, living touch of the creative "act," I must say that the subtle structuring of a shot, the refined nuances of lighting, and the strict calculation of tonal values found in the work of our best cameramen have long been capable of competing on equal terms with the best examples of the art of the past!

Let us, however, return to the portrait of Yermolova.

It was not by chance that I referred to the mirror as cutting the figure. To my mind, in that "cut" and in the montage-like juxtaposition of the results of that cut there lies the fundamental secret of the effect of this portrait.

I have written and spoken many times about montage as being not so much the sequence of segments as their *simultaneity:* in the consciousness of the perceiver, segment is piled on segment, and their incongruences of color, lighting, outline, scale, movement, etc., are what gives that sense of dynamic thrust and impulse which generates a sense of movement, ranging from the perception of purely *physical movement* to the most complex forms of *intraconceptual movement* when we are dealing with a montage that juxtaposes metaphors, images or concepts.

Therefore we should in no way be confused by the following reflections, which concern the *simultaneous conjoint presence* on one canvas of elements which are, in essence, *the successive phases of a whole process.*

Nor should we be puzzled by the fact that the various elements are simultaneously seen both as separate *independent units* and as *inseparable parts of a single whole* (or as separate groups within that whole).

Moreover, as we shall see below, the very fact of that unity of *simultaneity* and *sequence* proves to be a unique means of producing an absolutely specific effect.

But let us get down to business.

I said that the frame of the mirror "cuts" the figure. The figure is cut not only by the frame of the mirror; it is also cut by the line of the skirting-board, i.e., the line at which the floor meets the wall, and it is cut by the broken line of the cornice, that is to say the line, reflected in the mirror, at which the wall meets the ceiling.

Strictly speaking, these lines do not cut the figure: they go as far as her outline and politely break off; only by mentally extending them do we slice across the figure at various levels, thereby separating from each other the lower part of the dress, the bust and the head.

Let us extend these lines in fact, and "cut" the portrait into sections (see illustration).

When this is done, the straight lines which figure *as objects* in the picture (as do the frame of the mirror and the lines of juncture between floor and wall, wall and ceiling) function simultaneously, as it were, as the *edges* of individual film shots. Admittedly unlike the standard edges of film frames, they have irregular outlines but they nevertheless fulfill to perfection the basic functions of film shots.

The outline traced by the first line surrounds the figure as a whole; this is a "full-length shot."

The second line gives us the "figure from the knees upward."

The third, "waist-length."

And finally the fourth gives us a typical "close-up."

For purposes of greater clarity, let us go a little further and physically cut the picture up into a set of four shots. We will place them side by side and check out the features (apart from the difference of scale) which distinguish them. To do so, let us separate these "cut-outs" of the figure and study each one individually as an independent shot.

What, in general, distinguishes one shot from another, apart from the scale and the edges of the frame?

Above all, of course, the placing of the set-up.

Let us examine our "shots" in sequence, from the viewpoint of . . . the setup.

From which point, if one may so express it, was frame No. 1—"full-length"—shot?

We see that in it the floor is not shown as just a narrow strip, but as a large, flat, dark gray surface, on which the hem of the dress is disposed around the figure as a broad black mass: the figure has clearly been shot *from above*.

Shot No. 2. "Figure from the knees upward." As it now appears in the cutout, the figure has been placed *parallel* to the wall on which the mirror is fastened. As for the set-up, this frame would have been shot *head-on*.

Shot No. 3. When this part of the picture is detached from the rest, we see the upper half of Yermolova's figure against a background of a certain spatial depth: when cut out with this particular framing, that space is no longer perceptible as being a reflection in the mirror. The depth provided by the mirror functions as the depth of an actual spatial background.

This is a typical and well-known case in film-making practice, when a relative impression of space is produced by means of simply altering the frame. But much more important in this instance is the fact that, due to the relative positioning of the figure, the walls and the ceiling, the figure in this "shot" no longer appears to have been shot head-on: it has clearly been shot slightly *from below* (the ceiling can be seen overhanging the space above it).

Shot No. 4. The face is seen in close-up against a horizontal plane, which we know as the ceiling.

When is this kind of result produced in a shot?

Only, of course, when it is shot emphatically *from below*.

Thus we see that all four of the theoretical "shots" of our sequence differ from each other not only in the *scale* of what they depict but in the *displacement* of the set-up (the points from which the object is viewed). Furthermore, this movement of the set-up strictly duplicates the process of gradual enlargement towards a close-up: as the object increases in size, the set-up moves consistently from an *overhead* set-up (A) to a *head-on* shot (B), thence to a set-up that is *partly below*

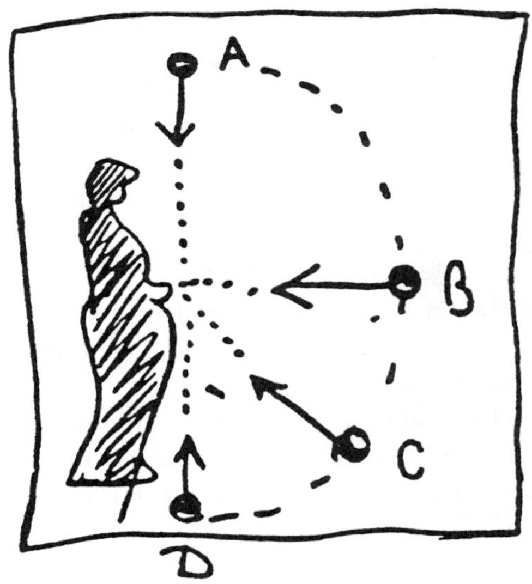

Figure 2.1.

(C), and the shooting finishes *from below* at the lowest possible point (D) (see fig. 2.1).

If we now imagine shots 1, 2, 3, and 4 connected in a montage sequence, then it transpires that the eye has described a complete arc of 180 degrees. The figure has been shot in sequence from four different viewpoints, and the combination of these four points gives a sense of movement.

But *whose* movement?

We have already seen some instances of a combination of various phases of movement in which the eye traverses the *object* of the shots in one single movement. We may take as an example the montage of the three marble lions in a sequence of poses on the steps of Alupka Castle. Combined by montage, they give the illusion of a *single lion leaping to its feet.*[5]

Here we seem to have a similar case.

In this instance, however, is the effect of motion *of the figure itself* produced because its four sequential positions are perceived as four succeeding phases of movement, thereby resulting in the illusion of a continuous movement by the figure as a whole? This is the source of the dynamism to be found, for example, in the figures of Daumier and Tintoretto,[6] where the separate parts of a figure are disposed in accordance with the various phases of a single, continuous process of movement; the eye, as it travels over these separate phases of "distributed" movement, involuntarily performs the leap from one phase to another and perceives this sequence of impulses as uninterrupted movement.

Exactly the same means are employed to create the basic effect of dynamism in cinematography, where the only difference is that the projector shows to the spectator, in sequence and in the successive phases, not just separate parts of the figure but the figure as a whole.

It is interesting to note that in order to convey movement *expressively,* the film-maker is not content to use this basic effect of cinematic dynamism alone; to transmit movement in a way that is gripping and expressive, the cinema has recourse to something similar to the method of . . . Daumier and Tintoretto. In this case—in montage editing—the cinema reverts to showing dynamics through the separate parts of a figure. The question, however, remains: is this the case in the portrait of Yermolova or not?

The answer, of course, is a categorical negative!

Because what has here been fixed on canvas is not a series of four successive positions of an object but four successive positions of *the eye of the observer.* Therefore these four points are not a function of *the behavior of the object* (as with the aroused lion and Daumier's lively figures) but are a characteristic of *the behavior of the spectator.* And this behavior reveals itself in a movement from a viewpoint that is "above" to one that is "below" the figure, as though moving to a point . . . "at the feet" of the great actress!

But the behavior of the spectator can also be defined as the *attitude of the spectator;* or rather, it is the attitude imposed upon the spectator by the artist and it derives entirely from the attitude to the subject of the artist himself.

It is this—the artist's attitude—which obliges him to have recourse to the particular graphic structure which most fully expresses that attitude.

I think that if a line is capable in some way of expressing a thought and an attitude towards something (which it does here), the line of the viewpoint along the arc ABCD entirely corresponds to the idea of "admiration" which one involuntarily feels when looking at the portrait of Yermolova.

But that is not all.

This basic "tendency" in the overall composition of the portrait is reinforced by two more powerful means of influencing the spectator.

These are the spatial structuring and the use of color (or rather the use of light), which also modulate in a downward arc along with the movement towards close-up and the shift of the "set-up" from "shot" to "shot."

A constant *expansion of space* takes place in the progression through shots 1, 2, 3 and 4.

No. 2 presses closely up against the wall with the mirror.

No. 3 is projected against the apparent depth of the room reflected in the mirror.

No. 4 stands out against a background of immense, boundless space.

Thus from shot to shot the ever-enlarging image of Yermolova herself dominates an ever-expanding space.

But at the same time the shots become progressively brighter.

No. 1 is completely dominated by the black mass of the dress.

In No. 2 the black part of the figure ceases to function independently, but instead tends to lead the eye towards the brighter area of the face.

In No. 3 the remaining areas of black now only cast shadows on the bright face.

In No. 4 the main part of the frame is wholly taken up with the face, which seems to glow from within.

This increase in the intensity of lighting from shot to shot, merging into a single uninterrupted process, is perceived as a *gradual brightening,* an *increasing illumination* and *animation* of the actress's face, which gradually advances out of the dim background of the picture.

Unlike the movement of the set-up, however, these two characteristics do not relate to any action by the spectator but to the apparent behavior of the subject portrayed: thanks to them, Yermolova seems illuminated by a growing inner fire and by the light of inspiration, and that inspiration seems to radiate on to the ever-growing number of her enthusiastic admirers.

Thus a reciprocal interplay is set up between the *admiration of the enthusiastic spectator* in front of the picture and the *inspired actress* on the canvas—in exactly the same way that the auditorium and the stage once merged as both were captivated by the magic of her acting. It is interesting that by his compositional method Serov expresses graphically almost *literally* the very same things that Stanislavsky says about Yermolova in words (I take the liberty of stressing those words which relate directly to our analysis): "in each part that she played, M. N. Yermolova always conveyed a *special* spiritual image, which was unlike the previous one and unlike any other."[7]

The chosen method of composition is undoubtedly "special" and "unlike any other." The montage principle of composition used here is profoundly original and individual.

(Just what a disaster can result from failing to use a "special" approach to the solution of a similar problem in painting we shall see from another example, also from the area of portraiture, which will be illustrated below.)

"The roles created by Yermolova live on in the memory *with an independent existence,* despite the fact that they were all *created from the same organic material,* from her *single spiritual personality.*"

It would be hard to find a more exact graphic equivalent of what has been said here than the way in which Serov has broken up the picture, as we have seen, into four parts that are autonomous yet which simultaneously continue to exist as a single, indivisible, organic whole!

Taken separately, these "levels" are like the "roles" which live on "with an independent existence," while taken together they constitute the single organic whole of the "full-length shot," i.e., "her single spiritual personality."

"All her movements, words, actions . . . were suffused with fire from within by an emotion that could be warm and gentle or fiery and thrilling."

This is the same feeling that is conveyed with such perfection by the gradual lightening that occurs from level to level, on which we remarked above.

"For our generation . . . Yermolova was a symbol of . . . *strength, emotional power,* genuine *simplicity* and *modesty.*"

There is "simplicity" and "modesty" in the "conventional," unpretentious painterly means that are used in the picture with such astonishing restraint, both in the pose of the actress and in the color resolution of the portrait itself.

There is "strength" in the enlarging of the face from level to level.

And finally, *emotional power* is conveyed as the *unity of opposites* within the compositional principle.

Like the *unity of the consecutive and the simultaneous.*

Like the *simultaneity* of the existence of the picture both as a *single whole* and as a *system of successively enlarging shots,* into which the picture breaks down and from which the picture is again reconstituted into a whole.

I am profoundly convinced that the compositional principle which we have analyzed was not, of course, "consciously" selected but arose for Serov purely intuitively. In no way, however, does this lessen the force of the strict logic of what he did in the composition of this portrait.

We are well aware of how long and agonizingly Serov struggled over the composition of his portraits; how much time he spent on ensuring that the visual solution of the *psychological* task which he set himself in the portrait should *wholly* correspond to the image that suggested itself to him at the meeting, or rather the "confrontation," with the sitter.

I quote at random from his letters.

"You know, I think, that for me each portrait is like living through an illness" (1887, to his wife).

"This evening I shall try and sketch the princess (Yusupova—S.M.E.) in pastels and charcoal. I think I know how to do her, yet—I don't know; with painting you can never predict anything beforehand" (1903).

"And then if I concentrate on one thing—even if it's just Girshman's nose—I find I'm stuck up a blind alley" (1910).

"Well now, it seems that I have finished my paintings, although as always I could keep working on them, I suppose, for an eternity, or at least for half an eternity" (1903).

And above all there is the invariable, the principal, the fundamental theme: *"The chief thing is—how to capture the character of the sitter."*

In this painful movement towards the fixing on canvas of the image floating dazzlingly and tantalizingly before the artist's eyes, the creative impulse gives rise to those amazingly complex and unyielding structures which later astonish us with their inevitability and immutability. [. . .][8]

Let us, however, return once more to the purely compositional aspect of the picture, whose effect has been to give us such a remarkably vital impression of the great Yermolova, and we shall find an astounding link with our initial example of the barricade. For there, too, two qualities emerged simultaneously: the depiction of a barricade together with a certain outline which revealed the essential, overall meaning of the barricade as an element in a struggle. By forcing the eye to follow its zigzags, the particular shape of that jagged line conveyed a *sense of conflict*. The feeling that it aroused was imprinted on our consciousness as the perception of a *struggle*. Every variation of the zigzag line AB from the straight line CD can be perceived as a thrust exerted on it from opposing sides, which with alternating success strike it at points d, d1, d2, d3, d4, d5 along the straight line and displace it towards points c, c1, c2, c3, c4, c5 (see fig. 2.2). The "alternation of success" may be seen from the adjoining column, which can be interpreted as a chart of the struggle between two forces.

Both sets of quantities are perceived simultaneously, and the result is the depiction of a barricade that is steeped in a feeling of struggle (not to be found to the same degree in a picture of a barricade which has not been treated in like manner).

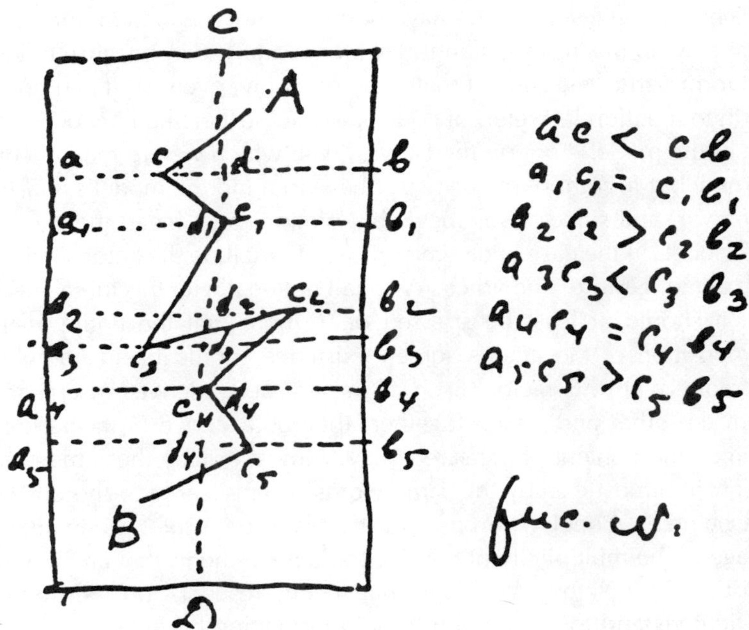

FIGURE 2.2.

In the portrait of Yermolova we have exactly the same thing—with the difference, of course, that the expressive message and the content of the drawing are not the same and the expressive aim is different. The variation between the two is not, however, limited to this.

The line CD is not actually drawn as such, nor even suggested, but is a line made up of a series of imaginary points that the eye follows as it moves; moreover, the plane of this imaginary line does not coincide with the plane of the picture, but is perpendicular to it (see fig. 2.1). Yet at the same time the line also derives from a more profound perception of the subject matter than the mere visual registration of its outward appearance. This deeper perception is inextricably linked with a more profound interpretation of the picture: its *meaning* is made up of a detailed apprehension of the subject plus our individual attitude to it. For a scrap-dealer the barricade is by no means an image of struggle but is a collection of second-hand goods suitable for resale (a bed, armchairs, shop signs, barrels and so on), while for a tourist it represents a heap of potential souvenirs!

We see in the portrait a complete repetition of the same multi-level construct noted above.

There is one level which I have purposely not mentioned, although I have by no means forgotten it. I shall not analyze it, because it does not form part of the subject matter of this study; even so, it can do no harm to mention it. I refer, of course, to the most elementary positioning of the model—not *on the canvas* (with which we are mainly concerned) but *in front of the canvas*. I have in mind the model's *real-life behavior,* and since this is inevitably motionless, I mean the *pose* of the model. In the case of cinema this would include the actor's behavior, mime, gesture, and voice. We shall not deal with this theme here, but it should at least be stressed once more that the entire visual composition of the actor's screen existence should be in complete harmony with this factor. Each of these aspects derives inseparably from the other and, taken together, they both derive from the idea, theme, and content of the screenplay. Almost exactly the same comment, in almost exactly the same words, is applicable to the pose of the painter's model. The pose must equally be a total, generalizing image of the multiplicity of positions and movements that are characteristic of the sitter. We know that in this respect, too, Serov was meticulous and took as much trouble in placing his sitter in front of the easel as he did in positioning the portrait on the canvas. See how much careful thought has gone into the poses of the Gruzenbergs, Miss Gershelman, or Lamanova. Or look at the pose of Yermolova herself. In the pose, of course, as in everything else about the picture there should also be a second level of generalization, above and beyond any generalization at the everyday, realistic level. I refer to the metaphor of pose and gesture (on which we have cited quotations from Engels and Gratiolet about people in action or actors), or rather the image—for example "the image of the hero," "the image of the leader," "the image of the owner," or "the image of the traitor"—which through the choice of pose and the use of the painter's medium should emerge from the straightforward anatomical depiction of the sitter.

Here, I think, lies the watershed between two different types of realists such as Serov and Repin.[9]

Repin stops at the point of realistic generalization. Here he is truly great: how vividly the "actors" in the scene of *Pushkin at the Examination* generalize their roles. A generalizing image of wider import, however, is beyond his powers. If he attempts one, the result is either allegory (what spaciousness) achieved by the *setting* of the scene, or else such appalling paintings as his version of the "inspired" Tolstoy (that full-length portrait of Tolstoy in which he is shown with arms slightly outspread and a face shining from within with a pink glow, like one of those paper lanterns used to illuminate a summer garden-party).

I have in mind Repin's portrait of Lev Tolstoy known by the title, *Tolstoy Renouncing Worldly Life*. It was painted in 1912 for the Moscow Society of Art and Literature. In it Repin set himself a task similar to that undertaken by Serov in his portrait of Yermolova. The portrait was an attempt to show the inner translucence, the other-worldly light shining within a great writer who has achieved the highest degree of spirituality.

We have observed the complex but consistent path followed by Serov in order to achieve his desired result by purely compositional and painterly means. Nor should we forget how Serov went to the extremes of "asceticism" in his use of pictorial effects by omitting even the slightest gesture by Yermolova: everything is intended to concentrate the picture's effect on the great actress's inner spiritual resources ("Her unfathomable spiritual depths," in the words of Stanislavsky). We have demonstrated above how consistently the sense of "inward illumination" and "inner light" were achieved in her portrait.

This is not Repin's method: he goes for it "head-on," in a direct "plain man's" fashion.

Whereas Serov—painting an *actress*, of all people—removed from his canvas everything theatrical, everything connected with the stage (up to and including such eloquent means of expression as gesture), not only does Repin above all emphasize gesture but *exaggerated* gesture—in other words, the pose. And who is his subject? One of the sternest of moralists and castigators of everything faked and theatrical, to say nothing of the merely false (one has only to recall Tolstoy's Savonarola-like intolerance of even Shakespeare). Yet here, with the artist trying so hard to be "monumental," the great sage (so often drawn by Repin himself in his plain yet truly monumental everyday simplicity) suddenly becomes a "saintly" little old man with his arms inanely stretched out at his sides!

Even worse, however, is the fact that Repin tries to convey the idea of "inward illumination" equally simplistically, with head-on literalism. As a result, instead of the head of a great sage we have something like a Chinese lantern, with the simulacrum of a literal, physical source of light inside it, a source of light whose pink glow shines through a pink-tinted face!

One cannot help recalling the words of Chekhov . . .

> The beer was served. Gvozdikov sat down, lined up all six bottles in front of him and, with a loving glance at them, started to drink. After three glasses he felt as though a lamp had been lit inside his chest and another inside his head: he had such a feeling of warmth, brightness and wellbeing. . . .
> After the second bottle he felt that the light in his head had been put out and it was growing dark.[10]

And this portrait was painted seven years after Serov had achieved such a brilliant solution of an analogous problem!

The error of Repin's method lies in his wanting to convey the *generalized* theme, i.e., a theme extending beyond the limits of simple depiction, by purely *depictive* means. The result is a work of appalling falsity. We have seen that an aim which "transcends" mere depiction—a generalization *about* what is depicted—should employ means which transcend the artist's normal methods. We have seen this in the very primitive example of the barricade, where the expressive character of the compositional outline is utilized. We have seen this in equal degree in a perfect example: the portrait of Yermolova. Reread once more the passage which describes how this "apotheosis" of the actress is realized, in particular the means whereby Serov achieves the sense of inner illumination of the face, as distinct from Repin's portrait of Tolstoy, where it has been attempted by crassly literal pictorial means, by a flat, empty picture of the old man's head, lit from within as though by "the light of thought."

Our reaction to this approach can only, of course, be one of bewilderment. Compare it with the mastery by which something no less elusive—the sense of a ballerina's "airiness"—is conveyed in [Serov's] portrait of Anna Pavlova merely by draughtsmanship and the use of background, for she is not depicted in flight when the quality of lightness would be conveyed by the pose itself. The same comments apply to pre-screen composition (in this respect the screen is, after all, only the more sophisticated brother of the painter's expanse of stretched canvas).

Here, too, *Yermolova* is equally perfect.

Let us repeat: what makes her portrait so expressive is the fact that we have before us in this picture the *simultaneous unity* of monumental *immobility* and a whole gamut of *dynamic movement:* the "zoom" effect of ever-increasing close-ups; the growing movement of space and light; the shifting viewpoint in relation to the subject.

This combination of contradictions within a unity also contributes to producing that thrill which grips us whenever we are fortunate enough to live through a direct experience of the dialectical process. It is also interesting to observe that the effect has been achieved without a departure from realistic depiction, which, despite everything, retains its representational integrity. [. . . .][11]

Let us return to *Yermolova* one last time and to that imaginary line joining up each successive viewpoint; this "all-round observation" of the subject, which we remarked in the portrait of Yermolova, is *exactly* what happens when we progress beyond the limitations of single set-up cinematography! It is a precise illustration of how in montage the elements into which an event is broken up are reassembled into the montage image of that event. To describe this complex dual process, in 1933 I invented the term *mise en cadre* (in all respects analogous to the concept of *mise en scène*).[12]

We shall return to this subject when we move on to the next section. . . .

There only remains to draw one further generalizing conclusion from the total phenomenon which we have investigated in such detail with all the examples given in the first section, and which stood out with particular force in the case of the portrait of Yermolova.

The simultaneity with which the construct exists at two levels—in the *whole* and in the *parts*—is the precise analogue of a fundamental characteristic of human perception in general, which has the ability to comprehend a phenomenon in two ways: *as a whole* and *in its details; immediately* and *in mediated form; complexly* and *differentially.* The terms we use depend on the area we choose to examine, but this peculiarity of human perception is to be found in equal degree in all aspects of man's activity and thought and it invariably permeates them. . . . At various periods of mankind's development, these two characteristics of perception have been distinct or separated from each other. Engels discussed this exhaustively in *Anti-Dühring.* Only when man reaches the appropriate age in his personal existence, in the existence of his species (social development), and in the existence of his society (the stage of dialectical philosophy which characterizes mankind in its maturity) does this separation merge into the unity of a new quality. The one-sidedness of the *child's* synthesizing mode of thought becomes the *adult's* analytical thinking, having acquired the differential principle. In the same way the mind of *man at the dawn of culture* evolves into the *mind of man in the epoch of a developed culture;* similarly, philosophy develops from *primeval chaos* into *materialistic dialectics.*

The curious feature about this process, of course, is the following: synthesizing perception is, of course, the lower stage of perception (*vide* Engels), whereas differential perception is a step forward (*vide* ditto). Observation which is capable of *generalizing* is, of course, the highest type of all. (It figures in science as the *generalized concept,* in art as the *generalized image,* belonging in equal degree to the highest category of man's intellectual activity; provided, of course, that one is either consciously or intuitively directed towards the progressive development or advancement of social conditions, to the degree and in the direction permitted by the social epoch.)

Here a contradiction seems to arise: the highest stage—the generalized image—seems *in visual terms* to coincide with the most primitive type of synthesizing perception. But this is only an apparent contradiction. In reality we have in this instance that very same "apparent reversion to the older stage" which Lenin mentions in discussing the dialectics of phenomena. The fact is that generalization is *a true synthesis,* i.e., simultaneously a synthesizing (immediate) and a differential (mediated) perception of the event (and a perception *about* the event).

A generalization from which the purely representational element has been removed would be a bare, non-objective abstraction dangling in mid-air. Such would be a third version of our barricade, so generalized as to be deprived not of the compositional outline (as distinct from the first version), but of the actual picture, and retaining only the "image-expressing" zigzag line of its contour. All the "pictorial" and "expressive" qualities would instantly evaporate from the sketch, while the zigzag itself might not be interpreted as a barricade but as . . . *anything you like:* as a graph of the rise and fall of prices, or as a seismographic trace of subterranean tremors, and so on and so forth (see fig. 2.3). It would be open to all these interpretations until the abstraction reverted (as in our case) to the representation of some concrete, objective subject matter.[13]

In a sketch that contains the full complement of elements, its main, fundamental characteristic is clear, namely that the effectiveness of our chosen examples rests on the fact that each element in them appeals to its own particular part of our perception and that the combination of them appeals to the totality of our synthesizing consciousness, drawing the spectator "from head to foot" into its effect.

It is this characteristic of human perception, of course, which deter-

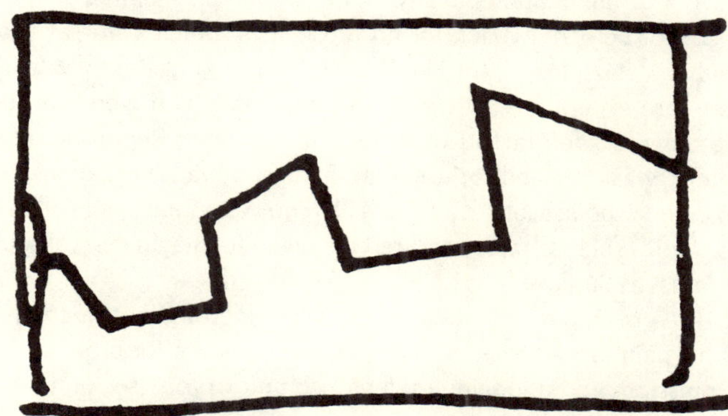

Figure 2.3.

mines both the fact of the structure and the existence of precisely this kind of structure in any truly complete and perfect human artefact.

In this drawing *the nature of the artefact is a reflection of the characteristics of human consciousness—of Man—within its formal structure alone.* This will be *as much reflected in the form of the artefact* as the reflection of Man is the prime condition of a vital and meaningful *content of the artefact.*

Having noted this we should not forget it while dealing with the immediate problems of montage, because we shall return again to the principle we have just enunciated.

Post Scriptum

I don't like Repin. That, however, has nothing to do with my analysis of the method that made his portrait of Tolstoy such a disaster. In judging it so unfavorably I am in the company of Igor Grabar, a fervent admirer of Repin's painting. Although he does not analyze the reasons for the ugliness of this particular work by Repin, he does not mince words in his criticism of it. In a chapter significantly entitled "Downhill," Grabar writes: "But worst of all, it must be said, is the portrait commissioned in 1912 by the Moscow Society of Art and Literature, and which was entitled by the artist *Tolstoy Renouncing Worldly Life.*"[14]

I think this quotation disposes of any accusation that I am prejudiced in my criticism of this portrait:

> We now come to a most essential factor in Repin's work, *his lack of imagination*—not only in *The Zaporozhians* and *St Nicholas of M* . . . , but in all Repin's work in general. Lack of imagination need not be a drawback for an artist; it is sufficient to say that neither Velázquez, Frans Hals, or Holbein had it. But they, with very rare exceptions, never tackled themes which were outside the range of their talents or beyond their ability; Repin, unfortunately, was attracted to just such themes: *Sofia, The Zaporozhians, St Nicholas;* later *Get Thee Behind Me, Satan,* and others. For topics such as these required the gigantic imagination of such an artist as Surikov. . . .
>
> Three of Repin's characteristics determined the entire content of his painting—a lack of imagination, a passion for problems of expression, and a longing to depict complex processes of human action, movement, and thought, chiefly as seen through their physical manifestations.[15]

Let us allow ourselves to take the *literal* meaning of that missing trait: "imagination." I believe that it should least of all be interpreted in the sense of "invention" or "fantasy." It has two main connotations: 1) an entering into the image of what is depicted, and 2) a transposition "into image" of what you are depicting. Hence, the portraits of Repin are really, if anything, an "atlas" (Grabar somewhere calls *The Zaporozhians* an "atlas of laughter") of types and prototypes, features great and small taken from nature as though to compile a textbook for an actor who might wish to play them (that is why on my bookshelves monographs on Repin are to be found among the books that are of use to actors, not among the books on painting at all!), whereas Serov's portraits are like a gallery of uniquely *personified* images of living people, acted out by the artist. Later, when discussing El Greco, we shall again come across the case of the artist as actor, putting his own role-playing into his works.[16] But in this matter El Greco will not be in the same class as Serov, who was a master of absolute self-personification in the image he created, whereas El Greco transposes "into himself" all the multiplicity of his subjects and models. It is to this second point, i.e., Serov's ability (and his method) not only to depict but to "imagine" what he depicts, that the whole of this section on the Yermolova portrait is devoted. Comparing Serov to Repin only serves to consolidate our position, and it is further confirmed by the characteristic, mentioned by Grabar, of Repin's lack of imagination. [. . .][17]

I would not like to leave the subject of Repin without having defined more precisely what I mean about the nature of his art. No one will deny that the realistic figures which he *depicts* are typical. But the point is that his work as a painter is limited to representative depiction. Repin does not typify his subjects by simultaneously depicting the man and generalizing his features into an image. Repin does something different: he copies from nature the features of people he has found who happen to be typical. Typicality is thus not achieved by artistic means but through the features of a model, conscientiously recorded by the painter. It is in this sense that the expression "a well-set scene" was appropriate when we used it with reference to *Pushkin at the Examination*, but apart from qualifying Repin as a skillful stage director we might also call him a good entrepreneur in the skill of type-casting his actors.

For the filmmaker, it would be difficult to find a more exciting description of typecasting than that relating to another realist artist: Surikov, in particular the case of the mathematics teacher who turned out to be the perfect "image" for Menshikov.[18] Surikov, however, differs from Repin in that he uses a large number of purely painterly means to create the image of a man and the image of the scene in which he is placed. The sense of "enclosure" comes out with special force in one particular scene, which is also thematically linked with imprisonment or enclosure. And this theme in itself brings us back again to Menshikov, this time not to his physical prototype but to the picture of his exile in Beryozova.

Descriptions of dead bodies being transported over long distances usually create a very powerful impression: those coffins enclosed one inside the other—an oak coffin, then a lead coffin, a covering over the oak, a covering over the lead—as in the engravings of Napoleon in his coffin after the shipment of his body from the island of St Helena; the body seems outlined by the heavy, quadruple contour of the coffins, from the inside one to the plain outer box surrounding the inner layers. I don't know whether the image of Napoleon on St Helena was hovering in front of Surikov's mind's eye when he was painting his picture, but whenever I look at *Menshikov at Beryozova* I involuntarily think of the prisoner of St Helena, whose wings have also been inexorably clipped by the walls of the tiny cottage, by the fence of the little surrounding garden, by the unyielding contours of the island itself and the vast watery space around it, to say nothing of the English guardships patroling the coast: such are the images of Bonaparte alive (if such an existence can be called living) or of the dead Bonaparte encased in the fourfold outline of his coffins! And that, to me at least, is how Menshikov appears, with his passionate, unbending nature, as through buried alive and fettered by his Beryozova exile in four coffins which clasp him one after another in their embrace—with only the slight difference that his coffins are not physically real but are a metaphorical effect achieved by means of the "concentric" rectangles of the composition which squeeze each other inward.

In the center of the composition is his tightly clenched fist, an image of the will-power by which he restrains his urge to hurl himself pointlessly into the fray. The first is "gripped" by the huddled group of his family, pressing closely in upon him for compositional reasons. The rough-hewn log walls of the cottage clasp the group in their turn. The dim light of a winter's day shines through the window, so that we sense that the cottage, too, is in the grip of frost, even before our eye is allowed to come to rest on the pitiless rim of the frame, which encloses the picture as a whole, reminding us of the famous prisoner in the reign of Louis XI, who for years was kept in an iron cage which allowed him neither to stand up nor so much as to straighten his back. With Surikov, this feeling stretches past the edges of his canvas and extends beyond this picture to others; *Menshikov* stands at the center of a whole cycle, which includes *Boyarina Morozova* and *The Morning of the Execution of the Streltsy,* as distinct from another cycle linked by thematic unity—*The Capture of the Snowbound Town, The Conquest of Siberia,* and *Suvorov Crossing the Alps.*

We shall find nothing analogous to this with Repin. In his pictures, typicality is achieved by other means; we have attempted to point out exactly what these means are. The typical as a simultaneous demonstration of both a phenomenon and a conclusion (generalization) drawn from that phenomenon; the typical, fully realized so as to embrace both objective representation and generalized image: this is not within Repin's powers. And that, perhaps, is the reason why he is so strong as a purely representational painter and why he is so popular with those who are looking for realistic depiction above all. Here, too, perhaps, is the secret of the diametrically opposite effect made by the two exhibitions, both held in the Tretyakov Gallery—one in 1934, the other in 1935—the first showing Repin, the second Serov. The general impression produced by each exhibition as a whole repeated in reverse the effect of comparing the separate, individual works. Each one of Serov's pictures, in its typicality and in its unexcelled ability to express character, surpasses Repin. The ensemble of the Repin exhibition—as a comprehensive, all-embracing "portrait of the epoch"—far outdoes Serov's incomparable gallery of faces, through each *separate* one of which there speaks the whole epoch. Why is this? I think it is precisely because a generalization within a picture, i.e., the element which goes beyond the limits of representation, is inaccessible to Repin; that everything he depicts, whether it is a pure tone or a pure color, is taken directly from nature. He never succeeds in mediating a generalizing statement on canvas. Only in the multitude (the unrestrained abundance of Repin's paintings sanctions the use of this archaism to indicate their quantity!) of the total collection can there emerge a generalization, of whose features each separate picture is no more than a single *stroke*. With Serov nothing like this occurs: each portrait, each picture by Serov, is its own world, capable of containing an idea in all its dimensions. *The Rape of Europa* alongside *The Girshmans, Lamanova* alongside *Peter* [the Great] remain autonomous worlds that do not merge with each other; whereas [Repin's] *The Church Procession* has much in common with his *Ivan the Terrible,* and nothing prevents *St Nicholas of Myra* from combining with the portrait of Rubinstein and *The Archdeacon* to form a general physiognomy of the period. This applies to Repin's entire *opus.*

Interestingly enough, the same thing occurs with the cycles of paintings within his total *œuvre.* His cycles are not of the Surikov type, that is to say they are not unified by linking images. With Repin, the cycles are formed by unity of subject matter. Most interesting in this regard is the case of one of Repin's last works, in which a cycle is made up of separate paintings intended to form part of one joint picture. These exist both as a cycle of several portraits and as the large work containing them all. Amazingly, whereas the collection of individual paintings produces the most striking impression, the picture which incorporates them all leaves us quite cold. Wherein lies the secret? In the fact that the work which unites them in one is a mere *collection,* a mere process of sticking them into one common *picture,* and is not a *generalization* into a single whole. Let me reveal that I am referring to Repin's picture *The State Council,* which is shown to the spectator in two forms—both as a completed picture and as a collection of superb portrait sketches, the studies that were made in preparation for the big picture.

The effect of the big picture is to leave us more than indifferent (not only because of the theme!) but basically because of its qualities of artistic composition—or rather because of its total lack of them. A glance at the great variety of the individual studies conveys an astounding effect, so strong, in fact, that I still recall the impression which they made on me the first time I saw them, and that was a long time ago, before the war, at the exhibition on the Field of Mars in Petersburg where they had their first public showing. Readers may make their own judgments on my age and the distance in time! I saw these sketches for the second time at the Repin exhibition of 1934, but this time alongside the completed picture. I tested my recollection of it, and was not only convinced that it was right but I think I also defined the secret of why the two forms of the work made such differing impressions. The fact is that when the spectator runs his eye over the individual portraits, he forms a generalized image: that of the collective face of the State Council, which comes across so clearly through the features of its members that there also emerges the face of the regime of which they are the supreme executives. Nothing of the sort comes out of the group picture itself. The figures and features are transplanted into it from the separate portraits in exactly the same way that spectators are seated in an auditorium—according to the numbering of their tickets—only here they are disposed according to rank, i.e., on grounds dictated by governmental statutes and decrees and not by artistic criteria at all.

Why is it that in the big picture the faces do not merge into a collective image? It is because in a picture that generalizing aspect and image have to be given by the artist himself. If he fails to provide it, the spectator is disorientated, and in order for him to assemble the elements of the picture into his own overall conception or generalizing image, he must take the finished picture apart, break it up into fragments and then consciously reassemble them; in other words he must do a "home-made" version of . . . the preparatory sketches, in which the artist's *strictly pictorial* mode of combining them—which goes no further than spacing out the individual figures!—at least does not disturb his own imaginative combination of his figures! The conclusion to be drawn is that the combination of the *separate portraits* on *pictorial* grounds not only fails to provide any new generalizing, interpretative element but even deprives them of that expressive force which, in each separate portrait, derived from the spectator's need to perceive each one mentally in a *montage-like* relationship with all the others. It is this compositional montage—this process of grasping the whole in a single action and simultaneously subordinating it to a rhythm which would define and generalize the theme of that action—that Repin the artist has failed to do. Please do not think that I am making some kind of "leftist," anti-realist demand: accusations of the kind I have made above cannot be made against the densely peopled canvases of Surikov (*Boyarina Morozova*), of Alexander Ivanov (*Christ Appearing to the Multitude*),[19] or of Leonardo da Vinci (*The Last Supper*). It is significant that *Christ Appearing to the Multitude,* which is also on view to the public as both a collection of individual heads and as a complete picture, *in no way* produces the effect that we have observed in the case of Repin. With Ivanov the individual heads are separate and are simply interpreted as disconnected portraits (one of the surprising features being that the head of Christ is copied from the [same artist's] head of Apollo). Yet the true power of a dynamic image emerges when these same heads, in the implacable hands of the painter, force the spectator to perceive an expressive image in the unique compositional structure with which he has linked them all. The whole scope of Ivanov's mastery of composition stands out with particular clarity in his sketches illustrating the scriptures, in which there are some quite unforgettable pictures such as *The Stoning* [of the woman taken in adultery] and others. The fact remains that with Repin the generalizing factor is not to be found within one picture but in the combination of a number of pictures, a process which the artist himself fails to carry out when putting them on to one canvas. Either the resulting picture does not work at all (as with The State Council) or the outcome is what happened in the portrait of Tolstoy.

Clearly I am not alone in reacting to *The State Council* in the way described above. N. Radlov, for instance, writing on a quite different topic, namely Repin's painting technique, has this to say when referring to "the group of works in which . . . the nature of Repin's talent stands out most plainly and obviously. These are," in Radlov's opinion, "Repin's studies for *The State Council*." He goes on to say:

> In both the ends and the means of pictorial representation this work entirely reflects Repin's talent and strength. These are a series of characteristic [portraits], seized rapidly and immediately, as was demanded by the shortness of the sittings, and therefore devoid of any attempt at typification or drawing theoretical conclusions. The method used here by the artist is one of simplified tonal distinctions without any attempts at expressive colouring or sophisticated draughtsmanship.[20]

Thus Repin's "talent and strength" lie in the graphic "immediacy" of what he records. His drawings, free of "typification" and "theoretical conclusions," i.e., of generalization by artistic means, best correspond to his "talent and strength." The other characteristics mentioned—the *simplified* tonality, the lack of pretensions to expressing coloring, and the *unsophisticated* draftsmanship—all mean that the studies not only create a generalized image by virtue of their *function*, but that on *structural* and *technical* grounds they are typical "montage" fragments.

Let us conclude our analysis of Repin with a final thought. A generalized image of Tolstoy, worthy of the methods used by Serov, which Repin failed to create in the portrait we have analyzed, nevertheless does exist in Repin's *œuvre*. But where? It is to be found in the generalizing image and representation of Tolstoy which emerges from the loving, heartfelt sketches and pictures in which Repin has purely graphically caught the great old man at a number of separate moments. In these innumerable works Repin managed to fix pictorially one *single* characteristic of Tolstoy at a time, catching *one* feature in each picture or sketch. The graphic artist can ask no more.

NOTES

1. Maria N. Yermolova (1853–1928) was the leading Russian tragic actress of her generation, best known for her performances in the plays of Ostrovsky and in the title roles of such classics as Lessing's *Emilia Galotti,* Schiller's *Maria Stuart,* and Racine's *Phèdre.* Valentin A. Serov (1865–1911), Russian painter, member of the Wanderers (see below, n. 4), did a series of portraits of figures from the artistic world, including Rimsky-Korsakov, Chaliapin, Gorky and Rubinstein. His portrait of Yermolova discussed here was painted in 1905.

2. Ivan A. Aksionov (1884–1935), Russian theatre critic and historian, specialist in Elizabethan drama.

3. K. S. Stanislavsky, *Moya zhizn' v iskusstve* (Moscow, 1962; reprint of 2d ed., 1928), 70–71. The abridged English translation by J. J. Robbins (C. Stanislavski, *My Life in Art* [Harmondsworth, 1967]) does not include this passage in chap. 8, "Russian Dramatic Schools."

4. Paul Signac (1863–1935), French neo-Impressionist landscape painter. The Wanderers were a group of naturalist painters, including Repin (see below, n. 9), who rebelled against the Imperial Academy of Arts in 1870. Their paintings were characterized by a realism imbued with an element of social criticism. They were committed to showing their works as widely as possible through touring exhibitions; hence their name *Peredvizhniki,* the Wanderers, or Itinerants.

5. See E's own analysis of this sequence in "The Dramaturgy of Film Form," *S. M. Eisenstein: Selected Works,* 1:172–74.

6. Honoré Daumier (1808–79), French caricaturist and lithographer. Jacopo Tintoretto (1518–94), Venetian painter.

7. For this and the three subsequent quotations, see n. 3.

8. Lacuna in the text.

9. For Serov, see n. 1. Ilya Ye. Repin (1844–1930), Russian painter associated with the Wanderers.

10. Chekhov's short story *Svidanie khotya i ne sostoyalos', no . . .* [Although the meeting never took place . . .] was written in 1882.

11. Lacuna in the text.

12. In his unfinished manuscript for the book "Direction" [Rezhissura]. The first published use of the term was in "'Eh!' On the Purity of Film Language," *S. M. Eisenstein: Selected Works,* 1:290.

13. Here it is tempting to suggest a link with the Constructivists who in Soviet Russia included Tatlin, Rodchenko, Gabo, and Pevsner. They espoused a nonobjective socially useful production art that differed radically from the Russian Realist tradition exemplified by the Wanderers. But the congruence would be incomplete and ineffective. The Constructivists aestheticised the physical structure of materials into a central theme of their work, to a greater degree than our examples of psychologically expressive structuring of a phenomenon.

14. Igor E. Grabar (1871–1960), Russian neo-Impressionist painter and art historian. His two-volume work on Repin was published in Moscow in 1937. This quotation is from 2:151.

15. Ibid., 2:78. Vasili I. Surikov (1848–1916), Russian painter associated with the Wanderers. Two of his most famous paintings, *Menshikov at Beryozova* (1883), discussed below, and *The Boyarina Morozova* (1887), hang in the Tretyakov Gallery.

16. E is here referring to his draft article "El Greco y el cine" [El Greco and Cinema], not included in the present edition. A French translation is available: F. Albera (ed.), *S. M. Eisenstein, Cinématisme: Peinture et cinéma* (Brussels, 1980), 15–104.

17. The manuscript breaks off at this point halfway down the page. The text that follows begins on a new page.

18. See above, n. 15.

19. Alexander A. Ivanov (1806–58) painted *Christ Appearing to the Multitude,* for which he produced over 300 preparatory sketches between 1833 and 1857. It is also in the Tretyakov Gallery collection.

20. N. E. Radlov, *Ot Repina do Grigor'eva* [From Repin to Grigoriev] (Moscow, 1923).

The Spatial Form of a Character

The Spatial Whole of the Hero and His World in Verbal Art: The Theory of Horizon and Environment

To what extent does verbal art have to do with the spatial form of the hero and his world? There can be no doubt, of course, that verbal art deals with the hero's exterior and with the spatial world in which the event of his life unfolds. What gives rise to considerable doubts, however, is the question of whether verbal art has to do with the *spatial form* of the hero as an *artistic form;* in most cases, the problem is resolved in a negative sense. To resolve the problem correctly, it is necessary to take into account the twofold sense of aesthetic form.

Inner and Outer Form

As we have already indicated, aesthetic form may be both an inner and an outer, or empirical, form. Or, in other words, it may be the form of the aesthetic object, i.e., the form of the world which is constructed on the basis of a given work of art but does not coincide with that work; or it may be the form of the work of art itself, i.e., a material form.[1]

On the basis of this distinction, one cannot claim, of course, that the aesthetic objects in the different arts (painting, poetry, music, etc.) are all the same and that the difference between the arts consists,

M. M. Bakhtin, ''The Spatial Form of a Character'' (fragment), in *Art and Answerability: Early Philosophical Essays,* trans. Vadim Liapunov, ed. Michael Holquist and Vadim Liapunov (Austin: University of Texas Press, 1990 [1921–24]), 92–99. Copyright © 1990, by permission of the University of Texas Press.

therefore, only in the different means used for the actualization or construction of the aesthetic object (i.e., the difference is reduced solely to the technical or instrumental moment). This is not at all the case. On the contrary, the material form, the form that determines whether a given work is a pictorial or a poetic or a musical work of art, also determines, in an essential way, the structure of the appropriate aesthetic object, rendering that object somewhat one-sided by accentuating some particular aspect of it. But in spite of that, the aesthetic object is many-sided and *concrete* nevertheless—as many-sided and concrete as that cognitive-ethical reality (the "lived" or experienced world) which is justified and consummated in it artistically. This world, moreover—the world consummated in the aesthetic object—achieves the highest degree of concreteness and many-sidedness in *verbal* creation (it is least concrete and many-sided in music).

To be sure, verbal creation does not produce an *external* spatial form, for it does not operate with spatial material the way painting, drawing, or sculpture does; the material it works with—language—is in its essence nonspatial (sound in music is even less spatial).[2] The aesthetic object itself, however—the object imaged through the words—consists not of words alone, of course, even if it includes a great deal that is purely verbal. And *this object of aesthetic vision* has an artistically valid *inner spatial form* which is imaged through the words of a given work (whereas in painting it is imaged through colors, and in drawing through lines—and, once again, it does not follow that the aesthetic object consists here of nothing but lines or colors; the whole point is that a concrete object is to be produced out of such lines and colors).

There can be no doubt, then, about the existence of a spatial form within an aesthetic object which is expressed verbally in a given work. A different question is *how* this inner spatial form gets actualized: whether it has to be reproduced in a purely *visual* representation[3] (a visually full and distinct representation), or whether the only thing that gets actualized is an emotional-volitional *equivalent* of it, i.e., a feeling-tone,[4] an emotional coloring corresponding to that form (visual representation can be intermittent and fleeting in this case, or it may even be entirely absent, being replaced by words).[5] A thorough elaboration of the question so posed exceeds the bounds of the present inquiry and has its proper place in the aesthetics of verbal creation. As far as our problem is concerned, a few brief remarks on this question should suffice.

Even in the visual arts, inner spatial form is never actualized as a *visually* full and complete form (just as the temporal form, for that matter, is never actualized as a phonically full and complete form). *Visual* fullness and completeness are proper only to the external or material form of a work, and the qualities of this external form are, as it were, transposed upon the inner form (even in the visual arts, the visual image of inner form is to a considerable extent subjective). The visual inner form is experienced emotionally and volitionally *as if* it were visually full and complete, but this fullness and completeness can never be a really actualized representation. Of course, the degree to which inner form is actualized in visual representation varies in different kinds of verbal creation and in different individual works.

In narrative literature, this degree of visual actualization is higher: the description of the hero's exterior in the novel, for example, must necessarily be recreated visually, even if the image produced on the basis of verbal material will be visually subjective with different readers. In lyric poetry, the degree of actualization is lowest of all, especially in the Romantic lyric. In lyric poetry, the frequently heightened degree of visual actualization (a habit inculcated by the novel) destroys the aesthetic impression. In all lyric poetry, however, we meet everywhere with the emotional-volitional equivalent of an object's exterior, that is, with an emotional-volitional directedness upon this possible, although not visualized, exterior—with a directedness that produces this exterior as an artistic value. That is why we must recognize and must understand the *plastic-pictorial* moment or constituent in verbal creation.

Man's outer body is *given;* his outer boundaries and those of his world are *given* (given in the extra-aesthetic givenness of life). This is a necessary and inalienable moment of being as a given. Consequently, they need to be aesthetically received, recreated, fashioned, and justified. And this is precisely what is accomplished by art with all the means at its disposal—with colors, lines, masses, words, sounds. Inasmuch as the artist has to do with man's existence and with his world, he has also to do with the givenness of man in space as a necessary constituent of human existence. And in transposing this existence of man to the aesthetic plane, the artist must transpose to this plane man's exterior as well, within the bounds which are determined by the type of material he utilizes (e.g., colors, sounds, etc.).

A poet creates the hero's exterior, the spatial form of the hero and his world, by means of verbal material; the meaninglessness of this exterior from within and its cognitional factuality from without are rendered meaningful and justified by the poet aesthetically, that is, rendered valid artistically.

The external image of the hero and his world, expressed in words—regardless of whether it is visualized (as it is to some extent in the novel, e.g.) or whether it is experienced only in emotional-volitional terms—has the significance of a consummating form, that is, the external image is not only "expressive," but is "impressive" artistically as well. All of the propositions we have advanced above are applicable here as well—the verbal portrait is subject to them just as much as the pictorial portrait. Here as well, it is only the position of being situated outside the hero that enables the author to produce the aesthetic value of the hero's exterior: the spatial form *of* the hero expresses the author's relationship *to* the hero. Here as well, the author must assume a firm stand outside the hero and his world and utilize all the transgredient features of the hero's exterior.

The verbal work of art is created from outside each one of its heroes, and, in reading, we must follow the heroes from outside, not from within. Yet it is precisely in the case of verbal creation (and in the case of music even more so, of course) that the purely "expressive" interpretation of the exterior appears to be especially seductive and convincing, inasmuch as the author/beholder's situatedness outside the hero lacks here the spatial distinctness it has in the visual arts (visual representation being replaced here by an emotional-volitional equivalent "affixed" to words). On the other hand, language as a material is not sufficiently neutral in relation to the cognitive-ethical sphere, where it is used as both self-expression and communication, i.e., is used expressively. And these expressive habits of using language (giving utterance to oneself and designating objects) are transposed by us into our apprehension of works of verbal art. Coupled with this, moreover, is our spatial and visual passivity during such apprehension: the words image, as it were, an already finished spatial given, and what is not evident is the *creation* of the spatial form from outside through lines and colors, that is, the action of constituting and producing the form from outside through a movement of the hand and of the whole body that conquers the merely imitative movement-gesture. The manner of utterance as well as gestures and the play of features, inasmuch as they occur in lived life, just as language does, possess a much stronger expressive tendency (the manner of utterance and gestures either express or imitate); the creative emotional-volitional tones of the author/contemplator can easily be absorbed in the tones proper to the hero as he lives his own life.

That is why it is necessary to emphasize especially that both content (i.e., what is put *into* the hero—his life from within) and form are unjustified and unexplainable on the plane of a single consciousness; that it is only on the boundaries of two consciousnesses, on the boundaries of the body, that an encounter is actually realized and the artistic gift of form is bestowed. Without this essentially necessary[6] reference to the *other*, i.e., as a gift to the other that justifies and consummates him (through an immanent-aesthetic justification), form fails to find any inner foundation and validation from within the author/contemplator's self-activity and inevitably degenerates into something that simply affords pleasure, into something "pretty," something I find immediately agreeable, the way I find myself feeling immediately cold or warm. By using a certain technique, the author produces an object of pleasure, and the contemplator passively affords himself this pleasure.

Without the application of the mediating value-category of the *other*, the author's emotional-volitional tones that actively constitute and produce the hero's exterior as an artistic value cannot be brought into immediate accord with the hero's own directedness from within his own lived life. It is only thanks to this category of the other that it becomes possible to transform the hero's exterior into an exterior that encompasses and consummates him totally, that is: to fit the hero's own directedness to meaning in living his life into his exterior as into a form; to fill his exterior with content and give it life; to create a whole human being as a unitary value.

Horizon and Environment

How are objects of the outside world imaged with relation to the hero in works of verbal creation? What place do they occupy in verbal creation?

There are two possible ways of combining the outside world with a human being: from within a human being—as his *horizon,* and from outside him—as his *environment.* From within me myself, within the meaning-and-value context of my own life, an object *stands over against* me as the object of my own (cognitive-ethical and practical) directedness in living my life; in this context, the object is a constituent of the unitary and unique *open* event of being, in which I partake as a participant who has an urgent interest in the outcome of that event. From within my actual participation in the event of being,[7] the outside world is the *horizon* of my active, act-performing consciousness. It is only in cognitive, ethical, and practico-instrumental categories[8] that I can (so long as I remain within myself) orient myself in this world as in an event and introduce a certain order into its composition with respect to objects; this is what determines the outward aspect, the "face," of each object for me—determines its emotional-volitional tonality, its value, its significance. From within my own consciousness—as a consciousness participating in being—the world is the object of my acts: acts of thinking, acts of feeling, acts of speaking, acts of doing. The center of gravity in this world is located in the future, in what is desired, in what ought to be, and *not* in the self-sufficient givenness of an object, in its being-on-hand, *not* in its present, its wholeness, its being-already-realized. My relationship to each object within my horizon is never a consummated relationship; rather, it is a relationship which is imposed on me as a task-to-be-accomplished, for the event of being, taken as a whole, is an open event; my situation must change at every moment—I cannot tarry and come to rest. The object's standing over against me, in space and in time, is what constitutes the principle of the *horizon:* objects do not *surround* me (my outer body) in their presently given makeup and their presently given value, but rather—*stand over against* me as the objects of my own cognitive-ethical directedness in living my life within the open, still risk-fraught event of being, whose unity, meaning, and value are not *given* but imposed as a *task* still to be accomplished.

If we turn our attention to the world of objects in a work of art, we should have no difficulty in ascertaining that the unity and structure of this object-world is *not* the unity and structure of the hero's lived *horizon,* and that the fundamental principle of its organization and ordering is transgredient to the hero's own actual and possible consciousness. A verbal landscape, a description of surroundings, a representation of everyday communal life, that is, nature, city, communal life-style, etc.—all these are not constituent features within the horizon of a human being's active, act-performing consciousness (his ethically and cognitionally acting consciousness). There can be no doubt that all the objects presented in a work bear and must bear an essential relation to the hero, for otherwise they would be mere *hors d'oeuvres;* but this relation in its essential aesthetic principle is not a relation that is given from within the hero's lived-life consciousness. What constitutes the center of the spatial disposition and axiological interpretation of all objects presented in a work is man's *outer* body and his *outer* soul. All of the objects are correlated with the hero's exterior, with his boundaries—his outer as well as inner boundaries (the boundaries of his body and the boundaries of his soul).

The object-world within a work of art is understood and is correlated with the hero as his *environment.* The distinctiveness of the environment expresses itself first of all in an outward formal combination of plastic and pictorial features: in the harmony of colors and lines, in symmetry, and in other purely aesthetic combinations that are independent of meaning.[9] In verbal creation, this plastic-pictorial aspect does not attain, of course, any externally intuitable fullness and completeness (in the form of a representation); what we get here are emotional-volitional equivalents of possible visual representations that correspond in the aesthetic object to the meaning-independent plastic and pictorial whole (in the present context, we shall not deal with the combination of painting, drawing, and sculpture). As a combination of colors, lines, and masses, the object has an independent status: it acts upon us alongside of the hero and around him. That is to say, it does not stand over against the hero within the hero's own horizon; it is perceived as an integral object and, as such, allows us to walk around it, as it were. It should be evident that this purely plastic and pictorial principle of ordering and giving form to the external world of objects is completely transgredient to the hero's living consciousness, inasmuch as colors, lines, and masses (treated aesthetically) constitute the utmost bounds of an object or of a living body, i.e., the point where an object is turned outward, where it exists axiologically only in and for the other, where it is part of the outside world, and where, from within itself, it does not exist. . . .

NOTES

1. The aesthetic object proper is the object constituted in *aesthetic* perception; it must be distinguished from the "material" artifact. See below in the section entitled "Inner and Outer Form." On the aesthetic object in this specific sense, see Waldemar Conrad's trailblazing phenomenological study, "Der ästhetische Gegenstand," *Zeitschrift für Asthetik* 3 (1908): 71–118, 469–511, as well as Roman Ingarden, "Aesthetic Experience and Aesthetic Object," *Philosophy and Phenomenological Research* 21 (1961): 289–313, and Mikel Dufrenne, *The Phenomenology of Aesthetic Experience,* trans. E. S. Casey et al. (Evanston: Northwestern University Press, 1973), part 1 (Phenomenology of the Aesthetic Object).

2. The spatial form of the disposition of a text (stanzas, chapters, the *figurae* of scholastic poetry, etc.) has only a minimal significance.

3. Representation in the sense of the German *Vorstellung.*

4. Feeling-tone (German Gefühlston): the feeling-tone of a sensation, i.e., the feeling associated with a sensation.

5. Even though the emotional-volitional tone is conjoined with words (is attached, as it were, to the intonated sound-image of words), it relates, of course, not to words, but to the object expressed in words, even if such an object is not actualized in consciousness as a visual image; the sense of the emotional-volitional tone is determined solely by the object, even if this tone develops jointly with the sound of words.

6. Essentially necessary: founded on principle (German *prinzipiell*). "Essentially necessary" is one way in which I shall translate the adjective *printsipial'nyj*—the Russian equivalent of the German *prinzipiell*. Other translations of the adjective used throughout this translation are "principled," "founded on a necessary principle," and "essential and fundamental."

7. The event of being: being is an ongoing event. "Unique" in the sense of once-occurrent. "Event of being (or Being)"; Being constitutes an ongoing event, has the character of an event. Cf. German *Seinsgeschehen.*

8. The categories of the true, the good, and the practically effective.

9. Independent of meaning: they are independent or outside the bounds of the meaning to which the hero is directed from within himself in living his life.

Painting and the Language of Theater: Notes on the Problem of Iconic Rhetoric

The relation of the phenomenon of art to the duplication of reality has been repeatedly addressed in aesthetics. In this regard the ancient myths about the birth of rhyme from echo and the birth of drawing from an outlined shadow are very significant. Moreover, the magic function of such objects as the mirror in creating another, *prima facie* world, which resembles the reflected one without actually being it, is just as significant for the self-cognizance of art as the metaphor of reflection or mirroring. The possibility of duplication is the ontological premise for transformation of the world of objects into a world of signs: the reflected image of an object is separated from natural practical relations (spatial, contextual, functional, etc.) and, therefore, can be easily included into representational relations of human consciousness. Reflection of a face cannot be included into relations which are natural for the object reflected. Thus this reflection can be neither touched nor caressed, yet it can be easily involved into such semiotic relations as insult or used for sorcery. In this respect it is similar to imprints or impressions, for example, footprints or fingerprints. Magical operations on human footprints, recorded in the extensive ethnographic studies of different cultures, are usually explained by the diffuse property of the archaic mind which is allegedly incapable of distinguishing between the part and the whole and believes the footprint to be essentially identical to the person who left it. However, it is possible to put forward a somewhat different hypothesis: the foot-

Yury Lotman, ''Teatralnyi yazyk i zhivopis: K probleme ikonicheskoy ritoriki'' (Painting and the language of theatre: toward the problem of iconic rhetoric), in *Teatralnoe prostranstvo* (Moscow: Sovetskiy Khudozhnik, 1979), 238–52.

print is and is not the person at the same time; it is excluded from everyday relations and motivates its own inclusion into a semiotic situation.

The semiotic situation, however, is latent as a pure possibility in the elementary act of the reduplication of an object. As a rule, it remains unrealized for the naive mind that is not predisposed to the perception of reality in terms of signs. The situation is different when a double duplication or a secondary duplication occurs. In such cases we clearly see the inadequacy of the object to its representation and the transformation of the former in the process of duplication, which naturally calls attention to the *mechanism of duplication*. In other words, it turns the process from a semiotically unconscious to a conscious one. The recurrence of duplication and the transformation of the reflected image during this process play a special role in visual texts. In verbal texts the conventional character of relationship between content and expression is considerably more apparent. This conventionality can be demonstrated easily, but it has to be neutralized in the process of creating poetic texts: poetry fuses the planes of expression and content into a complex construct of a higher organizational level.

Visual arts (and their potential semiotic kernel—mechanical reflection of an object in a mirror-like surface) create an illusion of identity between an object and its image. In this way another step is added to the process of creating an artistic sign (text): at first the conventional nature of any semiotic fact must be uncovered, that is, a text perceived as nonconventional must be comprehended in terms of conventional signs. In practice at this stage it means attributing properties of a verbal text to a nonverbal one. Only at the next stage a secondary iconization of a text takes place corresponding in poetry to the moment when properties of a nonverbal (iconic) text are attributed to a verbal one.

The role of the double duplication in this process (especially at the first stage) can be illustrated by the example of the function performed by the mirror at certain moments in the development of visual arts. We can say that at times the mirror played the same typological role in painting as verbal puns did in poetic texts: it turned the language of art into the principal object of the viewers' attention by revealing the conventional nature of visual discourse. As a rule the double duplication is confined only to a limited part of the canvas. In this case the degree of conventionality in the area of secondary duplication was increased, thus revealing the semiotic nature of the text.

For example, the pathos of Renaissance art was partly grounded in the assertion of the "natural" perspective as an embodiment of a certain fixed point of view.[1] However, in Velázquez's *Venus with Mirror* the introduction of a mirror within the traditional perspectival system makes it possible to show the central figure (Venus) from two points of view simultaneously: the viewer sees her from the back and also sees her face in the mirror. Point of view is identified as an independent structural element which can be separated from an object of naive perception and given as a conscious and autonomous entity.

In *Arnolfini Wedding* by Jan Van Eyck we encounter the mirror in a similar function: the central figures are seen *en face* on the canvas and from the back as they are reflected in the mirror. The complexity of the effect is reached by distorting the reflection: the spherical surface of the mirror transforms the figures thus calling attention to the specific nature of reflectivity. It then becomes obvious that every reflection is a shift, a deformation which emphasizes certain properties of the object and simultaneously reveals the structural nature of language into whose space this object is projected. The spherical, rounded surface of the mirror accentuates the two-dimensional, angular character of the couples' figures which seem to be drawn on a flat piece of glass placed into the illusory three-dimensional space of the room (the illusion of three-dimensionality is achieved through detailed and convincing treatment of objects). The system of mirror reflection and perspective is perpendicular to the image plane and leads outside the painting's boundaries. Here an effect is created similar to the one that Jan Mukarovsky observed in cinema. He noted that there are instances when the sound space overflows the boundaries of the screen space and gains a greater prominence (e.g., a carriage may be filmed in such a way that the horses placed on an axis perpendicular to the screen are not seen, i.e., they are photographed with the camera placed where the horses should be; if the sound track is edited to reproduce the clatter of horses' hoofs, then the axis of the sound space will be arranged as if it were perpendicular to the screen space). It is precisely the mirror and the perspective reflected in it that reveal the contradiction between the essential flatness of the canvas and the three-dimensional character of the represented world; in other words, it reveals the nature of the language of painting.

Combining the mirror with metastructural elements allowed Velázquez in *Las Meninas* to present the very nature of the language of painting as the object of perceptual cognition. (The artist is depicted in the process of painting while the subjects of his painting appear to the viewer in the mirror reflection behind him.)[2]

In all these cases, as in many others (e.g., the spherical mirror which opens up the side space in Quentin Massys's *Money Changer with Wife*), the mirror appears to separate the method of representation from the represented objects. This is achieved first, through the duplication of what has already been duplicated by the artist's brush and, second, by simultaneously introducing into the image something that, according to the accepted codes of the language of painting, has to remain outside the frame. The method of representation becomes the subject of representation. The accompanying process of language self-cognition is reminiscent of the analogous baroque literary phenomena.

The above-mentioned examples concern the particular cases of a more general problem of textual rhetorics.

Rhetorics, one of the more traditional areas of language study, is currently gaining new importance. The need to relate the findings of linguistics to those of textual poetics gave rise to neorhetorics resulting in extensive scholarly work. Without going in depth into all the issues, let us emphasize just one aspect relevant for this discussion.

A rhetorical utterance, in my terminology, is not equal to a simple message with the superimposed ''ornaments'' which once removed would leave the meaning intact. In other words, a rhetorical utterance cannot be expressed by nonrhetorical means. Rhetorical structure is not found in the plane of expression but in the plane of content.

A rhetorical text, as opposed to nonrhetorical, can be defined as a structural unity of at least two subtexts represented by means of distinct and mutually untranslatable codes. These subtexts can be locally ordered entities, and, therefore, different parts of the text must be read by using different languages, or it must function as different, evenly distributed layers. In this case the text presupposes a double reading, for example, everyday and symbolic. Rhetorical texts include all those with a contrapuntal conflict within the single structure of distinct semiotic languages.

A conflict within the area boundaries marked by a different degree of semioticity is characteristic of the rhetoric of baroque texts. In the clash between languages, one of them always functions as natural (nonlanguage) and the other as emphatically artificial. In the frescos of baroque cathedrals in Bohemia we can find the motif of an angel in a frame. The peculiarity of these images is attributed to the fact that the frame imitates an oval window while the little figure on a "windowsill" sits with one leg dangling as if climbing out of the frame. The leg that does not fit within the composition is sculptural. It is attached to the painting as a continuation. In this way the text functions as a combination of painting and sculpture; moreover, the background behind the figure imitates a blue sky suggesting an open gap in the space of the fresco. The protruding three-dimensional leg breaks this space differently and in the opposite direction. The entire text is constructed around the play between the real and nonreal spaces, on the one hand, and the conflict between the two languages of art, on the other hand. One of these languages appears to be the natural property of the object while the other appears to be its artificial imitation.

Classicism called for stylistic unity. The baroque shifts among locally ordered entities seemed barbaric. The entire text must be uniformly organized and coded. However, this does not mean a rejection of rhetorical structure. The rhetorical effect is achieved by different means—a multilayered linguistic structure. In the most common example, an object of representation is initially coded by a theatrical code and then by a poetic (lyrical), historical, or pictorial one.

In a number of cases (most typically in historical prose, pastoral poetry, and eighteenth-century painting), a text represents a direct reproduction of a theatrical sequence or scene. Depending on the genre, a scene from tragedy, comedy, or ballet can be turned into this mediating text-code. In such manner, for example, the painting by Antoine Coypel, *Cupid and Psyche,* represents a ballet scene according to all the conventions required from the spectacles of this genre by the eighteenth century's interpretative scheme. The biographical fact of this painter's involvement in theater is not sufficient to explain such mixing of codes since the same device can be found in the works of other contemporary artists including Watteau.[3]

Speaking of "theatricality" in painting of a certain period we must avoid reducing the issue to a superficial metaphor. The problem is firmly rooted in the very nature of theater, on the one hand, and in the principle of "mediating codification," on the other hand.

The following aspects of this dual problem can be pointed out.

In any act of semiotic cognition it is essential to distinguish between the signifying and non-signifying elements of surrounding reality. The elements without signification are considered to be nonexistent from the point of view of a given modeling system. The fact of their actual existence is downplayed since they are not relevant to the given modeling system. While actually in existence, they cease to exist for the cultural system. The principal and essential act of any semiotic modeling of culture is to delimit the layers of culturally relevant phenomena. A certain primary codification is required in order to accomplish this, and it can be achieved by identifying everyday situations with the mythological ones and real people with the characters of myths or rituals. At different stages of cultural development the function of a mediating code can be assumed by etiquette or ritual ("whatever has an equivalent in a ritual can be said to exist"), or historical narratives ("what goes down in history can be said to actually exist"). Theater, however, is especially active in this respect as it combines a number of aspects of the systems described above.

The type of portraiture with a model dressed in a theatrical costume was a common effect of theater as the mediating code between everyday objects and paintings. Such are the numerous eighteenth-century portraits of women in the costumes of vestals, Diana, or Sappho as well as the portraits of men à la Titus, Alexander of Maccedonia, or Mars. The fact that the theater (and not some indeterminate mass of cultural and mythological notions) functioned as the codifying mechanism is confirmed by the nature of the costumes. They corresponded to the theatrical props prescribed by the eighteenth-century theatrical tradition for the characters. The stylization through costume means that in order to be identified with a signifying type in the given cultural system, and thus to become worthy of the artist's brush, a real person must be likened to a particular theatrical character. Numerous examples support the notion that this codification has a reciprocal effect on the behavior of real people in everyday situations.[4] It is interesting to point out the cases where the stylized conventional costume in portraiture had an effect on real fashions. For instance, the portraits by Elizabeth Vigée Lebrun played an important role in the popularity of the antique Empire-style clothes *à la greque* in St. Petersburg.

Another aspect of the problem is the assortment of narratives and the consequent choice of the subjects of painting. In the process of selecting the subjects worthy of representation from the point of view of a given cultural system as well as the means of representation (the instances or states of the subject considered to be "painterly"), an important role is played by the preliminary codification in a system of different artistic languages, most frequently theatrical or literary.

In delimiting a picturesque situation, it is essential to segment the flow of time in which the given subject actually exists. The fragmented and frozen moment of representation is contrasted with the uninterrupted and continuous flow of time in which the subject is immersed. The notion of "life as theater" frequently functions as the psychological instrument in effecting this transformation. Theater imitates the dynamic continuity of real life and, at the same time, divides it into segments and scenes, thus separating the whole, discrete units from the continuous flow. These units seem to be self-enclosed and frozen in time. It is not a coincidence that such terms as "scene," "picture," and "act" are equally applicable to theater and painting.

Theater is positioned between the nondiscrete flow of life and its segmentation into discrete frozen moments typical to the visual arts. On the one hand, it differs from painting and approximates life with its continuity and movement; on the other hand, it differs from life and approximates painting where the flow of action is segmented and at each moment every segment tends toward a compositional order within the synchronous slice of action: instead of the continuous flow of the nonartistic reality we are presented with a series of discrete, immanently ordered pictures capable of instantaneous change from one pictorial realization to another.

The intermediate position of theater between the moving, continuous, real world and the still, discrete world of visual arts determined the possibility of the frequent exchange of codes between theater and everyday behavior, on the one hand, and between theater and visual arts, on the other hand. Consequently, life and painting communicate in a number of instances through theatrical medium, which functions in this process as the intermediate code, the translator-code.

As a result of the interaction between theater and everyday behavior, along with the permanent tendency in theater history to make stage life resemble real life, there is another permanent yet opposite tendency to make real life (or its particular realm) resemble theater. The latter tendency is especially prominent in the cultures that have developed distinct realms of ritualized behavior. If the origins of theatrical action can be traced back to ritual, during subsequent historical development a reverse influence has occurred: ritual has absorbed the rules of theater. In this way, for instance, the ceremonies of the Imperial court created by Napoleon I were not oriented toward the traditions of the royal court etiquette, which was destroyed by the Revolution, but rather toward the formulas developed by the eighteenth-century French theater to represent the Roman Imperial court. Talma played an active role in developing etiquette. Ballet invaded the sphere of military training and parade. Theatrical spectacle captured even such a seemingly alien sphere as military combat. Lermontov described the feeling of viewers watching "the clash of the battle": "Without bloodthirsty excitement, as though watching a tragic ballet."

If the era of Classicism sharply demarcated the areas of ritualized and practical behavior, it was characteristic of Romanticism to filter the norms of theatrical behavior into the realm of everyday life. On the one hand, the enclosed realm of "high" stately manners was abolished, and, on the other hand, the realm of the "middle" style of behavior was ritualized, such as the etiquette in love and friendship, and situations like "communion with nature" or loneliness "amidst a bustling ball."

The rise of the "theater of everyday behavior" changed an individual's self-perception. The poetic moments and situations of life were foregrounded and declared uniquely significant and even uniquely existing. During the nonpoetic moments the individual retreated backstage as if he ceased to exist for the "drama of life" until his next entrance. Thus, for example, during the time of Napoleon's wars the life of combat was significant and real for a Romantic writer (i.e., it could become the subject of various texts) only as a sequence of heroic, elevated, tragic, and moving scenes. Stendahl's and Tolstoy's descriptions of the war made such a striking impression on readers because these writers moved the stage area backstage and insisted that true life goes on behind the curtains while only an imaginary existence, a pseudolife, takes place on stage.

Besides certain situations, the true authenticity was also attributed to an assortment of stage parts typical of this era. In order to exist ("am kräftigsten existieren," as Lavater wrote to Karamzin) an individual must add a semiotic Being to his physical Being. Lavater had the simple duplication in mind ("Our eye is not structured to see itself without a mirror," he wrote). In certain periods this is achieved by identifying oneself with a model role considered significant in a given cultural system:

> . . . having absorbed
> Another's joy, another's grief,
> Imagining herself a heroine
> Of her beloved authors,
> a Clarissa, a Julia, a Delphina,
> In the quiet woods Tatyana wonders
> with the dangerous book.[5]

The choice of a role was accompanied by the choice of a gesture. There appeared the realm of "significant movements"—gestures as opposed to mere everyday movements without signification.[6]

The Romantic critique of Classicism as the Age of Pose does not mean the rejection of gesture—the sphere of signification was only shifted: those realms of behavior previously thought to be completely nonsignifying were ritualized and endowed with semantic content. Simple clothes, a careless pose, a touching motion, the ostentatious rejection of signification, the negation of gesture become the carriers of important cultural meanings, that is, transformed into gestures. In Lermontov all movements of the heroine are "full of expression" and "sweet simplicity" at the same time ("sweet simplicity" is the rejection of gestures, but the expressivity of these gestures, their meaningfulness, turns them into gestures of a new type.)

> . . . another thing
> Are the eyes of my Olenina!
> What thoughtful genius,
> What childish simplicity,
> What languid expressions,
> What bliss and dreams! . . .
> She casts them down with the smile of Lel—
> The triumph of modest Graces;
> Looks up—like the angel by Raphael
> Who contemplates Divinity.[7]

It is interesting that alongside the demonstrative assertion of "childish simplicity" as the highest value, a theatrical-painterly code is introduced to interpret the *meaning* of what has only a physical existence:

"the angel by Raphael" is a reference to *Sistine Madonna*, known to Pushkin from etchings (most likely, literary descriptions also played a role); Lel—the Slavic Eros (here perhaps Eros in general)—is a reference to the traditions of painting, theater, and ballet.

A triangle is formed: real individual behavior in a cultural system—theater—visual arts; within it an intensive exchange of symbolism and means of expression takes place. Theatricality filters into everyday life and influences painting; everyday life influences both, waiving the banner of "naturalism"; and, finally, painting and sculpture actively influence theater, determining the system of poses and movements, as well as the nonartistic reality, elevating it to the level of meaningfulness.

In this respect it is important that, while being transferred into another realm, a signifying structure maintains its links with the original context. Thus we have the "theatricality" of gesture in painting and life, "pictorialism" in theater and life, "naturalism" on stage and in painting. This dual connection with different semiotic systems produces the rhetorical situation containing a powerful source for new meanings.

Rhetoric—the transfer of structural principles from one semiotic sphere to another—is possible at the junction of other arts as well. In this process a very important role is played by the totality of semiotic processes at the dividing line between word and image. Thus, for example, Surrealism in painting can be interpreted in some sense as the transfer of literary metaphors and the principles of fantastic literature into the sphere of purely visual representation. But because the connection between literature and rhetoric seems obvious, we thought it would be useful to demonstrate the possibility of rhetorical construction that does not bear on the realm of words.

NOTES

1. P. A. Florenskiy, "Obratnaya perspectiva," *Trudy po znakovym sistemam,* vol. 3. (Tartu, 1967); B. A. Uspenskiy, "K issledovaniyu yazyka zhivopisi," in L. F. Zhegin, *Yazyk zhivopisnogo proizvedeniya* (Moscow, 1970); I. Danilova, *Ot srednikh vekov k Vozrozhdeniyu: Slozhenie khudozhestvennoy sistemy kartin kvatrochento* (Moscow, 1975).

2. Michel Foucault, *Les mots et les choses* (Paris, 1966), 318–19. Cf. Russian text (without the reproductions of paintings by Velázquez): M. Foucault, *Slova i Veschi* (Moscow, 1977), 45–60.

3. The phenomena of pictorial rhetoric also include the more subtle instance of intercoding within different genres and types of visual texts. Thus, the canvases of Antoine Coypel are often seen not only through the prism of theater but also the tapestry techniques; Doumier's paintings contain the traces of his graphics. This could be compared to the way in which film scenes in *Color of Pomegranate* (a film by Sergey Paradjanov) are subordinated to the structure of medieval Armenian miniature.

4. Yury Lotman, "Teatr i teatralnost v stroe kultury nachala XIX veka" and "Stsena i zhivopis kak kodiruyuschie ustroystva kulturnogo povedeniya cheloveka nachala XIX stoletiya," in *Statyi po tipologii kultury* (Tartu, 1973); Pierre Francastel, *La réalité figurée*, Paris, 1965.

5. From A. Pushkin, *Eugene Onegin.*—Our trans.

6. I. Danilova, *Ot srednikh vekov k Vozrozhdeniyu: Slozhenie khudozhestvennoy sistemy kartin kvatrochento* (Moscow, 1976), 50–51.

7. From A. Pushkin, *Yeyo glaza.*—Our trans.

Movement—Immobility

The following extract is part of a chapter from the book *Culture "Two"* by Vladimir Paperny. Written between 1975 and 1979 in Moscow, the book was published by Ardis (Ann Arbor, Michigan) in Russian in 1985. The first translation of this extract by Jamey Gambrell appeared in the journal *A-Ya* in 1982.

Culture "Two" considers the break in the Soviet architecture that occurred in the late 1920s and marked a transition between the cosmopolitan, revolutionary, and dynamic architectural discourse of the 1920s and the conservative, hermetic, and static discourse of the 1930s–50s. Paperny sees this break as symptomatic of a larger cultural change: "We will assume that the changes taking place in architecture and the changes taking place in other arts, economics, lifestyles, social organization, and journalistic lexicon follow certain general laws." To summarize these changes, Paperny introduces the terms "Culture One" and "Culture Two." The terms must be understood as theoretical constructs that describe ideal types transcending concrete historical periods. According to Paperny, the opposition Culture One—Culture Two is not limited to the Soviet period; the entire Russian history is characterized by the rhythmic succession of the two types of culture.—Eds. note.

"I have, says Culture One, henceforth freed myself forever from human immobility, I am in constant motion."[1] It is a culture of displacement, changing states, instability and unsteadiness. It is "eternal struggle," "permanent revolution," "the earth upturned." Here, as in

Vladimir Paperny, "Dvizhenie—nepodvizhnost" (Movement—Immobility), in *Kultura "dva"* (*Culture "Two"*) (Ann Arbor: Ardis Publishers, 1985 [1975–1979]), 47–58.

Tatlin's tower, you should not "stand and sit, you should be propelled upward and downward, drawn against your will."[2] Your eyes are "forced to shift from one detail to another that must be seen."[3] It is "an instance of creative tempo, rapid shift in forms; there is no stagnation, there is only turbulent movement."[4]

In this culture architectural constructions must be mobile—only because "the very idea of movement has a great potential for development."[5] Houses should be "able to turn to the sun, be collapsible, modular and movable . . . with flexible arrangement of rooms and 'furniture.'"[6]

Ideally "the change of residence by individual citizens—the city inhabitants—would not present any difficulties, complications, or inconveniences."[7] A man with a suitcase, a woman with a sack—these are the typical characters of this culture as it is usually portrayed in films, and they are not accidental.

Not only people but houses themselves take off from the ground. "The cabins of ships, airplanes and train cars" become the prototypical dwellings.[8] The house turns into "a glass box or a passenger cabin fitted with a door and put on wheels, the inhabitant inside." This cabin is placed "on a train (special tracks, numbered platforms) or a ship, and the resident goes on a journey without leaving the cabin."[9]

In fact, a "change of residence" in such circumstances is unnecessary. If you want, just "attach the wings and the wheels and take off, the house and all."[10] The space itself where people roam expands to near infinity:

> I'm off!
>> Right away!
>>> In five minutes
> I'll leap
>> the length of the sky.
> In this weather
>> the going is good.
> Wait for me
>> at the cloud—
>>> under the Big Dipper.[11]

The people of this culture are "the conquerors of infinite seas, oceans and land . . . The Deity, the Judge, and the Law for themselves."[12]

Some unknown force seizes people, houses, animals, and things, mixes all of it up and splashes it impetuously all over the earth.

Everything that can move,
and everything that doesn't move,
and everything that was barely moving,
   creeping,
      crawling,
         swimming—
all of it
   like a lava stream![13]

People suddenly break loose from their place, leave behind almost all of their belongings, and drift like rolling stones in the endless expanses of the former Russian empire. As if a trumpet call sounds over the emptied fields:

Hey!
   Provinces!
      Weight anchor!
After Tulskaya goes Astrakhanskaya,
   one mammoth after another,
they have stood still
      since Adam,
and now shifted
   and shove each other,
      rumbling with cities.[14]

The Sovnarkom address to the working peasants signed by Lenin sounds an alarm: "According to information received, peasants in some provinces increasingly wish to relocate . . . Those who sow and spread discord . . . will be severely punished."[15] It was naive, of course, to think that the global process of melting could be stopped by threatening the sowers of discord with punishment—they were not the problem.

Twice the government tried to cope with the dispersal of population. First it happened between 1918 and 1920. At that time, for example, voluntary relocation from one county to another was prohibited.[16] But precisely three years later it became necessary to lift the ban.[17] Similarly, in 1923 Moscow City Council demanded obligatory registration of visitors within twenty-four hours, but in the same year a decree of the All-Russian Central Executive Committee and Sovnarkom was passed to prohibit "demanding from citizens of Russian Federation the obligatory presentation of passports and registration papers which

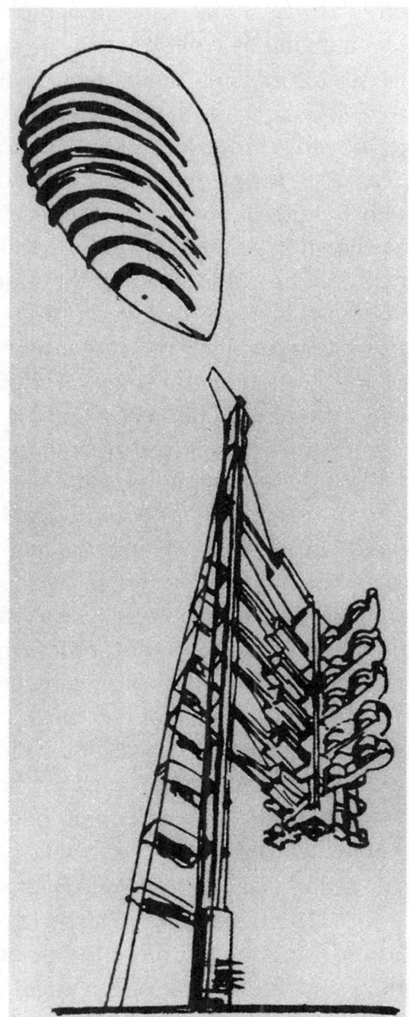

I. Yuzephovich, *Flying City* (1927–28).

would hinder their right to move freely and to settle in the territory of the Russian Federation.''[18]

In this period official efforts clearly contradicted the fluidity of culture, and for this very reason decrees which tied people down turned out to be so short-lived. In fact, many decrees of the 1920s directly encouraged fluidity. As a result almost everything in Culture One turned out to be unstable. Calendar and orthography were changed, time was constantly changing as well.[19]

The international system of time zones was in principle put into effect by a decree of February 14, 1919, but almost every year the clock's hands were moved, forward in the summer and backward in the winter.[20] This was done out of purely practical considerations—to save fuel—and such measures are not unusual. But the ease with which the time was changing and the abruptness with which it ceased to change in the next culture, indicates that the time in Culture One was no longer something granted to man from above, a Kantian *a priori* time. Time came down to the level of household measures, like the system of measures, weights, and physical units, which, by the way, also underwent changes in Culture One.[21]

On June 16, 1930, the time was moved an hour forward once again, next the effect of this decree was extended "until the special resolution of the USSR Sovnarkom," and finally "until revocation."[22] This revocation never followed. Time lost its plasticity again and froze one hour ahead of the international system.

The second attempt of the state to cope with dispersion happened to resonate with the natural waning of this process in the culture and, therefore, the attempt was realized with unprecedented thoroughness. The techniques to fix people in geographic space gradually became more and more developed. In 1926 measures were taken to "assist the conversion of nomadic Gypsies to a settled working way of life."[23] The same year the struggle for labor discipline began and employee service records were introduced in factories.[24]

In 1928 engineers, technicians, and agronomists were entered into a special registry.[25] In 1930 measures were taken in "the struggle with the flow of labor force," and among them the penalties against "the enticement of workers and administrative-technical personnel."[26] On June 23, 1931, Stalin set forth his "six conditions," one of which demanded once again to put an end to "the flow of labor force."[27] In 1932 a resolution was enacted authorizing dismissal from work for absence without valid reasons.[28] In the same year, in order to fight against "flyers" (the word sounds like a parody of Mayakovsky's *Flying Proletarian*), a decision was made to take away the food and consumer ration cards from any departing employee and to revoke his rights to housing.[29] In the same year an obligatory registration of all voluntary organizations was introduced.[30] Beginning in 1932 the internal passport system was gradually implemented.[31]

In 1935 a personal file was started for each student, and in 1938 a special "registration card" for each specialist with higher education.[32] In the same year "workbooks" were introduced (the same kind that exist today), and also the departure of kolkhoz workers from collective farms was forbidden.[33] In 1940 the "voluntary departure of employees from factories and offices" was forbidden once and for all.[34] And finally, on January 18, 1941, an order was passed requiring the prosecution of employees for twenty-minute tardiness.[35]

However skeptical historians may be regarding the state's preparedness for war in 1941, the culture was ready for it just in time.

It is apparent that Khlebnikov's "glass boxes," in which their "inhabitants" roam around the world, have no place in this culture. No wonder they are so well forgotten by Culture Two. The idea of Khlebnikov's "boxes" was revived only in the 1960s and by a man with the spirit most congenial to that of Culture One—S. O. Khan-Magomedov. He was the first to note the similarities between the projects of the English group *Archigram* to Khlebnikov's ideas developed more than five decades earlier.[36]

Thus the man of Culture Two loses his mobility in geographical space, but as a sort of unusual compensation the culture sets apart special individuals who take upon themselves the heavy burden of travel while relieving others of this necessity. All the famous expeditions of the 1930s—the rescue of the Chelyuskintsy, the drifting of the Papinintsy, Chkalov's flights over the North Pole, flights into the stratosphere—are described as something extraordinarily difficult and tortuous (as indeed they must have been) and yet joyous as well. Identifying himself with the superman who freely (although tortuously) soared over the net of parallels and meridians, the simple man also seemed to soar, experiencing all the torment, without noticing he was being tied down. A peculiar substitution occurred: instead of the real torment of being tied down, the man experienced the torment of empathy with the mastery of space.

But not just the sight of a man lifted off the ground makes Culture Two cringe. The sight of a lifted-off building provokes the same reaction. From this Culture's point of view, it is natural for a house to be grounded; and in the period after Word War II high rises were constructed precisely according to this principle, taking on the functions on the unrealized Palace of the Soviets. Among the architectural ideas and constructions most vehemently rejected by Culture Two are first of all the mobile living cells of Mikhail Okhitovich and the Central Union building on Myasnitskaya Street by Le Corbusier.

According to some memoirs, the transition of Moisey Ginsburg's architectural group from Urbanism to Deurbanism took only an hour and a half. In 1929 a man showed up in Ginsburg's studio, dressed in a plaid jacket and a derby hat; to Ginsburg's associates he looked like a cowboy. He walked around amid the renderings of communes that lay about and disappeared. This was Mikhail Okhitovich and he was only thirty-three then. The next day he returned and he and Ginsburg locked themselves up in Ginsburg's office. An hour and a half later Ginsburg came out and announced happily: "We will be Deurbanists."[37]

The essence of Okhitovich's theory was that "the city must perish . . . The revolution in transportation and the automobilization of territories overruns all commonly held ideas about the inevitability of density and the amassing of buildings and apartments."[38] In place of the city Okhitovich proposed individual collapsible living cells which could be transported on a developed network of highways and set up in any location in space. This idea, which clearly (though perhaps unconsciously) rhymed with Khlebnikov's glass boxes, provoked concern on the part of Le Corbusier. He immediately wrote to Ginsburg saying that "mind develops only in grouping of human masses." Ginsburg answered adamantly: "We have diagnosed the contemporary city. We say: yes, it is sick, terminally ill. But we don't want to cure it."[39]

What was actually new in Okhitovich's thesis as compared to the idea Ginsburg had supported until then? It was only the separation from the ground—the dwelling places had to be disengaged from the earth and freely distributed in space and connected by lines of communications. All the rest—communal preparation and consumption of food, communal care of children, that is, the virtual destruction of the family unit—had long since become the axiom of Culture One. Attachment to the land was not something of principal importance to Ginsburg; it was only the result of a certain inertia of thought, and as soon as he recognized this inertia the transition to Deurbanism was completed.

Culture One began with Khlebnikov's glass boxes and ended with the mobile cells of Okhitovich and Ginsburg. It is not surprising that as late as 1933 Le Corbusier still thought that "in Russia everyone was mad about Deurbanism."[40] In reality, by this time the journal *Sovremennaya arkhitektura,* where Okhitovich and Ginsburg used to be published, Deurbanism, and independent studios all ceased to exist. Okhitovich was criticized for "anti-Leninist methodological positions,"[41] most architects were employed by the Moscow city government, and under the leadership of Kaganovich were planning the reconstruction of Moscow, in other words, doing precisely what they did not want to do according to Ginsburg—"curing the modern city." In 1934 Okhitovich was expelled from the Party, although not yet arrested, and was working on the problem of "the national form of socialist architecture."

Le Corbusier's negative opinion of Deurbanism did nothing to improve Culture Two's relationship to his ideas and constructions. The house on Myasnitzkaya Street was rejected by this culture as a foreign body. It was an "alien house," "a cultural anachronism," and, most important, it was terrifying because it did not seem to have grown on the allocated place but it was as if it came from afar on its strange legs. This house is "somber and aloof, set on concrete pipes so that all its mass hovers over people, presses on them; it does not inspire one's vision but pulls it to the ground with lead weights," while the Soviet pavilion at the Paris exhibition is "the mighty movement upward . . . the rush toward a joyous future."[42]

We see that upward movement is now only possible as growth from the ground while detachment from the ground appears as heavy as lead weights. This heaviness was so tortuous that the first floor of the building, designed for parking, finally was walled in—this way it was not as terrifying for Culture Two.

The building on legs did not only come from afar, it was also an enemy. Architects saw in Le Corbusier's house "the hut on chicken legs"—the foreign masterpiece provoked associations with the hut of Baba Yaga, the witch from Russian fairy tales. This hut was capable of always turning its front to the fairy-tale hero and its back to the forest. Unfortunately, Le Corbusier's house faces the still unfinished Novo-Kirovskiy Prospect so that its "back" is turned to the viewers, and obviously it is not going to turn around. Nothing good could be expected from it.

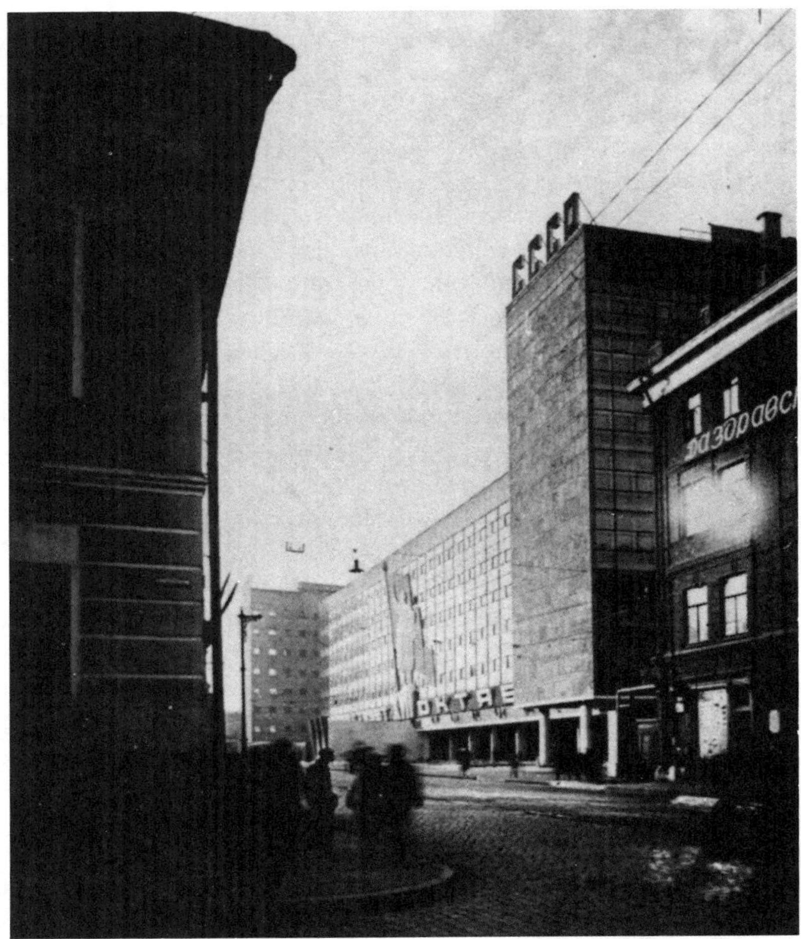

Building by Le Corbusier on Myasnitskaya Street, Moscow (1934).

The final blow to the house came from a seemingly unexpected side. In a poem by Osip Mandelstam, who did not fit into either culture, we find the following lines:

> Into the crystal palaces on chicken legs
> I will not enter even as a light shadow . . .[43]

Mandelstam was living in Moscow at the time (in 1931) and most likely had in mind the only crystal palace in Moscow—the building

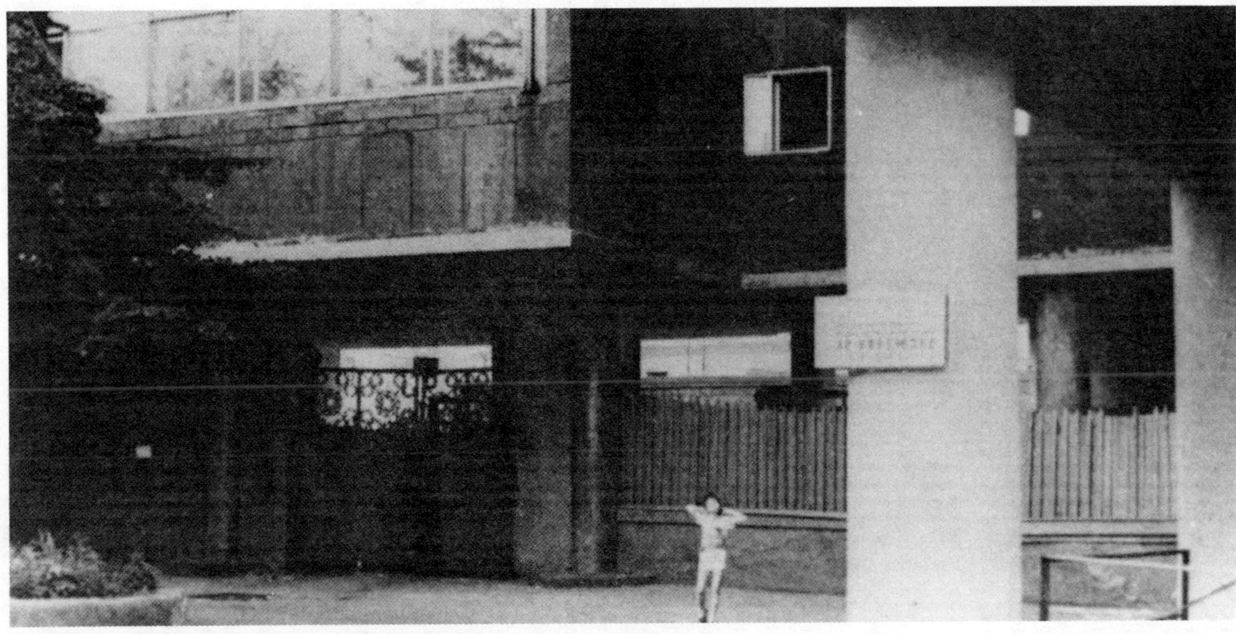

Building by Le Corbusier on Myasnitskaya Street, Moscow, with added fences (1979). Photograph by V. Paperny.

on Myasnitskaya Street. Three years later Mandelstam wrote the words that actually cost him his life:

> We live without feeling the country under our feet,
> Our words are not heard even ten feet away.[44]

It is sufficient to compare these lines with those written by Khlebnikov in 1921

> We are free people in a free land,
> We create laws, do not be afraid of laws,
> We mould the clay of our actions.[45]

in order to imagine the extent to which the "clay of actions" hardened in Culture Two.

The next wave of melting emerged in the mid 1950s, and perhaps its most striking expression was the idea of virgin land development. "We are beginning to plough the new field of art," wrote Ginsburg in 1924. This metaphor was realized literally by Vladimir Tatlin when, during the hungry 1920s, he cracked open the pavement in the yard of the Leningrad Academy of Art and planted potatoes in this field of art.[46] On the contrary, during the 1930s city streets were covered with tons of asphalt. In the 1930s–1940s new lands were occasionally developed (for instance, by the kulaks in Siberia), but this pathos was not culturally prominent. After 1954, when the decree about virgin land development was published, a whole subculture of nomads and tourists sprung up with its own style of life, clothes, and songs. These songs were about melting:

> I don't know where
> We'll have a chance to meet.
> The globe goes round and round
> Like a big blue ball.
>
> Cities and countries go by,
> Parallels and meridians.
> But there are no lines yet
> Along which we will wander in the world. (1950s)

During the 1960s the idea of Khlebnikov's mobile cells was resurrected in the architectural projects of the group headed by A. Ikonnikov.[47] Although the city, as seen by this group, is not nomadic, it does constantly change: "Surfaces easily change size, form, silhouette. They can be sensitive to wind, rain, the mood of inhabitants, time of day."[48]

The tourist subculture of the 1950s turned into the emigration of the 1970s. Many of the wanderers who sang the songs of melting in the 1950s left for Israel in the 1970s. The 1977 international competition for Theater of the Future can be considered the architectural culmination of Culture One of the 1960s. The five first prizes went to Soviet students who submitted projects for mobile theaters, and three of the winners had already emigrated to Israel.

In 1979 *Pravda* published an article by Doctor Likhachev who wrote: "Man is really a settled creature, even if he used to be a nomad. . . Without roots in native soil, in native land man would resemble tumble-weed."[49] In these words the overtones of a new hardening can be heard.

NOTES

1. Dziga Vertov, "Kinoki: Perevorot," *LEF* 3 (1923): 141.

2. N. N. Punin, "O pamyatnikakh," *Iskusstvo kommuny*, 19 March 1919.

3. Vertov 1923, 139.

4. Kazimir Malevich, "O Muzee," *Iskusstvo kommuny*, 23 February 1919, 2.

5. G. T. Krutikov, "Krugloe i polukrugloe zhilische," *Stroitelnaya promyshlennost* 9 (1928): 618.

6. K. L. Zelensky, "Ideologiya i zadachi sovetskoy arkhitektury," *LEF* 3 (1925): 100, 105.

7. P. A. Golosov, reply to a questionnaire quoted in S. Gorny, *Sotsialisticheskaya rekonstruktsiya Moskvy* (Moscow, 1931), 85.

8. Moisey Ginsburg, "Tselevaya ustanovka v sovremennoy arkhitekture," *Sovremennaya arkhitektura* 1 (1927): 18.

9. V. V. Khlebnikov, *Sobranie proizvedeniy*, vol. 4 (Leningrad, 1928–33), 279.

10. Vladimir Mayakovsky, *Polnoe sobranie sochineniy*, vol. 6 (Moscow, 1955–61), 356.

11. Ibid., 353.

12. V. T. Kirillov, *Proletarskie poety pervykh let sovetskoy epokhi* (Leningrad: Sovetskiy pisatel, 1959), 228–29.

13. Mayakovsky 1955, 2:120.

14. Ibid., 119.

15. *Sobranie uzakoneniy i rasporyazheniy rabochego i krestyanskogo pravitelstva RSFSR*, no. 59 (1920): appendix.

16. Ibid., no. 18 (1919): article 205.

17. Ibid., no. 36 (1921): article 188.

18. Ibid., no. 61 (1923): article 575.

19. Ibid., no. 19 (1918): article 289; ibid., no. 11 (1917): article 176.

20. Ibid., no. 9 (1917): article 142; no. 14 (1919): article 147; no. 21 (1919): article 258; no. 28 (1919): article 314; no. 9 (1921): article 63; no. 61 (1921): article 433; no. 17 (1922): article 182; no. 61 (1922): article 781; no. 32 (1924): article 287; no. 45 (1924): article 419.

21. Ibid., no. 66 (1918): article 725; no. 3 (1919): article 40; no. 35 (1922): article 417.

22. *Sobranie zakonov i rasporyazheniy raboche-krestyanskogo pravitelstva SSSR,* no. 33 (1930): article 362; Ibid., no. 51 (1930): article 534; Ibid., no. 10 (1930): article 113.

23. Ibid., no. 67 (1926): article 507.

24. *Sobranie uzakoneniy i rasporyazheniy rabochego i krestyanskogo pravitelstva RSFSR,* no. 55 (1926): article 430; *Sobranie zakonov i rasporyazheniy raboche-krestyanskogo pravitelstva SSSR,* no. 66 (1926): article 502.

25. Ibid., no. 31 (1928): article 275.

26. Ibid., no. 60 (1930): article 641.

27. I. V. Stalin, *Sochineniya,* vol. 13 (Moscow, 1951).

28. *Sobranie zakonov i rasporyazheniy raboche-krestyanskogo pravitelstva SSSR,* no. 78 (1932): article 475.

29. Ibid., no. 80 (1932): article 489.

30. *Sobranie uzakoneniy i rasporyazheniy rabochego i krestyanskogo pravitelstva RSFSR,* no. 74 (1932): article 331.

31. *Sobranie zakonov i rasporyazheniy raboche-krestyanskogo pravitelstva SSSR,* 1932, no. 84 (1932): article 516; no. 3 (1933): article 22; no. 11 (1933): article 60; no. 28 (1933): article 168; no. 46 (1933): article 273.

32. Ibid., no. 47 (1935): article 391; Ibid., no. 46 (1938): article 272.

33. Ibid., no. 58 (1938): article 329; *Sobranie postanovleniy i rasporyazheniy pravitelstva SSSR,* no. 18 (1938): article 115.

34. Ibid., no. 16 (1940): article 358.

35. Ibid., no. 4 (1941): article 63.

36. S. O. Khan-Magomedov, "Gorod buduschego i chelovek," *Sotsialnye predposylki formirovaniya goroda buduschego* 30 (1967).

37. S. O. Khan-Magomedov kindly informed me of this episode in 1978.

38. Mikhail Okhitovich, "K probleme goroda," *Sovremennaya Arkhitektura* 4 (1929): 130–34.

39. *Sovremennaya Arkhitektura* 1–2 (1930): 61.

40. *Architect's Year Book* 12 (1968): 238.

41. A. Mikhailov, "Rabota arkhitekturnykh organizatsiy," *Sovetskaya Arkhitektura* 3 (1931): 54.

42. E. Kriger, "Oblik velikogo goroda," in *Slovo o Moskve. Literaturno-khudozhestvenny sbornik* (Moscow, 1947), 336–37.

43. Osip Mandelstam, *Sobranie sochineniy,* vol. 1 (Washington, D.C., 1964–1966), 164.

44. Ibid., 2:623.

45. Khlebnikov 1928–33, 3:149.

46. *Druzhba narodov* 2 (1979): 224.

47. Vladimir Paperny with A. Ryabushkin and E. Bogdanov, *Zhilaya sreda kak obyekt prognozirovaniya* (Moscow: VNIITE, 1972), 31.

48. Ibid., 30.

49. *Pravda,* 10 November 1979.

Sots-Art

This is not a painting. This is a room. But not every room is meant to be lived in.

"They all come to see *Paradise,* hoping to find a philosophical analysis of the surrounding reality. They don't understand that the whole meaning of this painting-room is laughter and provocation. Yesterday, for instance, the underground millionaire Costakis came to look around and to check prices. Terribly embarrassed that he was not offered to buy anything. He said that in terms of investment *Paradise* is worthless. The reply was that with the exception of *Paradise,* which in principle can't be purchased, all Sots-Art is destroyed and exists only in slides. He, Costakis, works for eternity. He does not understand that our *Paradise* is like his collection: it exists only in Russia; because it can't be taken abroad, and because it can't be taken out, it is worthless. This is such queer modernism, which was not supposed to and could not exist here, but somehow it happened. What does it have to do with quality and use value? Anything can be added, heaped into this painting-room, into this *Paradise.* Maybe we could cut up a fake corpse and turn on the tape recorder with erotic sighs? Or maybe give the keys to lovers? But it would be easy to get framed for pornography, and today this is worse than 'anti-Soviet behavior.' By the way, the sporting goods store sells these wonderful plastic flies used for bait, and if you glue such a fly on a piece of sugar made from plastic and give it to every visitor of *Paradise* as a badge, how about it?"[1]

Zinovy Zinik, "Sots-Art," *Syntaxis* (Paris) 3 (1979): 74–102. Copyright © 1978 by Zinovy Zinik.

You find yourself in the space of a black parallelepiped, the lock clicks behind your back, and the eye of the unknown, but on such occasions inevitable deity, stares at you: one huge eye looks maliciously and suspiciously, another with reverie and even perplexity; the left side of the mouth bends down threateningly; the right side smiles charmingly. Transparent curtains stir: Why do they stir? Something is buzzing somewhere and you suspect that this is a tape recorder: Are you being taped? But so far you have not said a word. No, this is a fan. A sigh of relief. Then you will go along a little blue bridge (evidently taken from a children's playground) over a blue canvas river and notice that the river ends below the ceiling in a stream of blood from the belly of a baroque wax figure with the face of Prometheus, and further on it forks, turning into a stream of urine from an analogous wax figure of Confucius in the other corner of the opposite wall. And below this stream stands a silver-coated bust of a Roman citizen with the face of Taras Shevchenko or Taras Bulba, with an artificial fly on the forehead and spots of blood on the shoulder. And you will understand what you are being told: here urine is mixed with blood. The blood of ancestors with the urine of grandchildren, or vice versa. Yet none of it is real. You will turn around searching for truth and notice the traffic-controller in the urethra of Buddha and in the belly of the idol—children, tied together by a chain of light bulbs, dancing around a sunflower. (The light bulbs, i.e., the electrification of the belly, can be switched off by the visitor.) And also there is a smell here. It does not smell of Russia; neither of Pop Art. It's a different smell. But you are being surrounded—by the smells and the buzzing, newspaper and wax idols, and all of it is so-so, without a particular effort; with ideology but without attachments. And here you will turn around and see the plywood cut-out figure of a young man and a young woman, also Soviet, hand in hand, one palm greasing another, and a bottle of vodka and a huge key at their feet. You will notice the key right away, but you will not find a keyhole for it. And frantically looking for a keyhole, you will see a straightforward, classic portrait of Stalin on the background of the lunar surface. And you will understand that all this is neither a painting nor a room but the materialization of the brain work of a Soviet engineer, who studies yoga at night, tries to catch nirvana in the morning, and later, not having gotten enough sleep, goes to his classified job and votes for "fair wrath," "true indignation," and "justified pride." And you will knock on the door from the inside and (since you were locked on purpose but not forever) ask to be let out.

The living space of the picture-room *Paradise,* where a passerby finds himself, is literally cluttered with obtrusive ideologies, traces of myths, echoes of rituals, not counting the well-known religions and details of *byt.*[2] This clutter has a wry smile; and the deliberate eclecticism of consciousness is presented with impudent naivety as a new freedom—the freedom of a slave who had been beaten so frequently and variously that he already learned by heart all the devices of atrocity. And learned them so well that he is already capable of looking at this mockery from the outside, admiring its refinement, and smacking his lips in expectation of the sudden moment of pain.

There was a custom in Babylon: a slave who distinguished himself became the king for twenty-four hours. Afterward he was executed. The paintings we are talking about are such a twenty-four-hour reign of the slave. The idea of punishment in *Paradise* is presented literally: "Paradise" (the quotation marks here are not accidental) also includes a stool, from which one of the artists fell down while working on *Paradise.* Tilted as if falling down, with one leg glued to the floor, it enters into the painting-room as an uncomplicated symbol reminding us that every idea of spiritual power brings about punishment and that an artist's personality and his creative work are connected through the fracture of bones. The fact of fracture itself is staged into a derisive ritual, being performed in a chamber theater, and in this way enters into the painting. Moreover, this ritual is fixed in photographs with supplementary text, in *samizdat* fashion. Moreover: it is known to what consequences and judicial investigations such rituals and artistic presentations lead. (Incidentally, *Paradise* had to be taken apart on the demand of militia, and the studio with the picture room was taken away from the artists.)

Here, in this decisive (if not in the sense of prison then in the sense of emigration) work of the Famous Artists their main ideas clearly came together: the dialectics of the individual and the social, the myth of art and the creator, and time as an aesthetic criterion. Having taken into account the moral makeup of the Soviet individual, the spirit of Soviet everyday life, and the everyday life of Soviet spirit, this irony exists on the borderline with the traditional Russian *yurodivy* on church steps—the nobody's place.[3] I have in mind the Russian *yuro-*

divy who lives off charity yet does not demand, does not ask this charity: "his yellow eye is burning, everybody gives him on his own,"[4] but the *yurodivy*, having gotten this charity, instead of saying thanks, curses the giver; who pokes his crotch into your face and at the same time stretches out his hand for a penny; who simultaneously denounces the power of the rich and calls for humility; who can be stricken with an epilepsy attack, but his head, wallowing in the mud, winks at you soberly and cunningly; the blissful madman with the eyes of a mathematician, in whose life it is difficult to distinguish where artifice ends and where fate begins. Let us not forget, though, that the church steps were rebuilt into the main entrance of the Supreme Soviet reception room with glass doors.

"We were supposed to make big bucks at the pioneer camp on the Alley of the Cosmonauts. But my partner, a fool, used indelible pencil to mark squares for tracing of the portraits. We stamped out ten Gagarins, Marxs, Engels's, Lenins, and other outstanding members. We were already on the way to the payroll office when it began to rain. So, all the members turned into faces behind bars—the indelible pencil showed through. Now, this is exactly the merging of art and life. We work using stylistic hints: this is the style of a Stalinist painting, this is Cézanne's style. I grind out apples à la Cézanne like a genius and my partner wonderfully paints bottles à la Laktionov.[5] Laktionov's painting *Letter from the Front* had a great basin with soapy laundry water in the left corner of the original composition. So, Laktionov looked it over and decided to cut the basin out because it upset the composition. But we keep adding these basins. Of course, the impression is that the painting falls apart—there is no frame. What frame can there be when it's real life. We use conglomeration to imitate the principles of Soviet monumental style. Our Italian Renaissance and the National Renaissance is the mosaic in Moscow metro and the portraits at the May 1 demonstrations. A foreign correspondent showed up the other day, took pictures, and said: 'Our press needs your speeches, how you criticize your government.' We said: 'But out paintings talk for themselves. Stalin's executions—this was our, national, the first one in the world, Soviet happening.'"

Following the logic of the reverse movement of history the phenomenon of *yurodivy* consciousness is every day becoming the true model of the moral and spiritual makeup of the Soviet individual. When Solzhenitsyn took the burden of Russia's confession before the world (but did not pronounce himself the Russian Columbus yet), the primeval and tenacious popular mind, bread on the newspaper *Pravda* in the bathroom, first took him for a millionaire with hard currency in a foreign bank. The violoncellist Rostropovich (who then still had his Soviet citizenship) was perceived by the same *Pravda* reader as a good Soviet citizen, one of us, who procures hard currency for the Soviet government (perhaps from the same bank where Solzhenitsyn's money was kept) with his ingenious bow. And so, the *Pravda* reader heard rumors that the millionaire Rostropovich lets the millionaire Solzhenitsyn use his *dacha*. A Soviet individual nobly does not count his money. A Soviet individual counts somebody else's money. According to the information he has gathered, the critic of the petty bourgeoisie Heinrich Böll conducts high-level talks with the anti-Soviet millionaire Solzhenitsyn in the country house built with the money of the pro-Soviet millionaire Rostropovich (or, perhaps, "anti-Soviet?"). The most important thing is that the mind rushes about, trapped in the "anti-pro" problematic. From this point of view the concrete names are absolutely irrelevant: it is possible to imagine with the same success the meeting of Lenin and Herbert Wells at Tchaikovsky's *dacha* (or the meeting of Stalin and Goethe at Lenin's *dacha;* or the meeting of Gogol and Saltykov-Schedrin at Stalin's *dacha*). Soviet academic painting knew many such meetings at the imaginary *dachas* of Mao Tse-Tung, and there is an appropriate ceremonial canon––a heavy, velvet drape over an Italian window, abundant still lifes on the table, and the shaking of hands by the meeting's participants. It is first of all this canon which stands out and creates a parodic background for the painting by the Famous Artists uncompromisingly entitled *The Meeting of Solzhenitsyn and Böll at Rostropovich's Country House.* Simultaneously, we must look at their painting on an even larger scale, *The Meeting of Albert Einstein and Ivan the Terrible at the Country House of Zmey-Gorynych,* which makes a reference to the preceding *Meeting,* in order to be convinced not only that these meetings parody Socialist Realism, but also to realize the far-reaching concept of ideological duality of the world where such meetings take place. The general ironic mood of the ceremonial picture, with Solzhenitsyn's face made from aluminum foil and with the cover of the journal *Novy mir* (the real cover) under Heinrich Böll's arm, provokes a tormented smirk of understanding the duality of a dissident's position: adorned with a crown of thorns and a crown of laurels and inevitably denying his connections with what he fights and what he rejects so vehemently. Solzhenitsyn is here taken not as a concrete individual, not even as a writer, but as a certain ideological, iconic sign and a banner. In the long run, anyone who tries to refute his enemy, who tries to prove the enemy wrong, is forced inevitably to speak the language understandable to the enemy—in the same way as propaganda in the country of the opponent is conducted in the language of the opponent's soldiers. In one fable a hero, having killed a dragon, returns to the liberated town; but children dash aside from him in fear, and the hero does not understand what is really happening until accidently he notices his reflection in a puddle and is startled—on his shoulders, instead of a face, are the same terrifying heads of the dragon, which he has killed so heroically. To reject the language of official ideology which became the language of *byt* means to deny this *byt*. Yet precisely in this *byt* is our life, and, consequently, one has to deny himself, to withdraw, which is impossible because the meaning of one's existence is in the struggle with this *byt*.

In the framework of the paradox of dualism in one's relationship with oppressive official ideology it was customary to divide Soviet people into so-called orthodoxes and infidels.

But presently all this hierarchy of double-dealing is insolvent simply because the Soviet logic, or rather the temperament of thinking and ideology, is vague and contradictory. It evolved into maintaining in verbal form the traditional relations between "a slave because of laziness" and "a master because of boorishness." And the fact that the new executions were born from the words only proves the rule of inseparability of words and deeds in Russia. The words turn into life before one's eyes: for instance, a novelist sits before his working table and writes a line—"at this moment there was a knock at the door"; and the words come to life: at this moment a drunk yard-keeper and a major really knock at his door with a search warrant. According to the laws of Lenin's dialectics, words penetrate into life to such an extent that they become a form of relations in life and in labor camps; and form, as it is well known, is the soul of things, as labor camps are the soul of the Soviet system. Any attempt to establish a hierarchy of conformity, non-conformism and orthodoxy ignores this fact of the all-penetrating nature of official ideology, its inculcation into our mental life with the same intensity as the inculcation of chemical fertilizers into agriculture. The attempts to sneak this hierarchy of double-dealing into the harmonious Soviet reality are based on Western theories of totalitarianism, the totalitarianism from which one can get away by going to another room, moving to another country, and finally being killed by it, but remaining unsoiled. But here it is different. Here everyone is guilty. What can be done? To be witty and pronounce oneself a poet among Jews? But what to do if here all poets are Jews?

As far as painting is concerned: until now orthodoxy was identified with Socialist Realism and dissent—with the so-called underground art of nonconformism, where the prefix *non* confusingly sounds like *neo*. Supposedly, the orthodoxes profess monumental and optimistic motives inspired by the moral code of the builders of communism, and each of their paintings is a finished poster with an already written slogan. The others, completely rejecting Socialist Realism which they considered an imposition by the party and the government of a social order on independent artists, profess the traditions of "art for art's sake"—from Surrealism to Conceptualism; in other words they grow geraniums on windowsills and spit on the construction of communism. But in reality it is impossible to escape the double-dealing and compromises here as well. Here, too, there were pure abstract artists who earned their living by painting portraits of leaders and cosmonauts when not occupied by painting abstractions, and afterward they again would devote themselves to the beauty of abstract forms after having shut their window curtains to avoid the building superintendent. But, seriously speaking, it is impossible to separate an artist's style from the visual environment in which he lives. And, therefore, we find the technique of Cézanne (although just partially) in the works of the fathers of Soviet academism, just like the garish Repin suddenly shows up in the works of the Soviet "underground" artists—in a sense of the social importance of a painterly detail. The desire to set oneself off by dividing Soviet artists into orthodox painters and abstract nonconformists according to their style is connected with the same ideological moment: the desire to close one's eyes to the fact that Soviet (Stalinist) art penetrated and firmly took hold of the viewer as well as the artist, corrupting both of them, regardless of whom each considers himself to be.

"In Russia there is one great artist: an old woman in Lenin's mausoleum. But only a few know about her because she is an elite painter. She works in a secret institute at the Kremlin. There, they have a room:

if you pull apart the curtains there is glass behind, and behind the glass spare heads float in alcohol. A little below this there is a complete set of hands and other body parts to match. An entire institute. They came up with a special liquid that flows through the mummies of Dimitrov and Ho-Chi-Minh; their fingernails are growing even now, and if we do not deliver this liquid to Bulgaria and Vietnam it will be the end of their people's cults, and that is why they are at our mercy. But Lenin did not live long enough to see the invention of this liquid, and, therefore, the Kremlin institute employs the old woman who does all the work: every morning before the opening she comes to the mausoleum with a little brush and touches up and freshens up Lenin here and there. It seems to me that she was the one to work out the projects for the fiftieth anniversary of the October Revolution. For example, did you eat the sausage with Lenin's profile? It was called *figurnaya:* slice a piece—Lenin's profile, slice another piece—again Lenin on the cut. The sausage itself is red, and the profile is white, from fat. Or the cake with the busts of Marx, Engels, Lenin, and—no, our confectionery industry did not have the nerve to put out a chocolate Stalin. This was a manifestation of the government's concern for children: nutritious and educational. And I am not even going to talk about the journal *Soviet Pig Breeding* with the words 'Fifty Years of Soviet Power' across the whole cover. Or the calendar *Fifty Years of Soviet Circus?* In my view, this was simply sabotage."

The movement, ironically named Sots-Art by the Famous Artists, is devoted to the intervention of state painting into private life, and this intervention became the subject and the style in this series of paintings. Here painting does not follow the laws of perception but the laws of contraposition of a subject and a technique of representation. The intimacy of a theme is contraposed to the awkward monumentality of style and, vice versa, the refinement of painterly technique to the political "anti-aestheticism" of the image itself. While looking at these works one must keep in mind the carefully painted still lifes in the Soviet streets whose gigantic letters urge to eat fish sticks and hint at the fact that milk is a beneficial and tasty product, not forgetting, of course, about the expressivity of posters à la Repin about the harm of alcoholism in a local hospital. These are the sources of the artists' *Double Self-Portrait:* two profiles of precise resemblance—Komar and Melamid—on the red background, copying with precision the metro frescoes with double portraits of Lenin and Stalin, Marx and Engels. But here normal human faces are pressed into the ideological canon, into the pictorial symbol of everything Soviet.

Here is another example. Done in the manner of Western Conceptualists, the work parodies the specialists and experts of a May 1 demonstration design: on a piece of red cloth in a baguette frame the slogan YOU FEEL GOOD! is painted with letters reminiscent of demonstration banners. Pop Art was a reaction to the dominance of consumer goods in the Western world. Sots-Art of the Famous Artists is a reaction to the dominance of ideology in the Soviet world.

"You feel good!" you are told by Comrade Stalin himself, whose portraits the Soviets could see on the Kremlin wall; also in their homes, framed above the bed, next to the photograph of a father killed in the Civil War; and in other places too. Addressing Stalin as the Father-Leader-and-Teacher mixed in these hypostases the intimate-domestic, social-tribal and spiritual-political categories. Although the word "mixed" here is not quite appropriate: it did not mix but rather mechanically knocked together with nails and, therefore, managed to split consciousness—because the joining was not only vivisectional but also compulsory, forcing the brain to rush about in the unjoinable. The "social," ending up as compulsory ideology, intervenes—not infiltrating but busting in—under the cover of fine words (as a polite knock on the door often ends up in a search) and populates the "personal," turning this personal into a communal apartment. The original religious truths (if they were ever fixed in consciousness at all) began to double and multiply: duty becomes both the duty to children—and, therefore, one must steal to buy "milk for the kids"; and the duty in relation to strict social dogma—and, therefore, one must be executed for stealing. Duty, emptied of its religious understanding, turns into the ambiguous "this is how it must be" accompanied by winking toward authorities. Freedom is interpreted as the unconditional trust in authorities, as an inspired slavery. But the same freedom is also taken to mean the avoidance of social obligations—a quick condemnation of the twenty million people to penal servitude, so that the bosses would leave you alone and you could have a drink of vodka and some borscht with the wife and the children. When subordinated to the social, personal categories turn moral principles into a communal squabble about justice in relation to the issue of whose turn it is to clean the loo.

In the end, original religious (metaphysical) dogmas become meaningless because life and meaning are constructed not according to the laws in relation to the Absolute (regardless of how this Absolute is understood) but according to dialogical laws of avoiding a direct answer to a directly put (and not always directly) question. As though this is not a life, but an unwanted, unpleasant, evasive conversation you must take part in forever. Naturally, this leads to continuously intense doubling of consciousness: a person constantly feels not quite at home or like he has some screws loose. He is always partly at a demonstration, partly at a party meeting, and partly in jail.

On the International Women's Day an admirer sends his lady a postcard with a picture of mimosa on the hammer and sickle background, and factory administration is always ready to congratulate newlyweds with the certificate of the fiance's work achievements.

A poster reminding that we are moving toward communism, and not idiotism, hangs in the dining hall next to the announcement warning to wash hands before eating or, even better, next to a slogan in the factory dining hall: "Ask the administration for knives!"

One of the works by the Famous Artists, concluding the Sots-Art series, looks like a white canvas filled with parallel rows of multicolored circles; next to it is a table matching the circle of each color with a letter of Russian alphabet. All this looks almost like Goethe's theory of correspondence between color and meaning. A viewer is asked to perform the frustrating work of deciphering the horizontal rows of multicolored circles, letter by letter. And if you have enough patience, you will be rewarded by discovering that this color puzzle, which looks like a Pointillist painting, is in reality a quote from the Soviet constitution about the freedom of speech, press, and assembly.

An external, nonpainterly factor is introduced into the painting's style: the particular article of the constitution is of no importance, but the frustrated work of its unraveling is. A case itself is not important, it does not matter, what matters is which investigator is on the case; and not even the investigator but the transition from one case to another, according to the general Party line, which is what must be guessed. Words themselves are not important, what is behind them is—a jail or a successful career? Only in the light of these directives and the renunciation of the essence of words and deeds does the constant discussions about the IDEALITY of Russian man become understandable.

If before the Revolution the fools and the *yurodivys* were marginal and nontypical phenomena, throughout the years of construction and the strengthening of Soviet power the entire country turned into a giant and faceless, cruel and helpless *yurodivy*. And while turning into this *yurodivy* ever more consciously and persistently, the country attained an unknown and wonderful power which other nations and states cannot understand.

"Now these avant-gardists will be running around with their kitsch and neorealism. But we have our own native neorealism. More precisely we had it in the form of the ballerina statue with a raised leg by sculptor Motovilov, on the roof of a building on Pushkin square. She was standing with a raised leg like a dog while below Soviet people were walking by. But when foreigners started passing by below, the Moscow City Council ordered its removal: What if the foreigners will think that, pardon me, they are being pissed on from above? Only Mukhina remained for us, with her mammoth sculpture. Her naked *muzhik* and *baba* with hammer and sickle can only be compared with the works of Michelangelo.[6] Only he could afford something like that. When he made a heel, you had to notice it. His proportions were not sculptural but ideological. I, he said, do not make giants, I make great people. And if Mukhina's mammoth couple at the entrance to the VDNKh (Exhibition of the Achievements of the National Economy in Moscow) is to be photographed not from below, as we usually do it, but from the middle 'normal' level, you see horrible monsters with giant heads and tiny feet. Here meaning depends on a point of view. This is similar to the project of the Palace of the Soviets on the spot of Church of Jesus the Savior, where now the swimming pool is. Before that it was an old-believers' church, and the priest, when the Church was being destroyed to build the Palace, spat and cursed this place, and even now people keep drowning in the pool. So, for the Palace of the Soviets a statue of Lenin was planned of such a size that only one finger was ten meters long. But then they figured out that the head would be lost in the clouds, and if this head were to be figured out in correct perspective, the foundation would not hold it because of the ground."

"The Famous Artists of the 1970s, Twentieth Century, Moscow" is a pseudonym, parodying the anonymity of all the nameless creators of the monumental genre which veiled our eyes to such an extent that when a stranger looks into our eyes he will see only the reflected cries for anonymity. The collectivity of the pseudonym refers to the pseudocollectivity of the ideological Egyptian pyramids, the Kursk Arches and the Belamor-Baltic Canals, the cattle-breeding pavilions and the cosmonauts. You walk about in the midst of this anonymity, you live in it, you don't want to talk about it, but you do, and you are being dissolved in it as in the shadow of Mukhina's sculpture at the entrance to VDNKh until you are lost in this four-letter country. This anonymity stretching to the horizon cannot be owned and you cannot be personally responsible for it, just as you cannot take personally the dialog between the sickle and the hammer in Soviet sculpture. In this anonymity the notion of individual style vanishes and disappears. For this anonymity an individual style is not important but a technical device is, and it must be expropriated in the name of the great anonymous goal. The eclecticism of Soviet art is explained by this noncaring about the historical uniqueness of individual style; Soviet eclecticism proceeds from the assumption that all human history serves as manure for the bright edifice of communism. And in general, eclecticism is based on the assumption that a man's soul is mortal but his deeds will live for centuries, and these deeds must be pocketed for one's own needs.

Thus, *The Meeting between Solzhenitsyn and Böll at Rostropovich's Country House* has everything like a supermarket including the real lamp à la Pop Art hanging in the corner of the frame. This detail takes the picture outside of its own frame similarly, by the way, to how the social significance of its heroes (the significance understood through the eyes of an "average Soviet individual") takes it outside of the context of painting, turning it into a parody of Socialist Realism. A painting does not have a frame. The relationship to a painting is contained within it. It literally "speaks for itself." In Soviet language about Soviet language.

"Recently, on the occasion of the decree about improvements in the aesthetic appearance of the city, it was decided to set four lighted letters S-S-S-R on top of four apartment buildings near my house. But the workers had set up the first two letters, and then went drinking somewhere, and so now I look out my window everyday and see only the SS."

The work called *Ribbon* does not have an end. It is a "ribbon" consisting of 364 miniatures glued to the wall. "Reading" them you learn about the typical episodes in the life of a typical person who is the same age as the artists (since the character is still alive, the ribbon does not end). But this is not the only reason why the *Ribbon* is left open. *Ribbon* also depicts the character's consciousness which is eclectically made up of notions imposed from above and changing every five years with a new five-year plan. The identically varnished squares of the miniatures are painted in different styles. But the stylistic diversity cannot cover up the coma of similitude among the themes of these life episodes. Here the object of parody is the idea of professional difference among the Soviet artistic schools: regardless of the difference in style and the local virtuosity of technique, all the miniatures have the same scale and the same varnish. The life of the man from this "ribbon" becomes the succession of equally varnished styles that dictate behavior. In the style of every miniature we can read ideas that are historically connected with the period when the given style of painting reigned supreme. For instance, one of the miniatures, painted in the pure Socialist Realist style, depicts a search in the apartment of a Soviet intellectual with an inspector and witnesses present. This is a parody on the classical Soviet subject—the search of a Russian revolutionary by Tsarist police. In this way, the time of the character's life, presented as the succession of styles, looks like a series of flashbacks from the history of the society in which the character was "stylistically" dissolved.

But regardless of how important the concrete style of each miniature may be, it functions only as an allusion to a style, to its signs, to its criminal evidence. The circle of political ideas that go along with a style are more important than the style itself. This type of visual representation has to do not with style per se but with allusion to it, with its idea; this is not art but meta-art—it does not just appeal to vision but plays on the corresponding notions from Russian-Soviet mythology. It was this kind of meta-art that helped the masses read the mandate to increase the number of denunciations per capita in the appeals to fight surrounding enemies.

Every work of the Famous Artists enters in a dialog with the viewer, as it always was in Russia where art and politics can hardly be distinguished. Here we see the traditional inclination of Russian painting to leave the frame of a picture-monolog, the desire to transform (as a result of real political helplessness) painting into a weapon of struggle for human rights. For Russian Peredvizhniki this inclination turned into the romanticizing of the social primitive. They combined juicy social conflicts with dry and simplified painting technique, the tendency that later gave birth to Socialist Realism. This very inclination is parodied by the Famous Artists by reducing art to the role of an educator of blind and ignorant masses.

This is why it makes no sense to talk about the precision of composition or the structure of brush stroke in connection with the Famous Artists. Only one thing is demanded of form: it must provoke the prohibited conversation but not the prohibited actions, as it was with Peredvizhniki. Because freedom is the clarification of the past through conversation in the present. In the framework of this provocative speech, or meta-*yurodivy* behavior, so to speak, it is important to quickly select a fact which would provoke the viewer to a conversation with the image, to take hold of the interlocutor, to take him inside the frame of the painting or to open up the painting to include the interlocutor. Such style demands from the viewer a complicity with the work or, more precisely, a confession of the complicity. A Soviet individual is tormented by the desire to speak up and the fear to blab out. The feeling of guilt for complicity emerges only when the existence of the criminal reality, the complicity in which we can talk about it, is admitted. The Famous Artists make apparent the complicity of every viewer in this meta-art. But here, painting-dialog ends and painting-theater begins. A relationship with what is seen is included into what is being represented. "The whole world is theater and people are the actors"—this is so close to every Soviet individual who from birth plays a role prescribed by the Party and the government. Sometimes it is the role of a screw in the great construction, sometimes the role of a "great artist," sometimes the role of a dissident with a manuscript instead of a bomb and a hole in his pocket. And everybody works modestly at his post, joining in the triumphant hymn of the front-rank workers of Communist labor.

"The other day we organized the first Communist happening-*subbotnik*.[7] About twenty people showed up, not counting the whales of modernism. The program was the following: we put a giant red canvas against the back of the alcove wall, like a backdrop on stage, and in front of the stage—a small table like a conductor's stand. On the table were a microphone and a tape recorder, and both of us sat down behind it. And on the stage—Andrei with Lev and Ira with Vera—in white t-shirts and blue shorts with numbers, and with brushes in hand. The whole thing is that none of them had held a brush before with the idea to paint: their consciousness has not been marred by bourgeois art. The program of action was this: we sat down behind the director's stand with the newspaper *Pravda* in hand and read the editorial "The Scope of Housing Construction" into the microphone. Afterward the roles were distributed: each one of the numbers-participants took on the task of depicting a major moment of the text. One took on the depiction of the process of production; another—the relations in a labor collective, the third, for instance—salary funds. First of all, everybody gets used to the role according to Stanislavsky's system, thinking over the meaning of the text, putting oneself in the place of another actor and vice versa. Then, following our instructions, everyone went to the corner of the stage where we had cans with archetypical color mixtures, and each one dipped a brush in a typical can. Red color, for instance, corresponds to the labor collective. Then we put on the tape with the recording of the sounds of a May 1 demonstration, and everybody started daubing the best they could over the red background. We were going to donate the resulted collective masterpiece of Party-Spontaneous Marxism to the Tretyakov Gallery. The work was going great, we were giving instructions over the microphone, and suddenly the bell rang. We should not have opened the door, but we had nothing to conceal, so we opened it. A bunch of militia men burst in, dressed in civilian clothes, and their boss with them. He started shouting: 'Everybody in the car!' We, all together: 'You don't have the right!' He: 'I know when Soviet laws are broken!' And all the participants together: 'You say this before the witnesses?' He went crazy, and everybody was giggling because everyone, except us, of course, was sure that this was a continuation of the plot, that we had planned this. Maybe it was the continuation of the plot, but we did not plan it. Everybody was having a great time until we were actually taken to the militia station. And only after nearly falling asleep on a wooden militia bench did I remember—the tape recorder! Because when the militia men burst in, the tape recorder was on. It would have been enough to switch it from 'play' to 'record,' and what a document of the era we could have had!"

Now, not only from each event does there remain a painting—from each painting there remains an event, connected with and provoked by it. This always has been a part of the legend about an artist's life, and without this myth the reception of his paintings by posterity would be completely different.

Time is the prime perpetuator of the myth of the artist. Already in *Ribbon* time entered as a stylistic element: the style of each successive miniature was connected with the subjects of the image by the period of the style, and time was the aesthetic criterion of the completeness of *Ribbon* or, more precisely, its incompleteness. The structure of *Ribbon* is such that the author could have worked on it all his life, making, say, a miniature a year, and the completion of this masterpiece would be determined by the date of the author's death. The deadly inevitability of completion would create the impression of the painting's wholeness, where every miniature is just one more step toward and a rehearsal for the perfection that can only be achieved after death. It is possible to imagine the biography of practically every twentieth-century artist in the form of such a "ribbon," perfecting their styles from one painting to another.

Studying the artist's oeuvre, later generations find in the "ribbon" of his work the ups and downs on his way to the personal "I"; they look for predecessors of his (unconscious) style and even compile the registers of his followers. Death cuts short the monolog of his brush in the middle of a brush stroke. All his life he was supposed to be persecuted and incomprehensible, so that a century later the grateful descendants erect a monument for him on yet another Soviet square. This is a sham because every human biography is unique and its posthumous cementation in any form, even in the form of a diary written by a nineteenth-century schoolgirl, is also unique. The value of art, however, is not in the uniqueness and originality of style. Art is the unique personal interpretation of the canon of beauty, as religion is the private understanding of a religious code. Whether the canon of Stalinist art is good or evil is the question for philosophers and sociologists. But this is the only canon of beauty created by Soviet regime, and the business of a Soviet artist is to face it. The refusal to notice this canon leads into nothingness—to the half-baked modernism of Moscow basements and eventually to politics.

In the end, Russian culture is cluttered with names of the tragic martyrs in the name of art who did not move this art a single step forward.

The analysis of the relationship of an artist's biography to his art has led the Famous Artists to the period of Post-Art—paintings-exhibitions. These are "retrospective exhibitions" of fictitious, invented names in Russian-Soviet art. Upon entering the room, you find yourself at the exhibition of a "famous" artist, his paintings are hung on the walls, his biography is on a stand. It is a painting inside a painting, an exhibition within an exhibition, a peculiar theatrical Pirandellism. There is everything expected at an exhibition: paintings, letters, and documents, an art historical essay about this legendary biography. Nikolai Buchumov is nearly our contemporary who worked in the first quarter of the twentieth century but who, "as opposed to various wise guys" (as he writes about himself), did not discover anything. He does not remember his childhood; "I only remember the bitter smell of wormwood." Yielding to "the devilry of modernism," he painted a pink mermaid on the shore of a blue sea in a baguette frame (this picture was really found in the attic of an abandoned house on Arbat—this is how the idea for the painting exhibition emerged). But later, having come to his senses, he "ran away from the decadent cities" to be closer to earth and the smell of wormwood, and, leaving aside the social problems of the century, he started to paint like "a bird sings." Having moved to his native village, for the rest of his life Buchumov painted the same landscape from the same place and from the same point of view. Therefore, on the identical squares of his paintings at the "exhibition," we see the inevitable contour of his nose, because Buchumov followed nature in everything and he saw his nose through the corner of the eye. He painted four small studies a year, one for each season, and, because he knew beforehand when he would meet his death, he prepared the necessary number of canvases—forty-four, if I am not mistaken. This landscape, which he painted until his last sigh, is a tiresome view of miniscule changes on a sad stretch of a Russian plain, and the studies show the degradation of a lonely tree drying up from year to year. Of course, such painting exhibition is first of all a parody of the martyrs of pure art and of French Impressionism at the times of struggle against Zionism and class enemies in general, the martyrs who eventually turned into solid Soviet academic painters. Yet having come to the exhibition and having agreed to play the role of a visitor at this historical exhibition, you are pulled into a complicity with this act, with this *yurodivy* creation of greatness from nothing in your presence. Finding yourself at this exhibition, you pay your respect to the heroic deed of the artist who, regardless of the approaching illness and death, did not put down his brushes and gave all of himself to the purity of Russian landscape. The fact that this landscape turned out ugly is of secondary importance, or perhaps there is a great historical meaning which lies behind its ugliness. Time justifies everything, the names and the dates. One more, one less—what difference does it make for historical progress? And turning to another wall, you see one more painting exhibition: "Russian eighteenth century abstract artist, serf Apeles Zyablov." Huge, dark canvases in old frames are on the wall. Finished with a special American varnish, these canvases are covered by a web of small cracks, an artificial web that creates the physical impression of another time. But when this brown medley of the serf-genius is scrutinized, it turns out that it is nothing less than the works by Kandinsky! Each painting is meticulously dated from the eighteenth century, and this obvious dodgery makes a joke of the ephemeral documental evidences of inventions—from the steam engine of the brothers Cherepanov to the arithmetics of orthodox believers. The style of the legend about these Russian self-made artists is enriched by a copy of the Decree of the Russian Academy of the Arts which ordered the re-education of the half-baked abstractionist Zyablov through the diligent drawing of classical plaster casts around the clock under the observation of a policeman. After this, according to the "biography," Apeles Zyablov hanged himself. On the special stand of this "exhibition" there is an album of correspondence between Apeles Zyablov and his master, landlord, and tyrant. The eighteenth-century flowery style of these letters parodies the style of Stalinist historians who retroactively endowed nonexistent heroes with nonexistent heroic deeds. And, finally, on such occasions there is the necessary article by a Soviet art historian who saw in the stormy abstractions of the serf (of course, against Western interpretations of this resurrected genius) a call for the liberation of peasants, and in the tyrant landlord—an eighteenth-century Enlightenment figure and patron of the arts. By the way, the name of Apeles Zyablov was not made up. Such a serf-artist really existed. He decorated a fireplace in the house of a well-known nobleman, Struyskiy, who became famous for being the first in Russia to construct in his basement a torture chamber for entertainment. Apeles Zyablov is a real name, but it sounds ridiculous, and the names of the Famous Artists—Komar and Melamid—sound just as ridiculous. Self-irony of this painting exhibition is in equating the abstractionism of Apeles Zyablov with Sots-Art of Komar and Melamid—modernism is absurd next to a torture chamber. Entering such an "exhibition" we cynically justify by our presence the "great artist" and the torture chamber—from a historical point of view. From a historical point of view, too, interrogation records are also great literature. The Famous Artists took the route of self-parody. But in certain historical periods self-parody means self-elimination. One can go no further with such a way of thinking. Further, one has to move to faraway places or be moved into a halfway house—in a straight direction or in a direction unknown. The Famous Artists, casting away their pseudonym and having become Komar and Malamid once again, chose, as always, the unknown direction.[8]

"At first I was surprised why Lenin's statues are full figure while Marx is always just a bust—always cut in the middle. Then I guessed it: to conceal the traces of circumcision."

NOTES

1. The monologs, set in this text in quotes, are intentionally distorted and fully fabricated shorthand records of the conversations with "The Famous Artists of the 1970s, Twentieth Century, Moscow" to whose works this essay is dedicated. "The Famous Artists of the 1970s, Twentieth Century, Moscow" is a parody pseudonym of Aleksander Melamid and Vitaly Komar. However, the monologs in quotes should be rather understood as a second voice in a radio broadcast about their paintings of the Moscow period, as though this second voice belonged not to the painters but to their paintings.

2. *Byt* refers to the general conditions of everyday life.—Eds. note.

3. *Yurodivy*—a madman considered to possess prophetic abilities.—Eds. note.

4. From a song by Bulat Okudzhava.—Eds. note.

5. M. Laktionov—Soviet portrait and genre painter.—Eds. note.

6. Reference to the monument *Worker and Collective Farm Woman* by Vera Mukhina (1937).—Eds. note.

7. *Subbotnik*—an unpaid voluntary mass workday.—Eds. note.

8. The author refers to Komar and Melamid's emigration to Israel.—Eds. note.

Public and Artist in Russia at the Turn of the Twentieth Century

In May 1896, an all-Russian industry and art exhibition was opened in Nizhni Novgorod. The tsarist government saw the primary purpose of the exhibition as demonstrating achievements of Russian capitalism which had been developing at an unprecedented pace during this period. On the other hand, by showcasing the success in industrial development, the exhibition was to cover the overall political and economic backwardness of the social system of the country. The exhibition also had an extensive program of theatrical performances, entertainment shows, and concerts. The event provided a unique opportunity to watch, in immediate proximity to one another, buffoon shows and performances of the Maly Theater company, listen to wailing cries of Russian folk singers and concerts of opera and symphony classics, witness first cinematography experiments, and admire guest cabaret stars. Exhibits of handicrafts and professional fine arts could be also seen close by.

Notable paintings were exhibited in the Far North Pavilion decorated with Konstantin Korovin's[1] celebrated Northern frescoes as well as in a special room where Mikhail Vrubel's canvases could be seen. The art section of the exhibition proper, however, was poor, and this was noticed by many art critics. Some prominent artists were not represented at the exhibition at all, whereas others had their minor

Grigory Sternin, "Zritel i khudozhnik v Rossii na rubezhe XIX—XX vekov" (Public and artist in Russia at the turn of the twentieth century), in *Russkaya khudozhestvennaya kultura vtoroy poloviny XIX—nachala XX veka* (Visual arts and culture in Russia at the end of the nineteenth—beginning of the twentieth century) (Moscow: Sovetskiy Kkudozhnik, 1984), 28–52.

works on display. The exhibition premises were filled with works of small-time painters and sculptors who had no difficulty in having their works selected by academic juries as the authorities had entrusted the Academy of Arts with responsibility for organizing the art section of the exhibition and selecting exhibits.

For the above reasons, the Nizhni Novgorod exhibition did not prove to be an important event in the artistic life of Russia, and we could have refrained from dwelling on it at length had it not been for some circumstances which were responsible for making this exhibition an indicator of the difficult and contradictory development of Russian fine arts during the period.

The exhibition was noteworthy for two reasons. First, it took place at the very beginning of the period of time under examination, and, second, it was the first joint exposition of various art groups of this particular period. At the time of extremely intensive formation of artistic factions striving for a distinctness based on independent aesthetic platforms, such an exhibition was representative, even though in a relative manner, of the situation in art in general and the artistic power structure in the bitter ideological struggle in particular.

In this respect the large number of minor and weak works of art displayed at the exhibition is in itself a fact which calls for a careful examination.

Let us consider the exhibition and some related artistic events.

According to an estimate made by N. P. Sobko, over 2,200 paintings were exhibited at art shows organized by the Peredvizhniki (members of the Russian school of realist painters of the second half of the nineteenth century belonging to the Association of Travelling Art Exhibitions) from 1884 to 1894. During the same period, over 4,000 works of art were displayed at exhibitions organized by the Academy of Arts, that is, almost double the figure of the Peredvizhniki.

Of course, the number of the exhibited works of art, taken alone, cannot provide a complete picture of the place and importance of creative principles in actual artistic development. Nor is it in a position to furnish a comprehensive description of aesthetic interests of society. Nevertheless, these figures are at least indicative of claims laid by certain groups of artists to meeting requirements of their time and, consequently, to speaking on behalf of society.

In this respect, the above figures are primarily testimony to an increase which was taking place in public activity of late academic salon art. The figures indicate that as early as the second half of the eighties, when the Peredvizhniki continued to win major creative victories owing to their profound insight into fundamental problems of Russia following the reforms of 1861, epigonic academicism was tenaciously gaining ground at exhibition halls in the attempts to attract the attention of the general public.

By the mid-nineties, academicism had grown in its aggressiveness, a fact which affected in full measure the composition of the art section of the Nizhni Novgorod exhibition. The Peredvizhniki had 230 paintings on exhibit. Their major portion had been displayed at the twenty-fourth exhibition of the Association immediately preceding the Nizhni Novgorod exhibition. On the other hand, academic exhibitors and members of the St. Petersburg Society of Painters were represented by 325 paintings. As a result, superficial canvases were predominant at the Nizhni Novgorod exhibition. They were far from true realism, seductive in their melodramatic subjects or the banal beauty of landscapes.[2]

The exhibition of 1896 and its organizers' activities, however, revealed another aspect of the profound contradictions characteristic of the artistic life of Russia during the period under examination. We have in mind the notorious incident involving two big paintings, *Mikula Selyaninovich* and *Princess Reverie*, specially painted by Vrubel for the exhibition. A scandal broke out which was given sensational publicity. These works of art had already been put into places assigned to them in the exhibition pavilion. However, they had to be removed at the categorical insistence of the academic jury. The canvases were eventually exhibited in a building specially constructed for them on the exhibition grounds by S. I. Mamontov.

The controversy over the two paintings, which involved the most influential tsarist dignitaries, was a singular example of bureaucratic morals and manners of tsarist Russia. The bitter conflict was prompted by bureaucratic presumption rather than aesthetic considerations, as the acceptance or rejection of Vrubel's paintings for the exhibition became a matter of personal prestige for the Grand Duke Vladimir Alexandrovich, on the one hand, and then the Minister of Finance S. Yu. Vitte, on the other. Nevertheless, the incident was directly related to art and elicited a keen response from artistic circles. Vrubel's paintings and the incident provoked an animated discussion in newspapers. Prominent figures of Russian culture of that time wrote about them at length in their private correspondence.[3]

In the course of this dispute it became obvious that at the turn of the century Russian art was facing a new complicated problem. Sharp criticism of Vrubel's paintings by both democratic and academic circles, even if they had their own reasons for rejecting the artist's work, revealed another battle line in Russian culture. In other words, Vrubel's paintings gave rise to another bitter conflict in addition to incessant relentless animosity between democratic realism and late epigonic academicism.

As is generally known, young Maxim Gorky was among journalists and critics covering the exhibition of 1896. His reports of the exhibition were a regular feature in *Nizhegorodskiy listok* (Nizhni Novgorod Newsletter) and *Odesskiye Novosti* (Odessa News) in the summer of 1896. Fine arts, especially Vrubel's paintings, were given much attention in his news stories. Maxim Gorky kept coming back to them, arguing with critics who were contesting his opinion.

Gorky's judgment of Vrubel was precise and categorical. The young writer believed that Vrubel had "spoiled Rostand's beautiful plot and he was equally successful in spoiling the legend of Mikula."[4] Criticizing the plastic rendering of Vrubel's canvases and his portrayal of characters, Gorky regarded these paintings as a direct manifestation of the fashionable disease of decadence in art.[5]

As he gave reasons for his negative judgment of Vrubel's paintings, Gorky asserted one highly important fact. In his opinion, Vrubel's paintings could be appreciated only by a very limited number of connoisseurs, whereas "it is not artists, but the public who need art and, therefore, the public should be given such paintings that it can understand."[6] This idea ran through all reviews of the exhibition written by Gorky and shaped his critical position. Sociologically this problem was not new at all. What was new was the fact that it was becoming one of the main criteria in analyzing and judging the quality of works of art.

The need for works of art which could be understood easily and appreciated by the general public was in Gorky's opinion especially imperative, as he regarded art primarily as one of the most important means of human communication. He wrote, "Art should play a pedagogical role, its objective is to establish the fullest possible identity

between sensations and feelings."[7] In this respect, it is worth mentioning that Leo Tolstoy strongly insisted on a similar role of art in his
treatise which he published one-and-a-half years later but had started
working on much earlier, even though it was based on his own concept of the nature and significance of creative work.[8]

Acknowledging a gap which had been widening between art and
the democratic public in the course of the historical development of
human society and resulting in the failure of people to understand the
work of even major artists, Leo Tolstoy arrived at a conclusion that all
professional art was useless. He called it "the art of higher classes."
Gorky did not go that far in his newspaper articles of the Nizhni
Novgorod exhibition. He was more specific in pointing out an interde-
pendence that existed between art and the public. It is true that he
blamed no one else but Vrubel for making his paintings difficult to
understand. However, Gorky repeatedly criticized the backward tastes
of many exhibition visitors. In one of his reviews, he openly wrote of
"conservative aesthetic tastes of the masses."[9] In another instance,
while talking of the yearning of people "to somehow beautify their
dull, drab and hard life," Gorky commented with a feeling of pity that
in their need for beauty people often had to make do with Brocard
soap wrappers which were sold in large quantities by smart dealers
in rural areas. Thus, it was publicity of perfumery shops that served
as a means of aesthetic education of the people.[10]

The renowned Russian public figure N. A. Rubakin wrote in the
1890s, "The history of literature is not only the history of writers and
their works conveying certain ideas to the society but also the history
of those who read these works."[11] Such an idea can be fully applied
to the history of art. It could appear precisely at the time when the
course of historical development of the society itself was drastically
changing both the content and forms of the artistic and cultural process.[12] For Russia, such time arrived at the turn of the century.

During these years an extensive research was conducted on the
interests and needs of the rapidly increasing masses of reading public.
Publishing was developing in order to meet a substantial increase in
demand for literature of various genres. So-called people's theaters
were springing up. They had their specific repertoire and were catering
to the public in their specific ways.

Acknowledgment of the problem of art and public, similar to that
we found in Gorky's and Tolstoy's news stories and essays, was to a

considerable extent a result of a rapid increase in social activity of the masses. Tolstoy had good reason to point out that the need for a new approach to understanding the purpose and significance of art arose at this particular time when, contrary to all preceding periods, "in all people there exists, if only vaguely, an awareness of equality of all people."[13]

Even though the Russian reality did not radically change the established forms of artistic activity, it did bring to light very important new tendencies.

One of the characteristic features of the struggle for ideologically sound democratic art, which Russian artists had been carrying on in the second half of the nineteenth century, consisted in this struggle having always been accompanied by demands of a wide public appeal for the fine arts. Such were the objectives of the Peredvizhniki who, through their creative and practical work, were waging a bitter war against inertness and anachronism of ideological and aesthetic principles of academicism. At the same time, they were at great pains to break out of the caste system as well as to overcome the extreme narrowness of the social environment which provided existence to the art of orthodox academicians and to which their art was appealing. Right up to the mid-1890s, the Peredvizhniki were essentially the only group of artists that had succeeded in attracting considerably more of the public to their exhibitions. Even if, in terms of the number of works displayed at exhibitions during the preceding period, academic art was becoming predominant, in terms of attendance the Peredvizhnik exhibitions unquestionably were holding sway.

During the period under examination, there was, first and foremost, a drastic increase in the number of exhibition visitors. Nicholas Roerich wrote in this regard in the late 1890s, "Not long ago, two to three painting exhibitions were customary, sufficient, perhaps even burdensome. Nowadays, during the last 1897–1898 season, there were sixteen exhibitions plus the opening of a new art museum. And there is public everywhere, enough public. The number of paying visitors has increased from six to ten thousand to thirty thousand, excluding those with free passes and students. Nobody finds lengthy newspaper reviews of exhibitions boring. These facts represent a marked step forward. A pleasant surprise for both artists and all intelligentsia."[14] Figures given by Roerich have to be rectified as he fails to take into account the public who visited traveling exhibitions in provincial towns.[15] Nevertheless, Roerich was right as far as the general tendency was concerned.

The increasing role played by art in everyday cultural life had a prompt effect on the Russian press of the period and exerted great influence over magazine publishing and publishing policies in general.[16] Problems of painting, sculpture, decorative arts and crafts and their development were discussed by both metropolitan and provincial newspapers. Practically every art exhibition, as small as it was, gave rise to a lot of talk and discussion by newspaper reporters and professional critics. At times, a regular exhibition became the topic of the day and moved aside other news stories. Of course, newspaper chronicles of the Russian artistic life of those years contain a lot of ignorance, platitudes, and other things that bear no relation to serious art criticism. Moreover, even if criticism became more professional in general, its average standards deteriorated as compared to the preceding decades.

Russian magazines published in the late nineteenth and early twentieth centuries bear testimony to the same processes. The *Vestnik izyashchnykh iskusstv* (Fine Arts Herald) characterized by scholarly sturdiness and a clear-cut orientation toward research and scientific publishing work was replaced by two new specialized periodicals, *Iskusstvo i khudozhestvennaya promyshlennost* (Art and Artistic Industries) and *Mir iskusstva* (The World of Art). Even though these magazines differed significantly in their ideological positions, they were very similar to each other in being oriented primarily toward contemporary artistic life. They were part and parcel of this life and were deeply involved in the struggle and arguments which were carried on in Russian art during these years.

Changes taking place in the artistic life of Russia were evidenced even more by the publishing policies of *Niva* (The Field), the popular magazine which had the largest circulation in the country. It should be kept in mind that many Russian and foreign artists were obliged for the wide popularity of their works to this magazine as it featured an abundance of artistic reproductions. For this reason, *Niva* played a dual role in artistic life. It was efficient in taking into account artistic tastes of the milieu for which it was the principal home-reading material. At the same time, it greatly influenced development of these tastes. Extent of this influence can be demonstrated by the following figures. While in 1891 *Niva* had a monthly circulation of 115 thousand, by 1900 this figure increased to 235 thousand copies.

It is quite easy to determine the kind of artistic events persistently popularized by *Niva* during the period under examination. Russian and West European academicism, Russian and foreign late sentimental and idyllic genre paintings were printed in the magazine most often. Drawings specially commissioned by *Niva* were of the same nature. Magazine subscribers received regularly, as bonuses, oleographs which were framed and hung on the walls of homes of urban and rural lower-middle classes.

On the other hand, it was extremely significant that, in the mid-1890s, in order to improve and reinforce the art section of *Niva*, its publisher, A. F. Marx, a man of careful judgment who had a strong sense of readers' needs, offered, for the first time in the publishing history of the magazine, a full-time job to a professional artist and critic Igor Grabar. He was responsible for writing essays on paintings, features of artists' jubilees, and exhibition reviews, and he also participated in selecting works of art to be reproduced in the magazine. Of course, the critic had to reckon with the general orientation of the magazine toward the tastes of the lower-middle classes and, consequently, was not in a position to have any appreciable influence on the artistic policies of the magazine.[17] Nevertheless, it was undoubtedly at this particular time that the art section started to play a more important role in *Niva*.

A marked increase in the number of exhibition and museum visitors and a quantitatively rapid rise in demand for consumption of works of art were of profound importance per se. They were indicative of an important aspect of historical development of Russian society during the period under examination. The significance of these facts for the artistic life of Russia was amplified manifold by their eliciting a quick response from the artists and, thus, exerting a strong effect on the content of creative work. Moreover, one of the most specific features of the Russian artistic life of this period consisted in the art being exposed, as never before, to a powerful influence of public tastes and preferences. Formation of new aesthetic principles reflected the social and historical content of the period and, at the same time, a clash of highly specific artistic needs of a vast and extremely heterogeneous public. Of course, the relationship between art and its consumer was developing quite spontaneously, with various outside factors often interfering with the process.

How did art react to the increased democratization of the public? How did this social process affect Russian artistic life?

We want to start by considering facts that bore no immediate relation to the contemporary creative practice but were very symptomatic in their own way.

A centenary celebration of Karl Bryullov's birth was held in 1899. One could expect that the celebration would be limited to a few habitual anniversary articles. Heated arguments about Bryullov's work that had raged over the years were losing their poignancy and seemed to have become a thing of the past. However, the events took a different course.

The artist's anniversary was observed in several Russian cities. The most impressive celebration was held in St. Petersburg where a pompous jubilee session was organized by the Academy of Arts and the Society for Encouragement of Arts on December 12, 1899. An exhibition of Bryullov's paintings was also scheduled to coincide with the above session.

The fact that the Academy was celebrating the memory of one of its most prominent members was in itself not remarkable at all. Bryullov's name had always been surrounded with an aura of eminence in the academic milieu. Another fact was more interesting. P. V. Delarov opened the jubilee session with a welcoming address later published by the *Iskusstvo i khudozhestvennaya promyshlennost*. The opening address was followed by speeches delivered by Ilya Repin and Vladimir Makovskiy who indulged in ardent praises of the creator of *The Last Day of Pompeii*. It is noteworthy that Makovskiy, a professor at the Academy of Arts in those years, addressed the session on behalf of both himself and the members of the Association of Travelling Art Exhibitions (Peredvizhniki). In fact, Makovskiy's speech was marked in the official notice of the session as a salutatory address of the association. Thus, the Peredvizhniki were, in addition to the Academy of Arts and the Society for Encouragement of Arts, the third creative organization that was observing Bryullov's memory in such a demonstrative way.

The Moscow Association of Painters, the Moscow Society of Art

 Lovers, the Tretyakov Gallery, and other art societies and institutions did not take part in the celebration on various pretexts and only sent short messages of greetings.

It is worth remembering that Bryullov was one of the old Russian art idols whose deposition had been, in Stasov's opinion, of particular importance for the consolidation and publicizing of the principles of Russian democratic art of the second half of the nineteenth century. Negation of Bryullov's artistic heritage, at times indiscriminate and unjustified, had become a commonplace feature of the critics' writings. No Peredvizhnik would have thought of taking the Great Karl under his protection.

What values did Repin and Makovskiy find in Bryullov's heritage now, on the threshold of the new century?[18] Both of them emphasized, first and foremost, his remarkable gift of drawing which had enabled him to cope with the most difficult technical problems. At the same time, Makovskiy pointed out that Bryullov had been a painter "highly sensitive to beauty." According to Makovskiy, Bryullov's principal merit was the fact that his *The Last Day of Pompeii* had proven to be "the first painting that stirred up Russian society, made it look forward to the opening of an art exhibition, gave it the happiness of experiencing rapturous exaltation induced by a work of art . . . With Bryullov's arrival, Russian art became a social phenomenon essential for the cultural development of both Russian society in general and every individual Russian in particular."[19]

We are interested in the sociological aspect of the heated controversies that took place during the Bryullov celebrations. We have in mind here the problem of an artist's social standing which was brought up during the centenary. We have already quoted from Makovskiy's speech that commended Bryullov in every possible way for awakening broad public interest in art. Repin must have voiced similar sentiments, even if newspaper accounts of his speech contain no such direct statements. It is a known fact that while preparing for his speech at the session, Repin made the following notes: "A vast majority was enraptured by Bryullov's *Pompeii* . . . Bryullov is a social artist. It takes a perfect form and a sense of life (sincerity) to be understood by a majority of public."[20]

This was a fairly drastic revision of the historical appraisal of Bryullov's creative work. True, the positive meaning of this reversal came to nothing more than declarations of the importance of universally comprehensible art. Essentially, the reappraisal of Bryullov's work was motivated by many conflicting and even conservative factors which were immediately and precisely pointed out by Repin's opponents. Nevertheless, these declarations were of great importance per se, especially as the controversy was concerned with artistic culture of the first half of the nineteenth century, and different interpretations of that particular period with respect to its culture were used by opponents as weighty arguments in support of their social and aesthetic positions.

This came to light quite clearly when a centenary of Alexander Pushkin's birth was observed that same year, almost coinciding with Bryullov's jubilee. As a matter of fact, this coincidence was repeatedly emphasized by the press. Both the creative work of the great poet and the entire Pushkin period evoked special sentiments in the Russian public.

Initiatives undertaken by artistic circles during Pushkin's jubilee of 1899 included, in addition to the huge work to have the poet's literary writings illustrated, a special issue of *Mir iskusstva* (no. 13/14, 1899). The illustration section of the issue was made up entirely of Russian paintings and graphics of the first third of the nineteenth century— O. A. Kiprenskiy, A. O. Orlovskiy, A. G. Venetsianov, F. P. Tolstoy, and others. An expert selection of reproductions revealed a stylistic perfection and poetic clarity of drawings and paintings of the Pushkin era.

The magazine featured interpretations of Pushkin by nearly all major Russian "right-wing" symbolists of the period—V. V. Rozanov, D. S. Merezhkovskiy, N. M. Minskiy, F. K. Sologub. Each of them tried, in his own way, to portray Pushkin as a forerunner of modern trends and, what is most important, as a poet completely alien to the masses and beyond their comprehension. F. Sologub's article was of particular significance in this respect. He was extremely perplexed even by the fact of a preparation for all-Russian Pushkin celebrations. "Does Pushkin really have anything for today's crowd? Maybe he does have something banal and popular?"[21] The questions were answered categorically in the negative by the author of the article himself.

In the sociological interpretation of artistic heritage, a different point of view also came to light, and it was contrary to that expressed by Repin and Makovskiy in their appraisal of Bryullov's work. This advocacy of extreme individualism both as the highest creative virtue and a form of an artist's social existence was antidemocratic. By advocating a full autonomy of the artist from the masses of general public, by prophesying a doom to art if it elected to cater to tastes of a rapidly increasing number of exhibition visitors, this criticism also reflected a complex and contradictory relationship between art and public. "Poet and the mob" was perhaps the most multifaceted problem facing those involved in Russian artistic culture at the time. Some prominent figures of Russian art were struggling with this problem, looking for new ways to resolve these conflicts in art. This fact can be evidenced by the disappointments and hope experienced by Vrubel and Alexander Block in their incessant search of a direct relationship with the public.

Let us take a closer look at the concrete circumstances of the period.

The Peredvizhniki were entering the new era having developed successful forms of relationship between their art and the democratic public. The main reason for such a situation could be the fact that *raznochintzy* (intellectuals not belonging to the gentry in nineteenth-century Russia), who had been the principal consumer of the art of Peredvizhniki during the seventies and eighties, continued to hold an important social position at the turn of the century. It was this intelligentsia and some other social strata ideologically influenced by it that kept providing a firm basis for the Peredvizhniki in artistic life. Ya. D. Minchenkov, who was involved in organizational and creative matters of the association during this late period of its existence and who was regularly accompanying traveling exhibitions to provincial towns, wrote: "It was mainly intelligentsia who were attracted by art as well as *raznochintzy,* teachers, students and, lately, organized working masses for whom, like for students, the doors of the exhibition stood wide open."[22]

The Peredvizhniki, however, became aware of new complex sociological problems too. Reasons for these difficulties were clearly revealed by one cultural event of the period. In the spring of 1904, the Association of Travelling Art Exhibitions organized the First Popular Painting Exhibition. Characteristically for the period, exhibition locations included Nobel's plant. A newspaper reported: "The First Popular Painting Exhibition of the Association of Travelling Art Exhibitions opened on the premises of the Smolensk public school on Schliesselburg Road on March 29. For this exhibit, approximately thirty new pictures had been painted and some old paintings had been repainted. All of them were adapted to suit tastes of working class people . . . An influx of visitors proves the need for such exhibitions . . . During the first day alone, over 300 people visited the exhibition . . . The exhibition features paintings by V. Makovskiy, Myasoyedov, Volkov, Kiselev, Lemokh, Beggrov, Bogdanov-Belskiy, A. Makovskiy, Popov, Savitskiy, Kasatkin, Bogdanov, etc."[23]

There is an interesting detail in this short newspaper notice. While preparing for the popular exhibition, association members were trying to adapt their paintings to their new understanding of the goals of public education. Even more interesting is an eye-witness account of the results of these initiatives. Minchenkov recollected: "One day, the old Peredvizhniki had an idea to bring art closer to the working class and peasants, to send painting exhibits to factory districts and villages, markets and fairgrounds where peasant masses come together. The main person behind this initiative, which fully met the Peredvizhniki's objectives, was Myasoyedov. However, the association did not succeed in carrying his idea through. On Myasoyedov's instructions, remakes of old Peredvizhnik paintings were produced for the popular exhibition, all of the same size. To make them easier to be understood by people, the paintings were somewhat embellished. Main attention was paid to the subject matter of the paintings. Craftsmanship, technique, purely pictorial objectives were thought superfluous. The working class and peasants were presented with second-rate art of antiquated tendencies.

"The experience proved that it had been a mistake of the 'old men' who had lost touch with the popular masses and no longer had any sense of the spiritual needs of these masses.

"The exhibition was first sent to working districts of St. Petersburg and turned out to be a complete fiasco. Workers had developed a sufficiently high sense of art since their days at school when they had been taken to traveling exhibitions and museums. They demanded more from art. What they were offered by the Peredvizhniki at their popular exhibition did not satisfy them."[24]

Thus, if the eye-witness account is to be trusted, even the Peredvizhniki, who had done a lot for popularization of realistic art, at times made serious mistakes while sincerely trying to win a new public and did not fully understand its aesthetic interests.

Even more serious problems and controversies, however, were obstructing the search for contacts with the general public in the artistic life of Russia in the late nineteenth and early twentieth centuries. These problems originated first of all from the great social heterogeneity of the milieu which was increasingly claiming its right to take part in artistic life. An increasing number of workers could be seen among the public who, according to Minchenkov, had a sufficiently developed artistic taste.[25] At the same time, petty bourgeoisie was increasingly laying claim to the right to judge art. The influence of petty bourgeois tastes proved to be sufficiently strong. This influence was due to more than the mere fact that lower-middle classes were rapidly increasing the number of exhibition patrons. The main reason was the situation when opinions of these classes, which primarily came into existence as a result of the stratification of the Russian peasantry, were passed off as those representing aesthetic needs of people, their true ideals and preferences. These opinions were at times supported and shaped by the ideology of late Russian *narodniki* (populists). We want to give just one telling example.

Should a present-day art historian wish to determine the hit of the 1897–98 art exhibition season on the basis of press reports and eyewitness accounts of the period, he would be able to do this quite easily. There were no differences in opinion among the contemporaries. Of all the pictures exhibited, the most attention was attracted by a huge painting by Heinrich Semiradskiy, *Christian Dircea at Nero's Circus,* which was displayed at the sixth exhibition of the St. Petersburg Society of Painters. According to a contemporary critic, Semiradskiy's painting provoked "so much printed and verbal discussion that he is frightened to approach it."[26] Nowadays, the painting has been justifiably forgotten. The painting depicts a scene from ancient Rome. The bored emperor amuses himself by watching a young Christian woman dying in the circus arena. Similar to Semiradskiy's earlier paintings, for example, *The Christian Luminaries,* the plot of the picture allegedly raised moral problems. The portrayal of Nero's brutality was supposedly intended to condemn despotism. In reality, however, the subject matter of the work was exploited by the painter to demonstrate once again his perfect, but completely cold, craftsmanship in depicting naked bodies, marble, mother-of-pearl, ancient costumes. In a word, it was a typical specimen of one of the numerous versions of European late academicism openly catering to undemanding tastes of the bourgeois public. Incidentally, this fact also determined the characteristic turn of academicism to the era of Imperial Rome trying to draw a historical parallel to fin-de-siècle sentiments which were a fashion with the bourgeoisie.

Semiradskiy's painting would not have been worth mentioning, if it had not provoked an intense discussion in the press of an extremely timely issue of a possible contradiction between the actual quality of a work of art and its public appraisal by numerous exhibition visitors. Articles were published by art critics with a degree of generalization hardly justified by the historical and artistic value of this canvas. Such was, for example, a detailed article by P. P. Gnedich which had an interesting title, *G. I. Semiradskiy and Contemporary Art.*[27] Gnedich wrote about the author of *Dircea:* "He is a Marlinskiy of the seventies and eighties. This is an artist who does not want to capture the inner character of his hero but exaggerates his outward features with a conventional, even purely decadent falseness. It may appear strange that I call Mr. Semiradskiy a decadent, but I am absolutely positive about it. . . . His people have no flesh, no blood, no muscles, no life. They are mannequins made for exhibiting exemplary painted rags." Gnedich follows up with his main message: "Let many like him. Both Kukolnik and Marlinskiy were liked too. They had supporters who scorned *Belkin's Stories* and *Taman* and favored their idols. But the hour struck, trash daubery crashed down from false icon cases to be replaced by Turgenev and Tolstoy."

Gnedich was opposed categorically in the same newspaper by A. V. Amfiteatrov who wrote in defense of Semiradskiy.[28] He also tried to refute Gnedich's idea of a temporary success of unimportant works of art. He wrote: "I believe that to negate the taste that the crowd shows of its own free will, by its own instinct, and to impose on it the public tastes that are dictated by theoretical judgment, amounts to historical injustice. If we look into the depths of the history of art, we will notice without fail that all lasting masterpieces had been appreciated by the crowd at their true value, even if without finesse but with solidity, if not by critical judgment, but according to an eternal instinct of truth and beauty that is innate in the masses."

Of course, nowadays there is no necessity at all to examine this dispute in terms of appraisal of the painting itself. Time has proven its critics completely right. It is more important to emphasize another issue. By referring to the crowd and the eternal instinct of truth and beauty innate in the masses, Amfiteatrov was bluntly trying to assert absolute unconditionality of aesthetic principles of bourgeois art.

However, what made the problem so complicated was the fact that the critic's appeal to the masses was more than just a rhetorical device. It took into account, with a high degree of precision, widespread artistic tastes of the period. Suffice it to say that, according to the press, 28,000 people visited the exhibition of the St. Petersburg Society of Painters which featured Semiradskiy's *Dircea* during one month. Only a few most popular Peredvizhniki exhibitions had a comparable attendance.

The most serious art critics were aware of these facts. They realized that backward conservative public tastes which were shaped and strongly influenced by petty bourgeois ideology, and, of course, had nothing in common with genuinely popular aesthetic needs, played a significant role in the lush flourishing of eclectic salon academicism. Moreover, it was obvious that the great popularity of academic art was indicative of its significant objective strength. It was from this point that Sergey Glagol, one of the serious art writers of the time, tried to appraise the eighth exhibition of the St. Petersburg Society of Painters in a detailed review.[29] He emphasized his absolute rejection of such works of art but had to admit that the work of society members "represents the lives of dozens of people while thousands of other people sincerely admire it and are fully confident that it is genuine art worthy of every encouragement and praise." For this reason, "it deserves attention and should not be ignored or mentioned just briefly." Next, Sergey Glagol asked the question: "What is the matter here? What is the difference between these two arts, the art of St. Petersburg painters (members of the St. Petersburg Society of Painters) and that of the Repins, Serovs, Vasnetsovs, etc., and why is the majority of the public fonder of the former than of the latter?"

Due to a rapid increase in public activity of academic salon art, this problem was developing into a serious social and artistic issue.

Striving for more than popularity at regular annual exhibitions, more precisely exploiting it in every possible way, the salon academicism was looking for new ways to win the public over to its side. In this respect, the so-called popular painting exhibitions organized by the same St. Petersburg Society of Painters were highly demonstrative. The first and the second such exhibitions were held respectively in 1898 and 1901. They were held on the premises of the St. Petersburg Horse Guard Riding School in order to demonstrate that they were open to people of all walks of life. A critic wrote, "The St. Petersburg Society of Painters has rented a riding school and a commoner wearing galoshes and a headpiece can enter it without being embarrassed by etiquette and parquet. The admission fee is a nickel, the catalog costs as much, which is a good bargain, and over 500 excellent paintings have been put on display. As a result, people get a cheap admission and an earthen floor of the riding school while everybody gets to enjoy eternal beautiful art."[30]

In fact, the organizers of the exhibitions did not set for themselves a goal of exhibiting paintings specially produced for the ordinary public. These were regular pictures painted by society members. As can be seen from the catalog, however, under the guise of genuine or true art, the public was usually presented with samples of salon academicism, that is, the same substitute art. It was not a coincidence that Semiradskiy's painting mentioned by us earlier was to become a highlight of the first exhibition.

Even if the exhibition organizers were guided by motives which had little in common with genuine democracy, the exhibitions were visited by fairly large numbers of people. Press reports put the number of patrons at over 60,000, almost a record number for exhibition admissions of the period. *Niva* (issue no. 42, 1898) publicized the first exhibition (a highly noteworthy fact per se considering the main orientation of this periodical with respect to fine arts) by featuring a print which showed an interior view of the Horse Guard Riding School with paintings hung on walls and groups of onlookers. The artist tried his best to reproduce the "common-folk" look of visitors. Newspaper reporters also pointed out that the exhibition was visited mainly by ordinarily public.

Of course, it would be very important to get accurate information with respect to the concrete social composition of visitors of the Horse Guard Riding School and, proceeding from these data, to try to relate academic art to particular public tastes. Unfortunately, no such statistics were recorded at that time. Nevertheless, an approximate makeup of the public can be determined from sociological research into readers' interests which was extensively conducted during the period.

N. A. Rubakin assigned a special place in his classification to an extremely widespread genre of literature which he called "translated foreign trash." In terms of its distinctive features, this literature had a lot in common with late salon academicism of fine arts. The literature was distinguished by superficially entertaining plots, the authors' predilection for depicting the so-called beautiful life and melodramatic effects. Rubakin wrote: "The principal consumers of translated novels are, first, those who have only recently been getting used to a 'thick' book—merchants, shop-keepers, clerks, tradesmen, generally those . . . who seek nothing but entertainment from a book. These people are looking for 'adventures experienced by heroes' in a book, by heroes and nobody else. They . . . dig through catalogs for a long time looking for scary and intricate titles (*Armfuls of Roses, Gold and Blood, From Bridal Bed to Scaffold, Three Kinds of Love,* etc.)."[31] According to Rubakin, categories of readers interested in translated junk were those who, "even if they knew its true value," preferred it to better authors who "tired" them, or to ideologically intelligent writings which they found "disturbing."

As with any analogy, there are certain limits to comparing such literature to late academic painting. On the basis of information provided by Rubakin, however, even the limited similarity between them makes it possible to explain reasons for throngs of people who flocked to the exhibitions organized by the St. Petersburg Society of Painters. It equally enables us to understand who exactly were the people called "commoners" by newspaper reporters.

The above facts are indicative of one highly significant feature of Russian artistic life during the period under examination. It was the search for cheap popularity, a deliberate catering to undemanding artistic tastes that formed the basis of the relationship between the artist and the public in cases described by us.[32] To be exact, there was no search but rather an efficient exploitation of ostentatious professional devices which had proven popular with the public. We have already spoken of the complex social circumstances which determined the great popularity of such art. Epigonic academicism did a lot of harm by disseminating petty bourgeois banality and providing support to vulgar tastes and bourgeois psychology. As to the artists who represented this art, they were hardly guided by any profound ideological principles. Rather they were concerned with much more concrete and practical problems, how to make the best use of their popularity in order to retain their commercially sound positions in cultural life which were increasingly threatened by competition.

In the late 1890s and early 1900s, a new tendency came to light in Russian art which also exemplifies grave intrinsic contradictions of the social and cultural development of the country. Vrubel's debut in St. Petersburg, Diaghilev's first exhibitions and establishment of the World of Art group, development by the Moscow Association of Painters of its own style, and other artistic events were accompanied by an ever-increasing number of press reports and magazine reviews, letters and statements by artists themselves of a discord between art and the public. Mass publications which reflected tastes of the so-called general public or, in any case, claimed to do so, were blaming artists for this situation. On the other hand, specialized journals, first and foremost *Mir iskusstva,* saw the root of all evil in an inadequate aesthetic development of the masses, in their artistic conservatism. At the same time, another, more important border line was becoming apparent. Different camps were emerging which proposed their own ways to overcome this conflict, pointed out directions which Russian art was to take in its development, specified its place and role in social life. A brief survey of critical literature of the period is sufficient to provide support for the view that different social and artistic circles, while agreeing on the existence of the above fact, at times drew diametrically opposite conclusions from it.

Artists' complaints of not being adequately appreciated by the public were heard from all directions during this period. At times, these complaints were nothing but a pose or a show of bravado. In many cases, however, they represented very sincere and serious reflections on the artists' creative destinies. Here is one of such testimonies, a letter written in 1904 by a relatively unassuming painter and more than moderate innovator—F. I. Rerberg—which he addressed to V. G. Korolenko: " . . . everything has got mixed up and turned upside-down in our small world of art during these fourteen years. Most former ideals have been destroyed, many former idols have been toppled over and replaced by new ones . . .

"All of us had been Repin's disciples, his ardent admirers, and followers of the Peredvizhniki. Four years later, when I visited you in Nizhni Novgorod, I came there to arrange exhibitions on behalf of the Moscow Association of Painters, a group where we first spoke of the need for liberating art from tight conventional frames which the Peredvizhniki had squeezed it into. It was a happy time, a time of concerted faultless and selfless effort, a time when we had trust in our own strength, when we saw the light at the end of the tunnel.

"But soon we came to realize that the struggle was excruciatingly hard. A few great talents emerged from our group. Our exhibitions became fresh, full of variety and color. And yet, the more subtle and artistic are paintings at the exhibitions, the more you realize that our public has no need for art, that it is only able to appreciate funny stories and photos.

"This failure of artists and the public to understand each other at times makes our work simply unbearable. I know some very talented artists who have given up painting after they realized that nobody needs it. I am still confident that eventually people will understand our work, they will realize that it is necessary and useful, and yet it is incredibly difficult to live among people who are stubborn in their unwillingness to understand us, to be unable, for years on end, to hear a single word of encouragement, to see no interest in things we cherish . . .

"I am not familiar with your attitude to gods we worship now, but I anxiously hope that you are on our side. You are a favorite writer of most of those artists who search for truth and with whom I happen to work. You are such a great writer of life and we are so anxious to become painters of life, real painters, not just storytellers making use of recipes invented by the Peredvizhniki who still remain popular with both the public and most men of letters."[33]

To better understand the meaning of this letter, we should keep in mind that "a few great talents" who had emerged in the 1900s at exhibitions held by the Moscow Association of Painters included, in the first place, Vrubel and Borisov-Musatov. It is important to emphasize that neither artists nor the public are necessarily to be blamed for the conflict described here that is highly characteristic of the period if we consider it from a purely sociological point of view and leave the moral aspect out. Very often both of them were right in their own way, and perhaps it is this fact that made the situation so dramatic.

A considerable narrowing of social addresses of many works of art, or rather a forced resignation of the artist to this circumstance, represented, to a certain extent, a response to calculated speculative popularity of petty-bourgeois art. It was a protest against turning art into popular consumer goods, against a relationship between art and the public which prevented an artist from establishing a spiritual contact with people. These were the reasons why a tragic dilemma was developing in the work of many prominent figures of Russian culture of the period. This dilemma was conducive to a revival of romantic concepts of a genius and the crowd. It also strengthened the artist's sense of having been chosen by divine will. It is not my function here to analyze in detail a highly complex interaction of sociological factors and ideological and aesthetic quests which gave rise to the new art at the turn of the century. Only a detailed examination of artistic life of the period can bring us closer to a solution of this problem. And still, even the few facts described here make it possible to assert that the above conflict resulted in an increase of individualism in the artist's work. Polemics between the artist and the public resembled an argument between two people speaking completely different languages.

It was Vrubel whom his contemporaries regarded as a personification of decadence in fine art. His work was perceived as alien by orthodox advocates of salon academicism, a fact which was natural and logical, and by a democratic public and critics as well. The positions taken by the young Gorky and Stasov in his late years with respect to the artist were sufficiently demonstrative. In its essence, Vrubel's work was permeated with the dramatic tenseness of the period, its anguish and hope. In this regard, it was worthy of being assigned its rightful place among the greatest achievements of progressive Russian culture.

Neither Vrubel's work, nor his description of his creative projects that can be found in letters and memoirs dating from the period, provide any support for the belief that the artist was consciously trying to overcome his estrangement from the mass public. Contiguities of some of his works with Modern style, that quite often made concessions to petty-bourgeois tastes, were conditioned by entirely different reasons and were only indirectly related to his romantic ideas of an artist's mission.

At the same time, Vrubel did not revel in his "majestic solitude" at all. He was feeling it keenly and painfully as the deepest drama of his life and creative work.[34]

In 1907, proletarian critics represented by A. V. Lunacharskiy called Vrubel a "pathfinder, a recklessly daring one." Lunacharskiy also added that "often, more often than not, innovators and unrecognized geniuses are condemned to a lack of understanding and derision."[35]

The World of Art group took a significantly different position from a sociological point of view. Proceeding from their aesthetic credo, the group leaders declared, from the very beginning, that art was independent of any circumstances lying outside artistic activity. Even if Vrubel strongly disagreed with the Peredvizhniki in many respects, he thought them "infinitely right" when they argued that "artists have no right to exist if they are not recognized by the public."[36] On the contrary, members of the World of Art, particularly at early stages of its existence, insisted on an autonomy of artistic interests in everyday public life.[37]

We have already mentioned some articles published by the *Mir iskusstva* magazine during Pushkin's jubilee celebration.[38] Several years earlier, in 1892, Merezhkovskiy provided a mystical interpretation of his idea of a "supreme ideal culture" in his essay "Reasons of Decline and New Tendencies in Contemporary Russian Literature." He pointed to a deep gulf separating the crowd and genuine art which was growing deeper as artistic life was becoming more public.[39] Such assertions reflected, to a certain extent, some real problems in the social and cultural development of Russia during that period, even if they were idealistically misinterpreted. However, conclusions drawn therefrom contradicted the entire objective historical process. It was not a response to negative phenomena which emerged in the course of evolution of Russian artistic life, it was a reaction against the evolution itself associated with the new stage in the life of the country.

NOTES

1. ". . . the Northern Pavilion decorated with Konstantin's frescos must be the most vivid and talented at the exhibition," wrote B. D. Polenov, describing his impressions of the Nizhni Novgorod exhibition (Ye. V. Sakharova, *V. D. Polenov, Ye. D. Polenova: Khronika semyi khudozhnikov* [Moscow, 1964], 550). This fact was confirmed by another eyewitness—M. V. Nesterov. "The best pavilion is that of Far North (commissioned by Mamontov) featuring K. Korovin's paintings," he wrote in one of his letters (see Nesterov, *Iz pisem,* ed. A. A. Rusakova [Leningrad, 1968], 109).

2. Academicism publicized itself at this exhibition quite openly. This was exactly the way Makovskiy's painting *Minin in the Nizhni Novgorod Square* was presented to the public. Nesterov wrote: "Minin is exhibited in a separate pavilion and a separate thirty-kopeck admission is charged. All has been done by the author to the benefit of the painting. It has been taken care of like a deceased rich man would have been. First-class funeral; carpets, tapestries, an elevated platform for the public, advertisements" (Nesterov, 110).

3. Bureaucratic correspondence with respect to the incident constitutes two thick volumes (Central State History Archives, f. 789, schedule 12, file 3-3). In the dispute, many painters unreservedly took Vrubel's side. See, e.g., N. A. Prakhov, *Stranitsy proshlogo* (Kiev, 1958), 148–56; K. A. Korovin's reminiscences (*Konstantin Korovin, Pisma, Dokumenty, Vospominaniya* [Moscow, 1963], 192); V. D. Polenov's letters to N. V. Polenova (Sakharova, 550–52).

However, there were also artists who gloated over the controversy. S. A.

Vinogradov asked in a letter: "Is it true that Vrubel's paintings have been torn down? I like it. I really think this deposition of the 'genius' is just" (Manuscript Department of the Tretyakov Gallery, inventory 9/145, sheet 3 ob).

4. Maxim Gorky, "Beglye zametki. M. Vrubel i 'Printsessa Greza' Rostana," *Nizhegorodskiy listok,* no. 202, 24 July 1896.

5. Ibid., no. 250, 10 September 1896.

6. Ibid., no. 219, 6 August 1896.

7. Ibid., no. 250, 10 September 1896.

8. See L. N. Tolstoy, *Chto takoye iskusstvo?* (Moscow, 1898).

9. Maxim Gorky, "Beglye zametki," *Nizhegorodskiy listok,* no. 201, 23 July 1896.

10. See *Odesskiye novosti,* no. 3659, 13 June 1896.

11. N. A. Rubakin, *Etyudy o russkoy chitayushchey publike* (St. Petersburg, 1895), 1.

12. Of course, it is important to keep in mind that democratization of Russian cultural life was part and parcel of the European process and that Western artists were also very concerned with the same problem. In this respect, it is interesting to compare Rubakin's words with the following statement made by Emile Zola: "At times . . . I am more concerned with the behavior of visitors than the work of artists themselves as it is often just one word, one gesture that betrays which artistic tastes are prevalent" (E. Zola, *Chto mne nenavistno . . .,* vol. 24 of *The Collected Works* [Moscow, 1966], 189).

13. L. N. Tolstoy, "Chto takoye iskusstvo?" vol. 30 of *Polnoe sobranie sochineniy* (Moscow, 1951), 33.

14. R. Izgoy (N. K. Roerich), "Nashi khudozhestvennye dela," *Iskusstvo i khudozhestvennaya promyshlennost,* nos. 1–2 (1898).

15. In his report on the occasion of the twenty-fifth anniversary of the Association of Travelling Art Exhibitions, G. G. Myasoyedov pointed out that the annual attendance at traveling exhibitions in all cities and towns averaged from thirty to forty thousand a year (*Albom dvadtsatipyatiletiya TPKhV* [Moscow: Izd. K. A. Fisher, 1899], 11).

16. As a matter of fact, some contemporaries were inclined to consider increased interest in fine arts both as a special result of the described sociological processes and, at the same time, as certain general law of the spiritual development of society. For example, Repin wrote: "Indeed, our contemporaries are noticeably more inclined to perceive various ideas with their eyes, through the instrumentality of fine arts. The interest in books is being increasingly replaced by the interest in paintings" (I. Ye. Repin, *Vospominaniya, statyi i pisma iz-za granitsy* [St. Petersburg, 1901], 247).

17. At the same time, it is noteworthy that it was *Niva,* or rather its 1897 literary supplements, that carried one of the first articles that pointed out and supported new tendencies in art. This was I. E. Grabar's article "Decline or Revival?"

18. Repin's and Makovskiy's speeches at the Bryullov's jubilee have not been published. The Peredvizhniki's salutatory address is quoted from a copy

that was preserved among archive documents of the Academy of Arts. Repin's speech was known from newspaper reports of this jubilee session.

19. Central State History Archives, f. 789, schedule 12, 1899, file 3-16, sheet 214. Similar opinions of Bryullov could be found in a number of newspaper articles published in early 1900. For example, *Novosti i birzhevaya gazeta* (News and Stock Exchange Gazette) carried the item: "One can almost say with certainty that the appearance of Bryullov's principal painting *The Last Days of Pompeii* concurred with the manifestation of general public interest in art and the emergence of Russian art criticism and art literature. This fact is another testimony to the great cultural and historical importance of the author of *Pompeii*" (Az, "Yubileynaya vystavka Bryullova," *Novosti i birzhevaya gazeta*, no. 3, 3 January 1900).

20. Quoted from *Repin: Khudozhestvennoye nasledstvo*, vol. 1 (Moscow and Leningrad, 1948), 539.

21. *Mir iskusstva* 13–14 (1899): 39.

22. Ya. D. Minchenkov, *Vospominaniya o peredvizhnikakh* (Leningrad, 1959), 118. Under the unquestionable influence of the Peredvizhniki, independent art societies are established in provinces during this period. Goals set by them are the same as those of the St. Petersburg Association. For example, newspapers reported in late 1897 that a group of painters from Kazan had drawn up "[a] draft charter of the Society of Volga Region Painters whose objectives include both improvement of artistic taste in local communities and organization of traveling art exhibitions in all major towns of the Volga Region" (*Novosti i birzhevaya gazeta*, no. 344, 14 December 1897). In March 1903, a Society of Siberian Travelling Art Exhibitions was established. Its charter was signed by V. V. Mate, A. A. Kiselev, Ye. M. Bem, M. N. Pedashenko-Tretyakova and other artists (Central State History Archives, f. 789, schedule 12, 1903, file 3-22). The first Siberian Travelling Exhibition took place the same year.

23. *Novoye vremya*, no. 10084, 31 March 1904. The newspaper report is confirmed by archive documents which testify that the exhibition at the Smolensk public school stayed open for a week and was visited by over 1,000 people. Later on, it was sent to provinces and visited such cities as Saratov and Novocherkassk (Manuscript Department of the Tretyakov Gallery, inventory 69/464).

The Peredvizhniki must have arrived at the idea of so-called popular exhibitions long before this event. In November 1898, S. A. Vinogradov wrote in a letter that, during a regular Friday meeting of Peredvizhniki, Myasoyedov had raised the question of "a popular exhibition" which "should travel from village to village in a waggon . . . Pictures should be painted on double-side oilcloth in order to be resistant to rain and other elements" (Manuscript Department of the Tretyakov Gallery, inventory 9/163, sheet 3).

24. Minchenkov, 309–10.

25. In this respect, N. A. Rubakin's observation made at approximately the same time is also noteworthy: "The type of an educated factory worker can be seen quite often, especially during the recent years, and this is the type who

does not require any special literature. Moreover, such literature is harmful for him" (Rubakin, 192).

26. N. K. Mikhaylovskiy, "Chetyre khudozhestvennye vystavki," *Russkoye bogatstvo*, no. 3 (1898): 158.

27. Bectus [P. P. Gnedich], "G. I. Semiradskiy i sovremennoye iskusstvo," *Novoye vremya*, no. 7909, 5 March 1898.

28. Old Gentleman [A. V. Amfiteatrov], "Etyudy," *Novoye vremya*, no. 7912, 8 March 1898.

29. See Sergey Glagol, "VIII vystavka kartin S. Peterburgskogo obshchestva khudozhnikov," *Kuryer*, nos. 102, 108, 13 and 19 April 1900.

30. Serg. Pechorin, "Pervaya narodnaya vystavka kartin," *Novosti i birzhevaya gazeta*, no. 215, 7 August 1898.

31. Rubakin, 132–33.

32. Trying to explain the success of such paintings from the point of view of their psychological perception by the public, Nesterov wrote in 1897: "Banality and vulgarity are apparently a concession to the public that at times resents art and artists whose sublimity offends its excessively sensitive pride. The Kiselevs, Pimonenkos, Volkovs and Co. are good because everybody understands them and their existence does not irk anybody. You can talk freely in their presence without being afraid that you may say a stupid thing and look stupid or ignorant" (Nesterov, 119).

33. Manuscript Department of the USSR Lenin Library, f. 135, section II, k. 32, inventory 50.

34. See, e.g., Vrubel's letter to his sister written in January 1899, in *Vrubel, Perepiska, Vospominaniya o khudozhnike* (Leningrad, 1976), 62–63.

35. A. V. Lunacharskiy, "Vystavka kartin 'Soyuza russkikh khudozhnikov,'" *Vestnik zhizni*, no. 2 (1907). Quoted from A. V. Lunacharskiy, *Ob izobrazitelnom iskusstve*, vol. 1 (Moscow, 1967), 390.

36. Vrubel 1976, 38.

37. This contention does not necessarily mean that enlightenment goals were alien to members of World of Art, even if they interpreted these objectives in their specific ways. Their approach to publishing exemplifies this interpretation. We can judge this approach by a letter written by Alexander Benois in 1900 in which he voices his opinion regarding aims and purposes of an official publication of the Society for Encouragement of Arts: "If we examine carefully the attitude of an educated Russian society or even artists to plastic arts, we will notice one surprising thing. While there is some devotion to art in words, in reality you will find a profound indifference and an abysmal ignorance . . . Those few who care about art should do their utmost to help cast off the general indifference, to kindle, at last, the flame of enthusiasm in the crowd and to make it be enthralled by beauty . . . It is precisely these objectives that should form the contents of a magazine to be published by the Imperial Society for Encouragement of Arts which should awaken an awareness of beauty" (State History Archives of Leningrad Region, f. 448, schedule 1, file 1156, sheet 9-11).

A more detailed description of social orientation of members of World of

Art in Russian art culture of the period can be found in my article "Alexander Benois's 'My Memoirs' and Russian Artistic Culture in the Late Nineteenth and Early Twentieth Centuries."

38. It should be emphasized that painters of World of Art more than once dissociated themselves publicly from the adjacent literary magazine.

39. See D. S. Merezhkovskiy, *Polnoye sobranie sochineniy*, vol. 18 (Moscow, 1914).

Stalinism as Aesthetic Phenomenon

The following essay was first published in the journal *Sintaxis* (Paris) in 1987 and is translated here without any changes. Although the specific references to contemporary political and cultural situation in the (former) Soviet Union are no longer valid, this in no way affects the general argument of the essay.—Eds. note.

The culture of the Stalin era has begun to attract the attention of researchers only recently. For the authors outside of the Soviet Union and its sphere of influence and for the independent authors inside the USSR, the history of the 1930s–40s usually is perceived only as the history of the persecution of "real" art, as a monotonous and frightening martyrology. Indeed, the art and the literature of Russian avant-garde, which formed before World War I, blossomed during the short period of cultural and political vacuum immediately after the Revolution, and partly held out until the end of the 1920s, when it was once and for all suppressed in the Stalin period. Beginning in the 1930s, the culture of the avant-garde was practically outlawed and disappeared rather quickly from the eyes of the public. Many leading poets and artists perished; some were able to emigrate, the rest found themselves in the situation of total social isolation and have gradually learned not to show their works to even their closest friends. In the period after Stalin's death, the heritage of the Russian avant-garde gradually began to receive more and more attention from art historians as well as the public. This process, however, is far from being com-

Boris Groys, "Stalinizm kak esteticheskiy fenomen" (Stalinism as aesthetic phenomenon), *Sintaxis* (Paris) 17 (1987): 98–110.

pleted. A great deal remains unknown or has not yet received the recognition it deserves, in part because of the Soviet cultural politics which remains hostile toward the art of the avant-garde. Even now the Russian avant-garde is practically inaccessible to the public in the USSR, and its historical study is very difficult, although lately there is a weakening of censorship in this area, albeit a very slow one.

Compared to the achievements of Malevich, Rodchenko, and Tatlin in art, or of Khlebnikov and Mandelstam in poetry (just to mention a few most well-known names), the official culture of the Stalin period, which replaced the avant-garde, appears at first sight as something terribly wretched, mediocre, and provincial. Moreover, the methods by which it was imposed provoke natural aversion and elicit no desire to try to understand its own "inner world." This position of simple dismissal is quite understandable and widely prevalent, yet it is not productive. The official culture of the Stalin period cannot be considered only as a purely negative phenomenon, as a method imposed from above in order to strangle "true" culture. As with any other cultural movement, culture of the Stalin period should be first of all considered in relation to its immanent logic, and only after that as a tool of totalitarian control. Overwise the main question of any historical investigation remains unanswered: Why was this, rather than any other culture, "imposed from above"? Even if we assume that this culture has but an instrumental logic, this does not eliminate the question: What is the immanent logic that makes an art strive for instrumentality?

The art of the avant-garde was persecuted and destroyed during the Stalin period in the name of "the only productive artistic method of our times—the method of Socialist Realism." According to the official formulation, it consisted of the desire "to show life in its revolutionary development." However, the artists of the avant-garde were, as a rule, loyal to the Soviet regime and were not persecuted for opposing the politics of the leadership or going against "revolutionary development of life." Charges against them were, first and foremost, on the grounds of aesthetics. Such merciless aesthetic censorship, culminating in the murder of the followers of the "alien" aesthetics, leads one to think that the goal was the creation of a sufficiently thought-out and strictly defined artistic canon. This impression is made even stronger by the monotony of the artistic production and by the content of the critical discussions of these times. These discussions, for instance, are often devoted to paintings which appear totally trivial to the outside observer, infinitely removed from any likeness of a formal experiment, and 100 percent loyal in their political intention. However, criticism found that workers were depicted in the painting too "schematically" and "machine-like," in a way which "casts aspersions on the inner world of the Soviet worker—the builder of Communism," or, on the contrary, that they were too "idealized" and, therefore, the painting looks like a "poster" and does not express "the tension of labor." Also, the composition of a painting may seem too constructivist or too loose, the color too local or too "impressionistic," and so on. In all these cases, according to the criticism, it is the matter of "retreat from the principles of Socialist Realism" toward this or that "formal movement already overcome by the whole development of the Soviet art a long time ago" that was ill-intentionally revived by the artist. Any such charge easily developed into a political accusation, and if the artist persisted and "positioned himself against the collective" or "did not want to listen to friendly criticism," it could lead to tragic consequences.

After all this, a historian naturally expects to find a formulation of the principles of Socialist Realism that precisely would define its formal structure. Nothing of this kind, however, can be found in the literature of the Stalin period. In the beginning of the 1930s the Soviet artists themselves, frightened by the strengthening censorship, addressed the Party leaders on many occasions asking for precise instructions about how they should "create" and what method they should use. Every time the leadership refused to give them such instructions, pointing out that in the Soviet Union the artist is completely free to choose an artistic method: "His own conscience living one life with the people and desiring to represent its epochal achievements" should tell him which method to use. At the famous meeting with artists, preceding the first Congress of the Union of Soviet Writers in 1934, where Socialist Realism as the sole method of the Soviet art was finally pronounced, Stalin in response to the recurrent question of writers—"How shall we write?"—gave an answer which became the starting point for all further discussions about art in the Soviet Union—"Write the truth."

This answer and the following official instructions for art disclosed the real meaning of the "struggle with formalism" that had unfolded already in the 1920s: it was a matter of not only and not so much the struggle against this or that "formal movements in art" but against the artistic form as such. All Soviet literary and art criticism from that moment until now relied on this principle—"content dictates form" or "new form may appear only as a result of a new content."One of the motivations of this idea lies on the surface—the Party censorship did not intend to allow the artists to be able to hide behind their work, behind its form. On the contrary, all artistic creation was looked upon first of all as self-denunciation, as evidence of potential political unloyalty. Since the formal organization of the work of art was equated with the direct expression of an author's ideology, any original artistic form was perceived by the criticism of the 1930s as political crime perhaps even greater than "the representation of negative sides of reality" in the framework of the accepted aesthetic. The latter pointed out that an author, although deluded, in essence remained "our Soviet artist." The accepted aesthetic of Socialist Realism itself demanded first of all obscurity and elusiveness of the formal structure of a work of art, which had to maximally approximate the normal nonaesthetic vision of a collective.

This aesthetic elusiveness spread out even to such "abstract areas of art" as architecture. Thus, one of the leading architects of the Stalin period, Moisey Ginsburg, wrote the following at the time: "We are asked to give up imitating classical architecture, to give up constructivist modernist architecture, and to fight with their eclectic combination. But what is architecture under these conditions at all?" Yet architecture turned out to be quite possible, and later artists, with pride, described on the pages of books and journals how they fought any sign of artistic form in their works.

Thus, the aesthetic of Socialist Realism can be defined as a consistent antiaesthetic—in the art of the Stalin period, the refusal to define the purely formal criterions of artistic work was constructive. The distance, guaranteed by the artistic form, between art and life with its "truth," disappeared. The artist was absorbed by the collective, and his attempts to break away from "life" by creating individual artistic style were punished by the political police.

The hostility of the Socialist Realism of the Stalin period to artistic form is usually interpreted as a sign of artistic reaction which came after the stormy innovation of the 1910s and 1920s. This reaction is most often explained in sociological terms. Indeed, during the long Civil War and the repressions of the 1920–30s, the cultural strata of Russian society were for the most part physically eliminated, and the rest were kept away from an active participation in social life. The educational level of the Party leadership was extremely low, and big cities became populated with déclassé masses of peasants escaping from the politics of collectivization. Therefore, many authors now see in the art and literature of the Stalin period not only a return to the primitive realism of the nineteenth century but even to the folklore forms of consciousness, almost to the primitive magic culture of the Stone Age, which did not yet know the notion of an autonomous artistic form. (In this respect, Katerina Clark's *The Soviet Novel: History as Ritual* played a pioneering role.)[1] Obviously, the cultural regression of the Russian population after the terror of the Revolution, the Civil War, and Stalin's repressions was quite significant, but not significant enough to support the notion of the return to the uncivilized stages of culture, notwithstanding the cult of Lenin's relics in the mausoleum, the endowment of the leaders with magical power, or the belief of biology during the Stalin period in the possibility of the creation of live nature from lifeless matter through the "dialectical transformation" in laboratory conditions. The popular appeal of art, pronounced by the Soviet rule, meant pseudopopular stylization and mass propaganda using "magic archetypes" rather than the actual spontaneous expression of people's creativity. The most obvious refutation of the folklore theory of Stalinist culture is provided by the long, pointed, and quite intellectually reflexive discussions which accompanied the formation of Socialist Realism. Many of the things which today remain true—about Socialist Realism itself, about its relation to the art of the past and to contemporary Western art—were articulated in these discussions from the very beginning. It should not be forgotten that at this time in the West, art gradually withdrew from avant-garde as well, which did not mean a return to tradition—as in the art of Surrealism, Magic Realism, or New Objectivism, or in the movement closest to Socialist Realism, the art of National Socialist Germany. In all these movements there is a shift of attention from the original artistic form to the "new object of representation," which could be either an individual (Surrealism) or a collective dream (Nazi art). The conscious turn to myth does not mean the falling into "barbarism," as it is sometimes claimed, but only the transfer of the avant-garde artistic impulse from the area of artistic form directly onto reality.

The phenomenon of Socialist Realism is not an exception. It should be regarded as the next step in the development of the Russian avant-garde of the 1910–20s. The main thesis of this article is that the art of Socialist Realism represents not only the organic continuation of the avant-garde but also its culmination and in some sense its completion. The same can also be said about other forms of totalitarian art of the 1930s.

This thesis may appear unusual or paradoxical, but only at first sight. Indeed, for the first time nobody else but precisely the avant-garde, and not only the Russian avant-garde, pronounced as its goal the destruction of a distance between art and life and the refusal of a traditional aesthetic position in relation to the world. The early twentieth-century avant-garde was first of all a reaction to new technology which, intruding upon life, broke the traditional aesthetic unity of the world, but at the same time seemed to open the possibility for its total reorganization. The premise of the avant-garde became "God is dead"—now the artist must take his place and create new unity in place of the lost unity of Nature as the creation of God's art. Instead of representing reality, the avant-garde's goal was its final destruction and the creation of a new and better world out of its debris. But the creation of a new world was impossible without the subordination of all mankind to this goal, or at least of the population of the whole country with all its resources. From this naturally emerges the demand to grant an artist absolute political power, a demand heard in many of the avant-garde manifestos. It was the artistic avant-garde which first put forward the idea of the subordination of politics and technology to the single aesthetic project, with the goal of achieving new harmony of nature and society. In this way the avant-garde made the fatal step beyond its traditional boundaries and connected aesthetics with politics, transforming artistic form into a political program.

This demand had a particularly undisguised and persistent character in the Russian avant-garde, intoxicated by the unlimited possibilities opened to it at first after the Revolution. All works of Malevich and Rodchenko, as well as the poems of Khlebnikov or Mayakovsky, have essentially a projective character: they are not works of art enclosed in themselves but rather the projects for the future, which must be realized by the collective efforts according to a single plan designed by the artists. And it is the artists of the avant-garde who first started throwing political accusations at their artistic competitors for being "bourgeois" and "hostile to the new Socialist reality"—the accusations which already at that time could have cost their opponents their lives. However, relatively soon it was discovered that avant-garde artists could not expect from political authority that it would fully submit itself and carry out their projects. Having discovered this, Malevich, Kandinsky, and Khlebnikov became disappointed in politics and left it, but many others began to cooperate with the political authorities with the idea of creating a certain division of labor between the artist and the politician, a division characteristic of the 1920s. In this period LEF, the main organization of the Russian avant-garde artists, headed by Mayakovsky and Brik, passed to the second stage of the flirtation between art and politics, later called "engagement": the artist was ready to put himself at the service of politics because he did not see any other way to realize his initial project of a total artistic remaking of the world. In this he is ready to leave power to the political leadership, if it would accept his aesthetics even in a somewhat reduced form. The avant-garde of the 1920s once and for all turned political accusation into the means of struggle against its enemies and equated an aesthetic program with a political one. All the polemics of LEF and of related publications now read as a continuous political denunciation and as the most humiliating assertions of loyalty addressed to the authorities. But here as well LEF was not illogical—even in their most repulsive expressions, the artists of LEF remained first of all artists, most of all preoccupied by the triumph of their personal artistic project.

In nontotalitarian countries the relation between art and politics in the twentieth century usually was limited to the first stage of the total artistic project, which did not find the public's understanding, and to engagement, sometimes favorably accepted by the politicians. But in Stalinist Russia (as well as in Nazi Germany) the project of the avant-garde passed into its final phase: political power refused the favors of the avant-garde artist and itself started the artistic transformation of the world according to its own notions. The political leadership of the totalitarian countries accepted the challenge of the avant-garde. The avant-garde artist, however, did not receive political power. Instead, the political leader found aesthetic power. In essence, Stalin was the only artist of the Stalin era; in this sense, he was a successor of Malevich or Tatlin to a much greater degree than the later museum stylizations of the avant-garde. Precisely because of this the avant-garde was persecuted so severely in the Stalin period; it was perceived as a competitor in the struggle for aesthetic-political power which became one. At the same time the official artists of the Stalin era no longer were artists in the traditional sense. The question of form did not exist for them for the simple reason that reality itself became the total work of art, which the artist was left to "truthfully" copy. Individual artistic style could only mean in this situation the attempt to compete with the Party's style of forming the life itself. So it was not by accident that the Party's leaders were seen as most qualified connoisseurs and lovers of art to be approached for concrete instructions of how to "create."

Therefore, Socialist Realism simply cannot be considered as a mere revival of "kitschy realism" of the nineteenth century as it may appear at first sight. Nothing, except "formalism," was criticized in the Stalin period as ruthlessly as "dull bourgeois objectivism," that is, precisely traditional realism. Socialist Realism was no less projectile than the preceding avant-garde; it was realism in the sense of political realism, realpolitik. Avant-garde projects were rejected in the first place because they were unrealizable and neglected the reality of practical politics. Avant-garde is a reductive art, it resembles ascetic sectarianism, living by the hopes of a coming apocalypse. Socialist Realism, the art of the winners, wanted to take all reality inside itself, change it all, and "bless" it with the Socialist ideals. In its planning for the future, then, Socialist Realism sought to base itself upon what has been built already, on the "presence of the future in the present," as the saying went.

But "future in the present"—this was exactly what Stalin and the Party had the time to create. Stalin was pronounced not only the creator of everything which was achieved in the country but also the demiurge, to whom "we owe our childhood," "the air we breathe," the climate and the appearance of nature, which were subjected to radical remaking that destroyed the traditional ecological balance, etc. In connection with the twentieth-century totalitarian movements, the notion of aesthetization of politics is sometimes brought up. The notion silently assigns to the citizens of these countries the role of spectators. More precisely, we should talk about the aesthetization of all life of the country, for which the citizens were extras or stage workers, while Stalin was the sole author and spectator. The skyscrapers and the Moscow metro, the canals and dams were constructed only for him. Twice a year he watched, rejoicing crowds pass him by, and in them he saw "all of the country and its new man." The aesthetics of

Socialist Realism is, therefore, the aesthetics of Stalin's politics, which placed aesthetic goals first, even before itself.

In his art Stalin first of all looked toward the historical periods in which politics was most closely connected with art—antiquity and the era of European Renaissance, which were pronounced to represent the eternal aesthetic ideals of mankind. Much in the politics of that time is impossible to understand correctly without considering the purely aesthetic criteria which guided the decisions. The extremism of the totalitarian terror often appears irrational and, indeed, cannot be fully explained by pragmatic considerations, but it becomes understandable as the decision of an artist to eliminate from his work all that stood in the way of its perfection. Thus, for instance, after World War II a huge number of disabled veterans were removed from big cities so their appearance would not spoil the cities' image; they were placed on faraway islands, where they quickly died from starvation. It is possible to recount many similar examples. The aesthetics of that time did not know forgiveness, and everything that did not fit its style was simply ejected from life. But still, despite all its selectivity, the aesthetics of Socialist Realism were more liberal than the extremely reductive aesthetics of the avant-garde. It should not be forgotten that the intelligentsia first met the introduction of Socialist Realism with relief: it is better to look like the heroes of antiquity than to turn into the walking squares and triangles of the Russian avant-garde. Socialist Realism suppressed the diversity of contemporary artistic movements. But within itself it was more diverse and had more possibilities than any of them. And, it should be recalled, it was not a matter of the diversity of museum exhibitions but of the appearance of the future in which one had to live. Therefore, every detail in a Socialist Realist painting has such tremendous importance—because it was a matter of fate for everybody, whether she or he has a right to live in the future or should be thrown away as not fitting into the style.

The contemporary viewer, of course, is not able to experience again the risk and the dramatic nature of Socialist Realism which led to the death of so many. Now the paintings of Socialist Realism look banal, unremarkable, helpless. But in this respect they are not that different from, for instance, the famous Suprematist compositions of Malevich, which, if you forget about their projective meaning, also can be seen as a banal collection of geometric elements. Malevich wrote in his *Suprematist Manifesto* in 1915 that he broke through the ring of a horizon, which jailed the artist, doomed to copy natural forms like a convict in love with his chains, and that art is progressing toward creation as its own goal and to the domination over natural forms. Obviously, this tremendous artistic insight of Malevich is still valid even when the historical avant-garde remains twice compromised—in its attempt to establish a new world based on such insights, as took place in the East, and in the desire to reduce those insights to museum academism, as happened in the West. Socialist Realism finished the avant-garde precisely because, after the downfall of the totalitarian regimes, avant-garde art only lives in the memories and stylizations of its heroic era. The Socialist Realist painting does not have Malevich's visions of the Absolute. However, the pathos of the Absolute in Socialist Realism is transformed into reality itself, which the painting wants to depict and which is the "reality of the future in the present" and, therefore, more real than any empirical reality, that is, superreal or, if you wish, surreal. (It is not by accident that during approximately the same years a number of artists in France moved from Surrealism to Socialist Realism with remarkable ease.)

In the 1920–30s, the transition to the artistic transformation of reality itself led many to the idea of the necessity to give up art in general and, in particular, easel painting (this point of view was shared, for instance, by the theoreticians of LEF). Socialist Realism meant the victory of those who thought that easel painting and art as a whole was a special kind of activity which could not be given up. In part, this was because "the future in the present" was not completely realized, and art, therefore, did not lose its projective role. But art in its traditional role was preserved mainly because it covered up a certain emptiness in the very center of reality that was being created by Stalin—art was called upon to depict Stalin himself.

A well-known Soviet art critic, Tugendkhold, later himself accused of formalism and buried in oblivion, was one of the first to point, in his 1927 review of the first decade of Soviet art, to the gaping absence of the leader himself in the reality he created. In the same article he located already in 1924 the turn to realism in Soviet art and connected it to the death of Lenin, when it became clear "that something principal is missing . . . that it is necessary to forget different 'isms' for at least now and retain his [Lenin's] image for posterity." Later on, as the future was more and more thought of as already having taken place, art concentrated on the depiction of Stalin and his closest circle.

In the last years of Stalin's life, practically only those books, films, and sculptures that depicted Stalin were given the highest prizes and pronounced the classics of Soviet art. We may suppose that if this development were to continue, art would limit itself to the creation and decoration of huge buildings according to Stalin's taste as well as to the portrayal of Stalin, reaching in this way a synthesis of the avant-garde and classical understandings of art. In view of this, it is curious that at the second session of the Academy of the Arts of the USSR, which took place in 1952 under the sign of Zhdanov's campaign for the final liquidation of any independence of art, one of the speakers quoted with sympathy the message of Pope Pavel III (1539), according to whom an artist is different from the simple craftsman in that he "is a portrayer of saints, leaders, and other rulers."

This portrayal of Stalin—"native, wise, and dear"—gave Stalin the opportunity, as a creator of new reality, to see in it his own reflection, created by the "new man" (whom he himself raised), which every "real Soviet artist" was considered to be. Here it is already a matter of a certain apotheosis of the superhuman in a human, of a self-contemplation of an absolute creative spirit completing world history in the image of its greatest empire.

There is little left of this grandiose perspective in the Soviet Union. The Stalin period disappeared from sight; the statues were blown up, the frescos washed away, the paintings were painted over or hidden in the basements where they hung together with the paintings of the Russian avant-garde. The films are not shown, the books are not sold and not available in the libraries, where they are kept on "closed shelves" together with the books of the previous period. In today's Soviet Union the art of the Stalin period has taken its place next to the avant-garde in the archive of forgetting of the social unconscious. It is forgotten and repressed to an even larger degree than the avant-garde, since it is less removed from the present and is met with sympathy by neither the leaders nor the opposition, not at all understood in its historical specificity. Although the appearance of Soviet art changed significantly, Socialist Realism is still considered officially the sole and required doctrine of all Soviet art, a fact that indirectly confirms the insight of Stalin's theoreticians, who claimed that the essence of Socialist Realism is not in the form but in the content. The sacral Socialist Realist formulas all sound the same; speaking of "the appearance of the Soviet man—the builder of communism" and the necessity to reproduce this appearance in art; saying that all formalism is harmful; that "the content dictates the form"; and that art must be "humanistic, national in form and socialist in content." But the contemporary official Soviet art has already lost its projective and optimistic character—it is full of stylization, symbolism, and the dreamy idealization of reality. It still dreams about the great eras of antiquity and the Renaissance but only as a beautiful past, accessible only to individual recollection but not collective realization. And, therefore, in a certain sense it is no longer Socialist Realism—because it is finally no longer avant-garde.

NOTES

1. Katerina Clark, *The Soviet Novel: History as Ritual* (Chicago: University of Chicago Press, 1981).

Transparency Painting:
From Myth to Theater

1.

Due largely to Newton's discoveries, light became one of the principal categories in the eighteenth-century culture (hence the common name of this century is "siècle de lumières"). The cultural and aesthetic aspect of the influence of Newton's *Opticks* was related mainly to its main postulate, according to which all colors of the visible spectrum are contained in the complex mixture of the light ray, the single source of all the wonderful diversity of the visible world. It seemed that Newton's theory put an end to the centuries-old dominance of natural-philosophical notions that related natural colors to the mixture of light and shadow and could be traced back to Aristotle.[1]

According to Newton, light exists as an infinite number of different independent colors, and, moreover, it is a corpuscular substance: Rays of Light "seem to be hard bodies," small particles of material bodies having certain "Powers, Virtues, or Forces."[2] The proposition about the substantive nature of light, which astonished Newton's contemporaries, was perceived as the proof of affinity between light and God.[3]

The special role in the natural-philosophical reinterpretation of Newton's optics was played by the school of English so-called scientific poets—James Thomson, David Mallett, and Mark Akenside.[4] Newton was idolized by the poets of this movement, and his theory was described in natural-philosophical epic poems influenced by Mil-

Mikhail Yampolsky, "Transparantnaya zhivopis: ot mifa k teatru" (Transparency painting: From myth to theater). *Sovetskoe iskusstvoznanie* 21 (1986): 277–305.

ton's *Paradise Lost.* Milton has a whole number of passages, obviously Neoplatonic in character, which are mainly concentrated in the third book of the poem and celebrate God as light:

> Hail, holy Light, offspring of Heaven first-born!
> Or of th'Eternal coeternal beam
> May I express thee unblamed? since God is light,
> And never but unapproached light,
> Dwelt from eternity, dwelt then in thee,
> Bright effluence of bright essence increate![5]

These fragments belong to the most popular, well-known parts of the poem and are the source of numerous quotations in eighteenth-century poetry. Scientific poets frequently evoked these passages as well as the related plot of *Paradise Lost,* which tells about the victory of God (light) over Lucifer (darkness) through poetic descriptions of Newton's theory. Already in the beginning of the nineteenth century William Blake, who felt something of a lyrical hatred toward Newton, ironically summarized the new (old) myth from the point of view of painting:

> That God is Colouring Newton does show,
> And the Devil is Black outline, all of us know.[6]

The introduction of Newton alongside with God and Devil in the context of Neoplatonic poetry, influenced by Milton, was canonized by James Thomson, who created a number of, so to speak, "Newtonic odes" to sun and light. In the ode *To the Memory of Sir Isaac Newton* (1727), Thomson, comparing Newton to God, writes:

> Even Light itself, which every thing displays,
> Shone undiscovered, till his brighter mind
> Untwisted all the shining robe of day . . .[7]

The metaphor of a shining colored veil, thrown by light over the world, is most likely related to Newton's explanation for color of bodies, according to which a color is produced due to reflection and refraction of light by an extremely thin veil, like a film wrapped around bodies.[8] The model, which Newton used to explain the color of bodies, was peacock feathers with their rainbow gradations.

Rainbow, which was explained by Newton, as well as the peacock became the symbols of Newton's optics, and in this capacity they were transposed into painting. Rainbow is the principal element of

The Theory of Painting (1779) by Angelica Kauffmann, one of the allegorical wall paintings at the Royal Academy in London created at the end of the eighteenth century and functioning as a sort of symbolic treatise on the theory of painting. *Air* (from *The Four Elements*) painted by Benjamin West depicts a nude with two angels, one holding a veil and the other leading a peacock toward her.[9] By the beginning of the nineteenth century a speculative theory of harmonization of colors in painting formed on the basis of Newton's spectrum. In 1804 Edward Dayes claimed, for instance, that the colors of sunset "should follow the same sequence of colors that is found in the spectrum."[10] In 1817, at the Royal Academy, Benjamin West advised his students that colors be arranged in historical paintings to correspond with the order of colors in the rainbow.[11]

But, in reality, the cult of Newton had little influence on the language of eighteenth-century painting and functioned mainly on a purely speculative, allegorical level. At the same time, the theory of the picturesque, prevalent at the end of the eighteenth century, canonized harmonization of colors in landscape painting based on the shades of brown and sepia. The fashion of the so-called Claude glass, which became popular after 1740, is typical of this canon. Rather than enjoying nature directly, travelers preferred to look at its reflections in a mirror backed by a darkened brownish foil which diminished the brightness of light and color and created the illusion of a painted canvas.[12] It is also characteristic for the theory of picturesque to taboo white color, which symbolized the presence of light for the "Newtonic" poets.

The unproductiveness of Newton's theory for painting is not only related to the fact that it destroyed the established canons of the harmonization of colors, but also that it did not offer a new effective "practical" poetics instead. Other than depicting a rainbow or a peacock, painting could not find other devices to express the spectral content of color. Light in its pure form remained unattainable for painting. This explains the imbalance between the Newtonic-Neoplatonic revolution in poetry and the merely gestural cult of Newton among artists.

During the second half of the eighteenth century, a general reaction against the cult of Newton started to gain momentum in the form of anti-Neoplatonic sentiments. At first it was expressed as the critique of the cult of vision: in Germany Lessing called blindness the source of Milton's genius, while Herder wrote about the "tranquil darkness" that gave rise to the images of Homer, Milton, and Ossian.[13] Herder's *Plastic Arts* and Lessing's *Laokoön* with their cult of the bodily and the tactile actively expressed the anti-Neoplatonic reaction. Such works as the discussion about the blind in Diderot's *Letter on the Blind* in some way prepared the forthcoming critique of Newton.[14]

A popular thesis about the impossibility of seeing light was particularly important for the development of painting. A fragment from the third book of *Paradise Lost* turned out to be an important source here too. Milton ends his hymn to light with the motif of his own blindness:

> . . . but thou
> Rivisit'st not these eyes, that roll in vain
> To find thy piercin ray, and find no dawn;
>
> But cloud instead and ever-during dark
> Surrounds me . . .
>
> So much the rather thou, Celestial Light,
> Shine inward, and the mind through all thee powers
> Irradiate; there plant eyes; all mist from thence
> Purge and disperse, that I may see and tell
> Of things invisible to mortal sight.[15]

The inability of painting to fix pure light received justification in the numerous reminiscences of this fragment. Direct and lengthy contemplation of light became connected with the motif of blindness. And the utterly dark blackness that veiled Milton "like a storm-cloud" was paradoxically advanced to the level of the condition necessary to see light.

Milton's motif of blindness played an important role in the formation of the critique of Newton's theory at the end of the eighteenth and beginning of the nineteenth centuries. As a result, this critique was largely addressed not directly to Newton's theoretical propositions but mainly to the *perception* of light, to light appearing before vision.

There emerged a two-tier structure of "luminosity." In heavens, the kingdom of pure light, Newton's theory dominated while on earth, in the "degraded" kingdom of man, light and color functioned according to Aristotle's principles.

Physiological component (the inability to contemplate sun) in connection with theological component (the inability to contemplate God directly) finally created a two-tier view of the existence of light in the

world, which began to play a fundamental role in cultural consciousness at the end of the eighteenth and beginning of the nineteenth
centuries.[16] In this view, the physiological threshold of vision turned
out to be the link that restored the opposition between light and
shadow that Newton destroyed. Edmund Burke, for instance, claimed
that "a light as that of the sun, immediately exerted on the eye, as it
overpowers the sense, is a very great idea."[17] Therefore, for Burke
darkness is elevated to the ranks of sublime whereas "simple light,"
which does not produce a physiological effect of darkness, is bracketed out of the sublime. For Shelling pure light is idea. "It [idea] takes
off the *veil*, with which it clothed itself in matter."[18] Pure color is
invisible. In synthesis with objects, light becomes dull and appears as
color, that is, mixed with darkness.

The importance of a physiological component is significant for
Goethe's theory of color. Goethe explicitly called his theory *Doctrine
of Physiological Colours:* "Physiological colors are the beginning and
the end of the entire color theory and are explained at the start of its
account . . . The organ of vision, like others, is accustomed to average
stimulation. Light, darkness and the colors emerging between them
are the elements, from which the eye draws and creates its world."[19]
For Goethe, light and darkness are to a large degree homonymous
with the thresholds of visual sensitivity, and this is what unites them.
That is why Goethe describes color processes in terms of violence
done to the eye and the eye's reaction to this violence and understands
the effect of color as a reaction to strong stimulation.[20] In the conflict
between Goethe and Newton we are dealing with the scientific aspect
of the above mentioned two-tier structure of understanding light.
Heavens remain with Newton and the earth with Goethe. This explains why Goethe emphasized the practical value of his theory and
why Shelling made this characteristic remark: "It is well-known that
none of the new artists, who thought about their art, ever employed
Newton's theory of colors. And this was enough to prove how little
this theory has to do with nature, because nature and art are in essence
the same."[21]

Debates concerning the fate of theories about light and color directly and keenly touched a number of artists at the end of the eighteenth and early nineteenth century. Turner, whose art presents a particular interest in this context, carefully studied the scientific poets and
even devoted his own poem to Thomson.[22] Starting in 1798 he began

to sign his landscapes with quotations from Milton. We are not just talking about a simple interest but about a profound reinterpretation of the light-color problem by this group of poets. Starting from the 1810s, the motif of direct contemplation of the sun, understood in the dramatic categories of Milton, finds its way into painting.[23] In 1814 John Martin, whose art we will discuss further on, sent to the Royal Academy a painting *Clytie* based on a motif in Ovid. Ovid tells of the nymph Clytie who was in love with Apollo and turned into a sunflower doomed to eternally look at the sun. In 1823 Martin completed a series of mezzotints illustrating Milton's *Paradise Lost*. In one of the illustrations, *Creation of the World*, the figure of God is almost indiscernable as it is dissolved in a powerful stream of light that cuts through the primordial chaos. Turner, in an 1837 illustration to a poem by Campbells similarly depicts God as an almost invisible contour in a stream of light. In all these works "luminosity" erases the discernability of the bodies engulfed in light. This motif reached its culmination in Turner's *Regulus* (1828, repainted in 1837) and *Angel Standing in the Sun* (1846). Regulus, a Roman taken prisoner by the Carthoginians and unwilling to betray Rome, was punished—his eyelids were cut off, and he was blinded by the sun. The painting represents the unbearable sunshine from Regulus's point of view. Contemplation of the sun is understood here as "violence" done to vision, as a traumatic shock.[24]

Turner accompanied *Angel Standing in the Sun* with lines from the poem *Voyage of Columbus* (1810) by Samuel Rodgers (1763–1855). The key to the meaning of this painting, however, is to be found in the description of an angel standing in the sunlight from the third book of *Paradise Lost*, where this image is treated in the context of the problematic of superhuman vision and unveiled light. In Milton's poem Satan is likened to light that shines incredibly bright:

> . . . far and wide his eye commands,
> For sight no obstacle found here, nor shade,
> But all sunshine . . .
>
> . . . and the air,
> Nowhere so clear, sharpened his visual ray
> To objects distant far, whereby he soon
> Saw within ken a glorious angel stand,
> The same whom John saw also in the sun.[25]

Superhuman vision, the removal of veils and shadows, the absolute transparency of atmosphere (in the categories of Aristotle, and later Shelling) allow to see something monstrous and unbearable—an angel prophesing the end of the world.

The image of blinding, as the extreme negative expression of the veil metaphor, became a kind of "aesthetic myth" at the turn of the nineteenth century.

2.

The metaphor of veil has its roots in the popular allegory of truth, which, in its turn, is a later version of the story by Plutarch about an inscription, found supposedly on the pediment of the temple of Athena (Isis) in Saiss: "I am the past, the present, and the future, and no mortal has yet removed my veil."[26] This inscription was also reported by Proclus, who made a crucial addition: "Sun was the fruit that I bore."[27] Subsequently, the story about the sculpture at Saiss became closely associated with the sun and partly with the moon.

In Ripa's *Iconology* sun is identified with Truth, which needs to be veiled. According to Ripa, allegory functions as such a dimming veil. The lunar aspect of allegory is based on the comparison of Isis to Diana who was traditionally identified with the moon. The stable interpretation of Osiris as sun and Isis as moon was formed by the seventeenth century.[28] In the previously mentioned wall paintings at the Royal Academy in London, the central place was occupied by a vignette, *Graces Unveiling Nature* by Benjamin West, which represents three graces in the clouds holding a veil over the many-breasted Diana (or Isis).

The Isidic allegory of truth enjoyed popularity especially at the end of the eighteenth century and became one of the classical topoi of Romantic culture. Sensational excavations in Pompeii, where the temple of Isis was found, had in part influenced this phenomenon. A great number of texts made reference to the discovery. Among other factors we should also consider the interest in Egyptian mysticism that had grown during the eighteenth century, the adaptation of Egyptian mysteries by Masonic rituals, and the Egyptian expedition of Napoleon.

The allegory of truth as Isis was canonized in the well-known poem of Friedrich Schiller, *The Veiled Statue of Saiss* (1795), which told the story of the death of a young man who dared to look at Isis. The impossibility of contemplating deity is connected with the solar aspect of the myth and is interpreted unexpectedly in terms of the two-tier system of light. In this respect, the statement by the scholar and mason Alexander Lenoir (1812) is quite revealing: "Osiris is pure light, whereas the power of Isis is effective over the sublunar substance which is subjected in turn to day and night, life and death, water and fire, beginning and end."[29]

For instance, the motif of veiled Isis as the embodiment of nature is characteristic of Novalis in *Students in Saiss*. The veiled goddess appears in *America* (1793) by William Blake as well as in his other works. In this essay it would be impossible to give a full account of the omnipresence of Isidic allegory in Romantic culture. We will focus only on a few solar-lunar interpretations of this allegory among the Romantics.

Mythology of the sun and the moon is crucial, for instance, for the poetry of John Keats, whose two most important poems, *Endymion* (1817) and *Hyperion* (1818–19), developed the lunar and the solar myths correspondingly. In Keats's poetry truth is associated with celestial bodies covered by veils, which in their turn are described as clouds.

However, Blake used this image many times before Keats. Characteristically, he compared his titanic heroes to clouds and constantly referred to divine veil directly as clouds. Shelley, who was inclined to Neoplatonism and to a large degree was influenced by eighteenth-century poetry, also used the veil metaphor.[30]

Let us once more point out the set of stable meanings. The light of sun (or moon) is equated with truth; veil clouds hide this truth (Shelley in *Ode to Liberty* [1820] even compares clouds to tyranny). No matter how painful the sight of light-truth is (blinding in Shelley, torturing and mournful in Keats), it must penetrate the veil, it must show through.

The showing of light through a screen became one of the principal mystical motifs in the culture of the eighteenth and the first third of the nineteenth centuries. By the nineteenth century it turned into a stable cliché and took on more and more conventional theatrical forms. In Thomas Moore's *The Epicurean* (1827), a significant part of which is devoted to Isidic mysteries defined by Moore as "theatrical spectacles, which formed a part of the subterranean Elysium of the Pyramids," the motif of the transparent screen plays an important role.[31] Here, in a number of passages, the veil of Plutarch turned into a simple "theatrical" curtain behind which a powerful flood of light was shining. In another passage the veil metaphor is treated as illusionistic spectacle: "The veil, which had before shrouded the face of the figure, became every minute more transparent, and the features, one by one, gradually disclosed themselves. Having tremblingly watched the progress of the apparition, I now started from my seat, and half exclaimed, 'It is she!' In another minute, this veil had, like a thin mist, melted away, and the young Priestess of the Moon stood, for the third time, revealed before my eyes."[32]

In this fragment from Moore, as in many Romantic writings, the natural-philosophical subtext of the allegory is obvious (priestess—moon, veil—fog), yet the entire scene is treated as a theatrical illusionistic attraction.

In a similar key, and probably not without Moore's influence, Edward Bulwer-Lytton interpreted the same metaphor in his famous novel *The Last Days of Pompeii* (1834). The novel is a kind of an anthology of the cultural myths of the 1820s–30s—here we have Naples, Pompeii, Vesuvius, the theme of blindness of the novel's heroin Nydia, Isidic mysteries, etc. In this banal intertwining of all subjects, an honorable place is given to the illusionistic spectacle that shows through a mystical cover. The action takes place in the house of Arbaces, the priest of Isis: ". . . the Egyptian seized the hand of Apæcides, and led him, wandering, intoxicated, yet half-reluctant, across the chamber towards the curtain at the far end; and now, from behind that curtain, there seemed to burst a thousand sparkling stars; the veil itself, hitherto dark, was now lighted by these fires behind into the tenderest blue of heaven. It represented heaven itself—such a heaven, as in the nights of June might have shone down over the streams of Castaly. Here and there were painted rosy and aerial clouds."[33] A celestial melody is heard—the indispensable attribute of all literary mysteries: ". . . the veil was rent in twain—it parted—it seemed to vanish into air."[34] Next follows a traditional description of a dazzling phantom palace where fountains "cast up a spray, which, catching the rays of the roseate light, glittered like countless diamonds" (i.e., all the solar symbolism, donned in Milton's "sources of light" and in Newton's "iridescent rays").[35]

For Bulwer-Lytton, and this is particularly important, the allegorical aspect remains in the background while the first place is occupied by the illusionistic theatrical transparency, a curtain sky with clouds, upon which a powerful flood of "theatrical" light creates visions. In *The Last Days of Pompeii* we encounter a vulgarization, a theatrical debasing of the Romantic allegory developed by Schiller, Novalis, Keats, and Shelley. But it is a vulgarization of the metaphor's material embodiment. More than once in the same novel Bulwer-Lytton describes a celestial mystical transparency, once even calling it "phantasmagoria," that is, a magic lantern show. Such a "phantasmagoria" show also takes place at the Temple of Isis, where on the back of the altar appeared "an indistinct and pale landscape, which gradually grew brighter and clearer as she [Ione] gazed" through a "curtain," and then "the scene was succeeded by the representation of a gorgeous palace."[36]

The stable association between veil and clouds also has another side. Clouds traditionally were understood as the place of manifestation of visions, as an endlessly changing text, upon which transforming pictures constantly appear.[37] These visions were provoked by the different regimes of solar or lunar lighting. The eighteenth-century poetry already formed a repertoire of cloud visions—in most cases they were the visions of a city (understood as the City of Sun, or Heavenly City), a palace, or mountain peaks.

Clouds as veil and as a screen started to attract growing interest. Luke Howard gave the first classification of clouds, later used by Goethe and Ruskin.[38] Goethe's work strongly influenced the Dresden Romantics. In the manifesto of this group of artists, *Letters on Landscape Painting* (1815–35) by Carl Gustav Carus, Goethe's meteorology was reinterpreted in terms of "natural mysticism" and declared the method of scientific cleaving through nature's mystical veil to the Divine Mysteries,[39] that is, it is directly connected with the veil metaphor. Johann Christian Clausen Dahl created a series of cloud studies under the direct influence of Carus.[40] Dahl influenced another German Romantic, Karl Blechen, who in 1828 was working on his cloud studies in Italy as well. This pilgrimage of German artists to Italy "for clouds" is particularly telling, since Italy, in contrast with Northern countries, was justifiably considered to be the country of cloudless sky. Italy, and particularly Naples, as the carriers of local cultural myth associated with luminosity, almost inevitably provoked among artists certain motifs and an interest in the problems of light. Thus, the first changes in the poetics of Dahl's style were apparent in his landscape painting *The Bay of Naples*. Dahl also returned with remarkable persistance to the motif of erupting Vesuvius (1823). Turner, who devoted more than 500 studies to clouds, interpreted them first of all as a transparent screen that dims light yet lets it through. Ruskin, who wrote his *Modern Painters* as an explication of Turner's theory of painting, devoted hundreds of pages to clouds. In the same book he also discussed in detail the veil metaphor, relating it to the problems of the theory of painting:" . . . when the earth had to be prepared· for the habitation of man, a veil, as it were, of intermediate being was spread between him and its darkness, in which were joined, in a subdued measure, the stability and insensibility of the earth, and the passion and perishing of mankind.

"But the heavens, also, had to be prepared for his habitation.

"Between their burning light, their deep vacuity, and man, as between the earth's gloom of iron substance, and man, a veil had to be spread of intermediate being; which should appease the unendurable glory to the level of human feebleness, and sign the changeless notion of the heavens with a semblance of human vicissitude.

"Between earth and man arose the leaf. Between the heaven and man came the cloud. His life being partly as the falling leaf, and partly as the flying vapor."[41]

3.

All of the above gave rise to a completely new problem in the history of painting—materialization of the principle governing the penetration of vision and light through the layers of medium that contain an image. It is as though under the influence of light rays images formed in the very substance of the medium and demanded a certain "piercing" energetic impulse both in order to be developed and to be perceived.[42]

Ruskin criticized previous painters for perceiving the world as colored surfaces. Taking as the basis of his criticism Wordsworth's comparison of sky to abyss in the second book of *A Walk in Chamouni*,[43] Ruskin pointed out that we look "not at the sky, but *through* it,"[44] while with the old masters clouds never appear "filmly" and light always falls on them rather than being contained within them.[45]

Ruskin writes about "transparency,"[46] about the clouds' "spongelike power of gathering light in their bodies."[47] Light as Newtonian substance appears to sight only at the moment of its coming through the transparent screen. Without a screen the ray of light remains invisible. Only coming through the opaque, through shadow, does light produce color. The idea of a transparent screen is directly connected with Goethe's color theory. But it should not be forgotten that, as the expression of the philosophical veil metaphor, transparency also functions as a physiological measure of the ideal Newtonian light, as the condition for the appearance of light to the imperfect human eye.

Turner experimented with the representation of the perception of light and atmosphere on paper and canvas. This explains his preoccupation with clouds, fog, stormy sky, and water. This also explains his interest in watercolors where a white sheet of paper—the pure medium—functions as the "source" of light. And, finally, this explains his persistent attempts to place the sun directly into the canvas "against" the viewer's eye, "behind the transparent atmospheric layer."

In the 1810s the desire to arrest movement of light in the medium also produced a tendency to transform the canvas or paper itself into transparency. Light was expected to manifest images upon these "bodies." Clouds were not only introduced in painting as objects of representation but also became a metamodel for painting itself. These tendencies made painters turn their attention to the examples of transparent painting on glass. After a decline in the eighteenth century, production of stained glass picked up in the beginning of the nineteenth century. In 1809 Dille (Henri-Louis Bop, 1776–1855) opened the first exhibition of glass painting, where he substituted the mosaic construction of ancient stained glass by "traditional" painting on one large piece of glass similar to a canvas. Dille's reviewers praised him for the fact that "these paintings have the solidity of nature. An eye cannot find in them the glass upon which they are painted."[48] Many followed Dille's example, and soon glass painting became a permanent feature at every painting exhibition. It enjoyed particular popularity in England, where following the fashion stained glass was used to decorate houses (libraries and dining rooms) and carriages. Here emerged the school of historical stained-glass painting whose members worked on transposing copies of masterpieces of world art onto glass. It was thought that the transparency technique would bring additional qualities to traditional painting.

English stained-glass painting of the first half of the nineteenth century utilized enamels on white glass in such a way that "real light" never touched the viewer's eye, and the gradations of light and shade were represented by the varied layers of enamel (in the same way as on a canvas). That is why English stained glass was criticized for being dull.[49] Only in 1847 Charles Winston discovered the reason for this dullness: the new stained glass did not let through a single ray of light, whereas the tiny bubbles in the ancient stained glass collected the rays of sunlight which were almost invisible to the eye but created the effect of sunshine.[50]

The experiment with stained glass was of fundamental importance for painting. One of the protagonists of painting's adventures with light, John Martin, started as a glass painter. After having abandoned this work much earlier, he still declared: "Glass painting must have surpassed all other branches of art in splendour, as it is capable of producing the most splendid and beautiful effects, far superior to oil-painting or water-colours, for by the transparency we have the means of bringing in real light, and have the full scale of nature as to light and as to shadow, as well as to the richness of colour which we have neither in oil-painting nor in water-colour."[51] The first painting to bring Martin popularity, *Sadak in Search of the Waters of Oblivion* (1812, after Shelly), is a direct imitation of the effects of glass painting on canvas. Martin achieved the illusion of real light coming through a thick purple glass. The effect of stained glass was so obvious that Coleridge noted: "It seems to me that Martin never looked at Nature except through bits of stained glass."[52]

This kind of vision became typical for many Romantics who often turned to images of precious stones in their descriptions of color. W. Steinert relates this tendency of the German Romantics to their interest in stained glass.[53]

In *Sadak*—Martin's first experiment in transposing stained glass onto canvas—the scene of action is a volcano slope running with burning lava. The volcano became the favorite subject of paintings which imitated transparencies. This choice was most likely motivated by the inability of new stained glass to represent direct light. The volcano had been already described by the poet David Mallet as inverted underground sun and associated with the end of the world and the dying-out day star. Thus it came to be seen as the "dim" light, the effects of which easily could be represented in glass painting.

The interest in volcanoes as a spectacle first began in Naples in the circles of William Hamilton (1730–1803), an English ambassador who attracted the attention of artists frequenting his salon (1764–1800) to

Vesuvius.[54] For instance, Hamilton incited an interest in volcanoes in Joseph Wright of Derby whose studies of volcanoes had a significant influence on English painters. The volcanic motifs were also assimilated in the neo-Isidic mythology (the connection between Vesuvius and Pompeii as well as the notion that volcanic fire is the breath of Typhon, the principal mythological enemy of Isis).

Already at the end of the eighteenth century, imitation of the volcano effects with colored glass was attempted on several occasions. For instance, we can find a description of the "prismatic lantern with pieces of different color glass" used to recreate the feeling of volcanic light at home.[55] Volcano is the same "prismatic lantern" for Martin. Fire and volcano eruptions became the principal sources of light in practically all of Martin's catastrophic visions, even when they are not depicted directly on the canvas. A gust of blinding fire through a thick layer of clouds or smoke—such is the characteristic feature of the majority of his works as noticed even by his contemporaries: "He rarely borrows his techniques from nature; his paintings do not resemble its creations . . . but are rather artificial and, like all mechanical achievements, they are marked by great precision and inevitable monotony. Six out of seven subjects by this artist are depicted under the cover of clouds with one central light source, and on the whole they are characterized by chemical red hues."[56] Chemical red hue is the color of transparent glass Martin inevitably brings to his canvases.

Belshazzar's Feast (1820)—the most famous of Martin's paintings—is constructed on the same principle. It represents the enormous palace of Belshazzar flooded by a blood-red shining light. Above the palace are the fiery clouds pierced through by lightning.

The different motifs of "luminosity" are brought together in this painting. As already mentioned, the motif of the burning, shining palace is related to the vision of the sun—the Heavenly City or—in an inverted form—the pandemonium. Some scholars see the source of Belshazzar's palace in Keats's *Hyperion,* although it is more likely that Martin represented the general stereotype of the vision of a city in clouds.

Along with the palace motif, the classic motif of blinding light is present in this work—the guests recoil being blinded by the shining letters. To describe the effect, the artists used the word "to emanate," a Neoplatonic term. Later, Edgar Quinet, who was sensitive to these kinds of transpositions of meaning, repeated the image of the letters

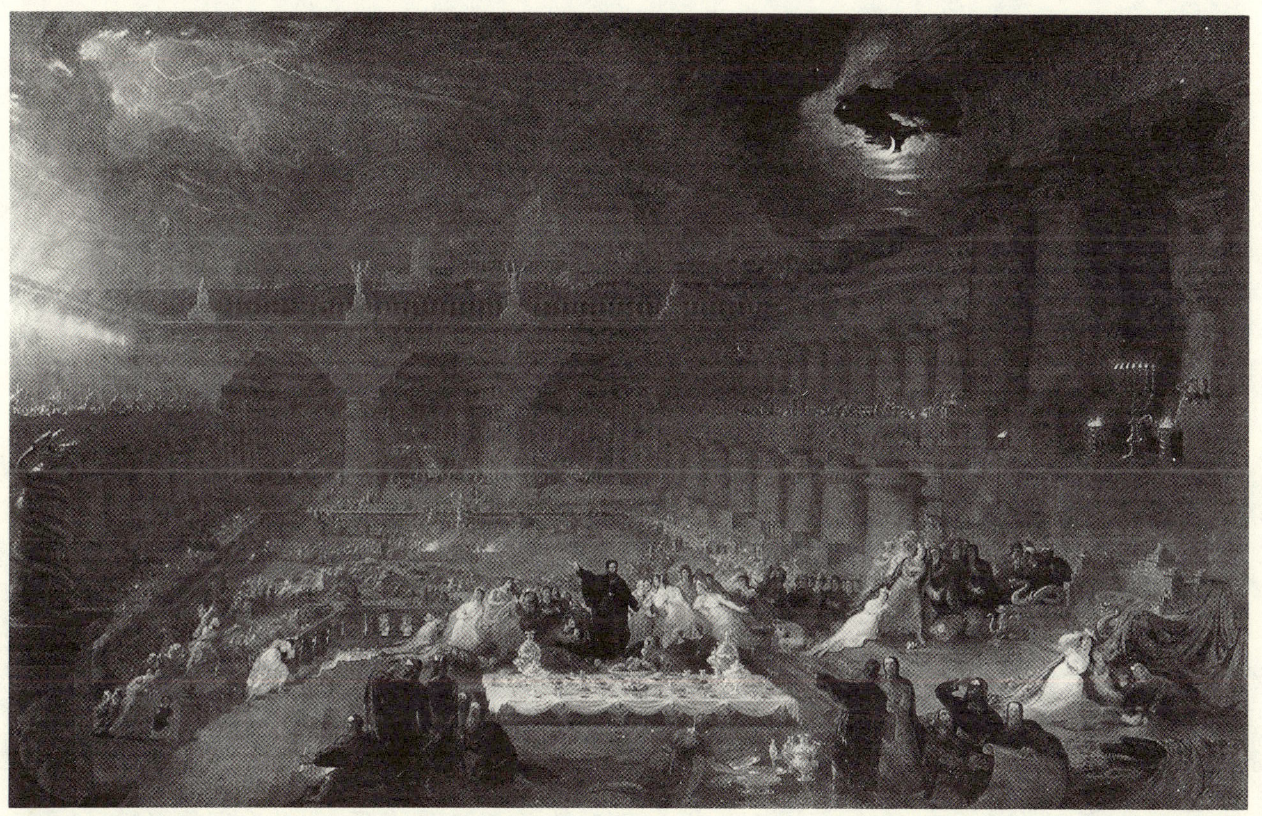

John Martin, *Belshazzar's Feast* (1820). Oil on canvas.
Collection Mrs. R. Wright.

shining over Babylon in a different context—as divine (transparent) language: "The light of night illuminates the inscriptions of Semiramis engraved upon the rocks of the Assur mountain. Each word shines from here like a fiery balde that writes the Divine language upon the stones."[57] Charles Lamb, who devoted an entire essay to *Belshazzar's Feast,* emphasized the transparency character of the burning inscription: "These letters are nothing but a lit transparency," and noted that their obvious "transparency" completely strips the scene of mystical character and moves it into the ranks of theatrical tricks.[58] In the same essay he tells an anecdote about a reception held by the Royal Prince where "an inventive gentleman Furley from Covent Garden" scared the public by a phantasmagoric transparency, on which "the shining golden letters spelled: Brighton—Earthquake—Swallows alive."[59]

For the ironic Lamb, the transparency character of Martin's work was a testimony against its painterliness and for its theatricality. Martin himself foregrounded the connection of the painting to transparency by making its copy on a glass which was displayed in the window of the exhibition hall and was meant to attract the public. The glass version emphasized the luminous character of the inscription, and for contemporaries this established an inseparable link between the painting and theater. Richard Redgrave described this glass set in the wall: ". . . the ray of light really shined through the terrifying inscription: the effect was striking although it undoubtfully belonged to theater more than to art."[60] Constable called *Belshazzar's Feast* "Martin's pantomime."[61]

The common perception of Martin's painting as a kind of theatrical performance was based largely on the ideas of Martin himself who published an explanatory booklet in conjunction with the exhibition. In the booklet the narrative of the painting was presented as a libretto of an opera in three acts, and the characters—Belshazzar, the Queen, etc.—even had their own lines. The libretto was accompanied by a diagram which with the help of a number system described the proper sequence of looking at the painting. In this way, *Belshazzar's Feast* was presented as a diachronic, stretched in time narrative rather than a synchronic text of a painting.

4.

Dioramas were the next step in the process of theatricalization of transparency painting. Here the flow of time, which was only present in the embryonic state on the canvases influenced by the aesthetics of transparency, became truly realized. Robert Barker, the inventor of panorama, is considered to be the first to realize the idea of using light effects for the demonstration of paintings.[62]

But it was the inventor of diorama, Louis Jacques Mandé Daguerre, who first used the double system of lighting. Some windows lit the canvas from the front, while others, with the help of a complicated system of mirrors, supplied the transparent lighting. With this system, by changing the lighting and shifting accent from the front to the back source, Daguerre could represent the change of time naturalistically and to demonstrate natural effects of light. The very first reviews of Daguerre's diorama noted that "the light and shadow change here as if clouds were passing over the sun."[63] But the most remarkable of Daguerre's inventions was painting with the so-called double effect. A canvas was painted on both sides with transparent and nontransparent oils. When the lighting was shifted from the front to the back, the transparent oils of the front side of canvas disappeared while the image painted with nontransparent oils on the back side of canvas and invisible under the front light would "develop." In this way, the subject of a painting changed due exclusively to the play of light. The diorama *A Midnight Mass at Saint-Etienne-du-Mont* (1834) caused the greatest sensation. This is how the journalist Gustave Deville described it: "At first it was daylight, the nave full of [empty] chairs; little by little the light waned; at the same time, candles were lit at the back of the chair; then the entire church was illuminated, and the chairs were occupied by the congregation who had arrived, not suddenly as if by scene-shifting, but gradually—quickly enough to surprise one, yet slowly enough for one not to be astonished. The midnight mass started, and in the midst of a devotion impossible to describe, organ music was heard echoing from the vaulted roof. Slowly dawn broke, the congregation dispersed, the candles were extinguished, the church and the empty chairs appeared as at the beginning. This was magic."[64]

A diorama show lasted about fifteen minutes. To be fully manifested, light demanded a passage of time since only while changing could it be maximally perceived as a substance that gives rise to spectacle.

Church interiors were the favorite subject of dioramas (the effect of stained-glass lighting was used here) and linked this spectacle with the tradition of mysteries. The German Romantics, who were very interested in the effects of transparencies, often interpreted church as spiritual vision. Caspar David Friedrich painted the vision of a church several times: *Vision of Christian Church* (1812), *The Cathedral* (1818), etc. The transparency effects can be found in the paintings of cathedrals by other German Romantic artists as well.

Friedrich had completed several transparencies for the Russian Empress and used the motif of a Gothic cathedral among other subjects. He also prepared the transparency *City in the Moonlight* which has apparent references to the visions of moonlit cities characteristic of his paintings as well as the paintings of the artists of his circle.[65]

The cultural myth that gave rise to dioramas became significantly overshadowed by purely theatrical, spectacular effects. Yet they still retained in a rudimentary form the remnants of archaic cultural mystery, a fact noted by the contemporaries. For instance, G. de Nerval in his review of the diorama *The Flood* exhibited by Charles-Marie Bouton, the coauthor of Daguerre, called it "a spectacular mystery performed by the elements," and perceptively traced such motifs of this diorama as the fantastic city with obelisques and pyramids as well as the rainbow to Milton's *Paradise Lost* and, even further, to the apocryphal *First Book of Enoch*.[66]

As a theatrical presentation of painting, the diorama absorbed mystery motifs into its ritual. The diorama by K. B. Gropius in Berlin was arranged as a house in Herculaneum. A viewer approached the painting after walking through dark interiors lit by dim red light that shone through mysterious transparent images.[67] The very movement toward the painting imitated the ritual of initiation with its necessary passage through dark corridors toward the final apparition of brightest light.[68]

At the same time, dioramas were making their way into theater. Since the late 1810s the evolution of stage lighting was closely linked with the development of theatrical painting. In 1817 gas lighting capable of widening the range of light effects was introduced at Drury Lane. And after 1820 dioramas and transparencies became the traditional elements of pantomimes, which were also created on the principle of mystery. Prior to James Robinson Planche's reform classic pantomime included the so-called dark scene as a preparation for the ending of blinding light.

Luminous painting developed as a complex symbolic system rooted in the philosophical questions of the eighteenth century. The transformation of philosophical and aesthetic experiments into the material of theatrical spectacles certainly vulgarized the symbolism and the meaning of artistic explorations. To a great extent this completed a long period in the evolution of painting, which was from now on forced to overcome the burden of vulgarized superimpositions by rejecting the already elaborated subjects. During the 1820s–30s motifs associated with the problematic of light were gradually transposed into theater where they became superannuated and died out.

There is a number of illustrative examples of such migration of motifs into theater. For instance, in 1833 the Ambigu Comique in Paris staged *Belshazzar's Feast,* the finale of which was the imitation of Martin's painting.[69] In this context, the "lawful" copying of Martin's *Feast* by Hyppolyte Sébron, a student of Daguerre, appears quite logical. Sébron recreated the *Feast* for a diorama of 2,000 square feet in diameter. The diorama effects transposed Martin's painting into a time dimension. Martin himself was outraged and perhaps considered Sébron's work as an unbearable vulgarization of his canvas. He sued Sébron but lost the case.[70]

By the middle of the nineteenth century, dioramas became one of the principal codes for the contemplation of nature with attention inevitably paid to light effects and transformations. In the eyes of those "infected" with the consciousness of transparency, nature turned into a spectacle with a well-defined time span, not unlike a show. Ruskin's old-age habit seems like a parody—every evening in his estate at Brentwood he would sit down in a specially placed armchair to contemplate sunset. As the legend goes, before each "show" a servant entered the room and uttered the same words: "Sunset, Mister Ruskin," as if he was announcing the arrival of an honored guest.[71]

As the code of transparency became the code of nature contemplation, it attained the status of "realism." A reversion took place as a result. Nature itself was perceived as the faithful copy of a vulgar spectacle. Perhaps this is the reason why Baudelaire and Gouthière were critical of nature. They represent the generation of aestheticians formed during the period when the transparency spectacles were exceptionally popular. And Whistler's famous statement about the "vulgarity of sunset" can be understood in the context of the theatricalization of nature by such conservatives as Ruskin who was Whistler's antagonist.

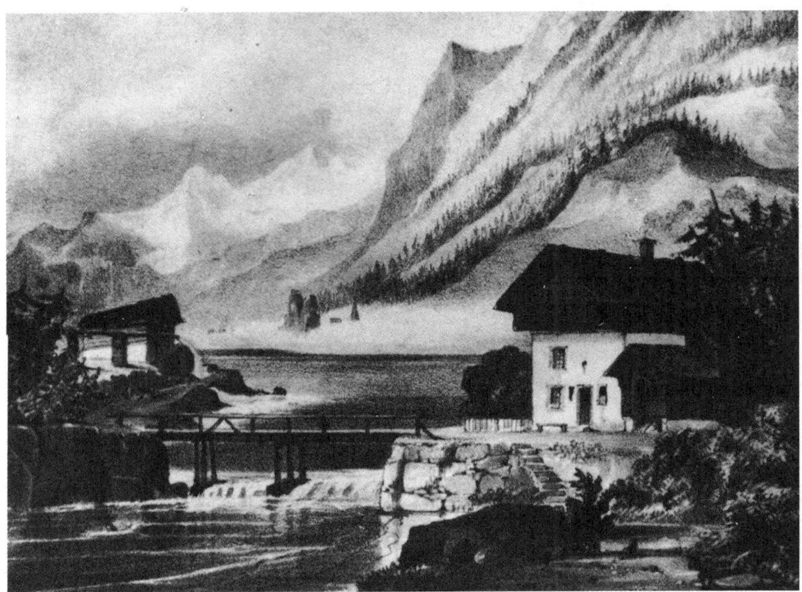

Dioramic colored lithograph of an Alpine village (c. 1836). Daylight scene by transmitted light.

In any case, the superimposition of dioramic code onto the "natural" contemplation of nature meant the end of experimentation with transparency in painting. It is logical that Impressionists, who continued to explore the problematic of light, completely ignored the motifs associated with the myths of luminosity. Volcanoes and palaces on fire were completely transposed into theatrical arsenal; nature was freed from mythological attributes and was prepared for a direct contemplation.

Meanwhile the history of transparency spectacles had just began. The development of an image under the effect of sun rays, which had mesmerized a number of painters at the beginning of the nineteenth century, took almost magical forms in photography. After leaving dioramas, Daguerre started working on the effects of light on chemical solutions and invented the daguerrotype. Turner followed closely the work of American photographer John Edwin Mayall and, most probably, was planning to involve him in the proving of his light theories.

But the tradition of transparency turned out to be especially important for cinema and its spectacle of a shining-through image that soars

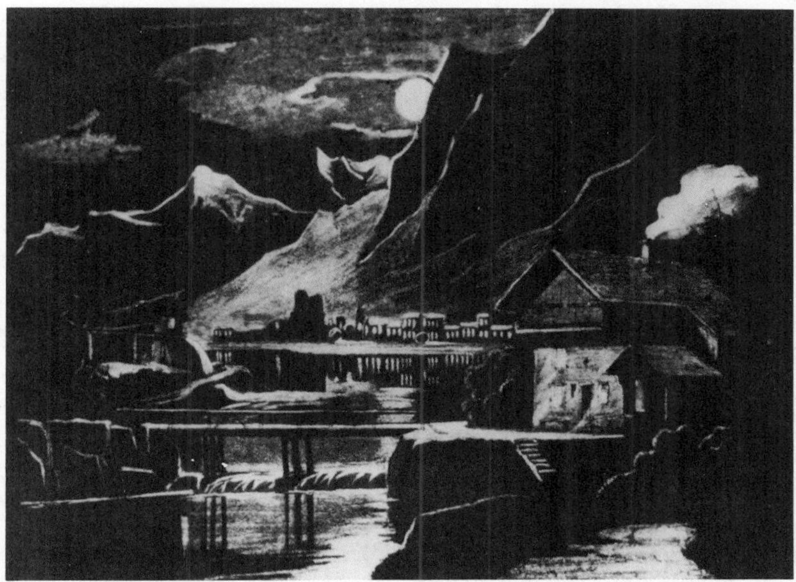

Dioramic colored lithograph of an Alpine village (c. 1836). Night scene by reflected light.

in the flood of light in a dark auditorium. It is in cinema that light, as the creator of time dimension, was used in a true, unfolding narrative. It is curious that early films still relied on the painterly motifs of luminosity: the fall of Pompeii, volcano eruptions, and the pantomime mysteries of Méliès. Griffith realized the cultural myth of light with a particular intensity. In 1914, while filming *The Avenging Conscience,* Griffith almost recreated the history of transparent painting when he asked his operator, G. W. "Billy" Bitzer, to shoot a long series of "cloud studies" and then used the white clouds as the background for visions of angels and the dark clouds for visions of demons.[72] Martin's *Belshazzar's Feast* became one of the iconographic sources for the "Babylon scene" in *Intolerance* (1916).[73] Here Griffith also includes the symbolic Temple of Holy Fire while the goddess Ishtar, whose symbolism is important to the film, does not just call to mind Martin's lunar symbolism but is most likely associated directly with Isis.[74]

The French director Abel Gance referred to cinema as the "cathedral of light," as if reminding us of the long history of transparency.[75]

NOTES

1. The definition of the phenomenon of color from the struggle of light and darkness is, to some degree, a later development of Aristotle's ideas, since in a direct form it is not present in the corpus of Aristotle's texts. But, according to A. F. Losev, it is one of "possible interpretations of Aristotle's principle, fully in accordance with the corresponding methods of Antique thought and Antique terminology." Losev summarizes Aristotle's ideas in this way: "In color we find at least two planes: light and darkness (or the medium of the diffusion and propagation of light), and these two planes are in the state of active conflict or struggle. In yellow or red color light, strenuously overcoming darkness, represents the active element; in blue it retreats, as though already not encountering any resistance from the side of darkness; in green both conflicting elements are in the state of peace, calm, and equilibrium" (*Istoriya Antichnoy Estetiki. Aristotel i pozdnyaya klassika* [Moscow, 1975], 302).

2. Sir Isaac Newton, *Opticks, or A Treatise of the Reflections, Refractions, Inflections and Colours of Light* (New York: Dover, 1952).

3. A. H. Bogolyubov, *Robert Guk* (Moscow, 1984), 95.

4. Marjorie Hope Nicolson, *Newton Demands the Muse: Newton's "Opticks" and the Eighteenth Century Poets* (Westport, 1979).

5. John Milton, *Paradise Lost* (New York: Odyssey Press, 1962). The eighteenth-century Neoplatonism turned to other thinkers and poets besides Milton, in particular to Dante (Blake) or Neoplatonists of the Italian Renaissance. These appeals, however, had a more local and less systematic character. Milton dominated everyone. Thus in this text we limit ourselves only to Milton's "myth"—the most productive for theatrical tendencies in culture.

6. *The Portable Blake* (Harmondsworth, 1977), 588.

7. *The Poetical Works of James Thomson* (New York, n.d.), 409.

8. This hypothesis was the result of an uncritical transposition of the phenomenon of color on thin film, as explained by Newton, onto all natural objects.

9. For the story of the creation of these paintings see E. Croft-Murray, "Decorative Paintings for Lord Burlington and the Royal Academy," *Apollo* 83 (1969): 11–21.

10. G. E. Finley, "Turner: An Early Experiment with Colour Theory," *Journal of the Warburg and Courtauld Institutes* 30 (1967): 359.

11. Ibid.

12. Christopher Thacker, *The Wildness Pleases: The Origins of Romanticism* (London: Croom Helm, 1983), 142–43.

13. E. M. Wilkinson, L. A. Willoughby, "The Blind Man and the Poet: An Early Stage in Goethe's Quest for Form," *German Studies. Presented to W. H. Bruford* (London, 1962), 29.

14. The philosophical context for the discourse on blindness in the eighteenth century is discussed in K. MacLean, *John Locke and English Literature of the Eighteenth Century* (New Haven, 1936).

15. Milton 1962.

16. M. M. Davy, A. Albécassis, M. Mokri, J. R. Renneteau, *Le thème de la lumière dans le Judaïsme, le Christianisme et l'Islam* (Paris, 1986).

17. Edmund Burke, *Filosofskoe issledovanie o proiskhozhdenii nashikh idey vozvyshennogo i prekrasnogo* (Moscow, 1979), 109 (Edmund Burke, *A Philosophical Enquiry into the Origin of Our Ideas of the Sublime and Beautiful* [Notre Dame: University of Notre Dame Press, 1968], 80). In his discussions Burke also relies on Milton.

18. F. V. Shelling, *Philosophiya iskusstva* (Moscow, 1966), 212.

19. Johann Wolfgang von Goethe, *Izbrannye sochineniya po estesvoznaniyu* (Moscow, 1957), 523. (*Theory of Colours* [Cambridge, Mass.: MIT Press, 1970].)

20. "Every color specification causes violence to the eye and forces it into opposition," Goethe 1957, 290; "When you look at a dazzling and absolutely colorless image, it leaves a strong and long impression whose fading is accompanied by color effects," ibid., 284.

21. Shelling 1966, 214.

22. About Turner's attitude toward scientific poets see A. Livermor, "J. M. W. Turner's Unknown Verse-Book," *Connoisseur Year Book* (London, 1957): 78–86; J. Lindsay, *Turner: His Life and Work* (London, 1981), 72–87.

23. M. R. Pointon, *Milton and English Art* (Manchester, 1970).

24. Perception of the world through the eyes without eyelids had been introduced into painting a little earlier (1810), as pointed out by Kleist, Brentano, and Arnim in the description of the painting *Monk on Sea Shore* by Karl David Friedrich: ". . . the impression is as if the canvas was seen by a person whose eye lids had been cut off" (H. von Kleist, C. Brentano, A. von Arnim, "Verschiedene Empfindungen vor einer Seelandschaft von Friedrich, worauf ein Kapuziner," *Meine süße Augenweide. Dichter über Maler und Malerei* (Berlin, 1977), 277.

25. Milton 1962.

26. Plutarch, *Plutarch's de Iside et Osizide* (Cardifi: University of Wales Press, 1970).

27. For the discussion of details, in particular concerning the place where the inscription was located, see Plutarque, *Isis et Osiris*, Notes par M. Mennier (Paris, 1924), 44.

28. J. Baltrusaitis, *La Quête d'Isis: Essais sur la légende d'un mythe. Introduction á l'Egyptomanie* (Paris, 1967), 78, 109.

29. Ibid., 59.

30. M. H. Abrams, *The Mirror and the Lamp: Romantic Theory and Critical Tradition* (New York, 1953), 126–32.

31. *The Poetical Works of Thomas Moore*, vol. 5 (Leipzig, 1842), 220.

32. Ibid., 281.

33. Edward Bulwer-Lytton, *The Last Days of Pompeii* (New York: Dodd, Mead & Co., 1946), 67.

34. Ibid.

35. Ibid.

36. Ibid., 121.

37. Hubert Damisch, *Théorie du nuage: Pour une histoire de la peinture* (Paris, 1972).

38. Luke Howard, *Essays on the Modification of Clouds* (London, 1803); and "Wolkengestalt nach Howard," *Goethes Werke in Zwölf Bänden*, vol. 12 (Berlin, 1981), 283–303.

39. Carl Gustav Carus, *Briefe und Aufsätze über Landschaftsmalerei* (Leipzig, 1982), 60–64. Carus saw the infinity of the sky as an attribute of God. See below in connection with the theme of "abyss."

40. Hans Joachim Neidhardt, *Die Malerei der Romantik in Dresden* (Leipzig, 1976), 165–66.

41. John Ruskin, *Modern Painters*, vol. 5 (New York, 1866), 109.

42. The energy theory of light, moving through "charged" ether, was developed by Lorentz Oken: Lorentz Oken, *Erste Ideen zur Theorie des Lichts, der Finsternis, der Farben und der Wärme* (Jena, 1808), and was assimilated by the Romantics, particularly Coleridge.

43. On the symbolic meaning of abyss as poetic meta-image see J. Purkis, *The World of the English Romantic Poets: A Visual Approach* (London, 1982), 149; J. T. Irwin, *American Hieroglyphics: The Symbol of the Egyptian Hieroglyphics in the American Renaissance* (New Haven, 1980), 79.

44. John Ruskin, *Modern Painters*, vol. 1 (New York, 1883), 120.

45. Ibid., 309.

46. Ibid., 281.

47. Ibid., 5:120.

48. *Moniteur*, 12 mars 1808. In *Histoire de la peinture sur verre*, by E. Lévy (Bruxelles, 1860), 218.

49. L. Lee, *Appreciation of Stained Glass* (Oxford, 1977), 76.

50. C. Winston, *An Enquiry into the Difference of Style Observable in Ancient Glass Painting, Especially in England, with Hints on Glass Painting* (Oxford, 1847).

51. William Feaver, *The Art of John Martin* (Oxford: Clarendon Press, 1975), 15.

52. *Table Talk*, 31 May 1830. In Feaver (1975), 15.

53. W. Steinert, *Das Farbenempfinden Ludwig Tiecks. Ein Beitrag zur Geschichte des Naturgefühls in der deutschen Dichtung* (Bonn, 1907), 29.

54. R. Fothergill, *Sir William Hamilton: Envoy Extraordinary* (London, 1969).

55. Thacker 1983, 192–93.

56. "Mr. Martin's Exhibition," *The Repository of Arts, Literature, Fashions, Manufactures, etc.* 127 (1822): 300.

57. Edgar Quinet, *Ahasvérus* (Paris, n.d.), 36.

58. Charles Lamb, *Barreness of the Imaginative Faculty in the Productions of Modern Art: The Essays of Elia and the Last Essays of Elia* (London, 1929), 266.

59. Ibid., 267.

60. T. Balston, *John Martin 1789–1884: His Life and Works* (London, 1947), 58.

61. J. Seznic, *John Martin in France* (London, 1964), 48.

62. G. Bapst, *Essay sur l'histoire des panoramas et des dioramas* (Paris, 1891), 7.

63. Helmut Gernsheim and Alison Gernsheim, *L. G. M. Daguerre 1787–1851: The World's First Photographer* (New York, 1956), 14.

64. Ibid., 32.

65. E. Wundmann, "Zum Landschaftstransparent der hintergründen Romantik," *Caspar-David-Friedrich-Almanach* (Berlin, 1941), 13–16.

66. G. de Nerval, *Diorama. Oeuvres*, vol. 2 (Paris, 1958), 773.

67. E. Stenger, "Daguerre's Diorama in Berlin," *Beitrag zur Vorgeschichte der Photographie* (Berlin, 1925), 22.

68. Bapst 1891, 9.

69. M. Meisel, "The Material Sublime: John Martin, Byron, Turner and the Theatre," *Images of Romanticism: Verbal and Visual Affinities,* ed. K. Kroeber and W. Walling (New Haven, 1978), 218–19.

70. Gernsheim, 43.

71. W. Gaunt, *The Aesthetic Adventure* (Harmondsworth, 1957), 119.

72. L. R. Phillips, *D. W. Griffith: Titan of the Film Art: A Critical Study* (New York, 1976), 109.

73. B. Hanson, "D. W. Griffith: Some Sources," *Art Bulletin* 4 (1972): 504–11.

74. Lillian Gish, *A. Pinchot, the Movies, Mr. Griffith and Me* (New York, 1970), 170–71.

75. A. Gance, "Le temps de l'image est venu!" *L'art cinématographique,* vol. 2 (Paris, 1927), 96.

Things and Words:
Toward a Lyrical Museum

. . . To give Things the innermost essence,
Of which they know nothing.
. . . Transient, in our transient selves, they
Search for redemption.

R.-M. Rilke, *Ninth Duino Elegy*

1. What Is a Lyrical Museum?

Usually Things are displayed in museums for three reasons. They can be very rare or ancient, unique and valuable in themselves; in this case we have a museum thesaurus, a treasury like the Oruzheinaia Palata or Museum of the Diamond Fund. Or these Things are important as samples typical for an entire family or class of similar Things; then we have a museum catalog, a systematic collection found in the museums of technology, mineralogy, or zoology. Finally, Things can be neither very unique nor very typical but interesting because of their association with a prominent figure; then we have a museum memorial which reconstructs the surroundings of a famous writer, scientist, or general. To be sure, these three functions of a Thing—as a curiosity, as a sample, and as a relic—can be interspersed and combined in actual museum practice; but traditionally they bestow on Things a museum status and promote them into the rank of exhibits.

The project for a museum to be discussed here does not belong to

Mikhail Epshtein, "Vesch i slovo, o liricheskom muzee" (Things and words: Toward a lyrical museum), in *Parodoxy novizny* (Moscow: Sovetskiy Pisatel, 1988), 304–33.

any of the above-mentioned types. Its displays are the Things of everyday life, in general use, without a particular monetary, historical, or artistic value; they are encountered everywhere and do not usually interest or surprise us. What is essential to such Things is not their typicality but the individual existence marked by the habits and ideals of their owners. Yet these displays do not command value as memorabilia because their owners are ordinary people whose names are unknown, who are still living, and who are not ready to be memorialized.

What kind of museum is it where ordinary Things are on display, and what right does it have to draw attention to them? In fact, besides the monetary, historical, or artistic value bestowed on a few selected Things, *every* Thing, no matter how insignificant, can possess a private or *lyrical* value. This latter value depends on the degree to which a given Thing had been lived and thought through, on the extent to which it had been assimilated to the selfhood of its owner. If certain crucial meanings can be discovered in it and communicated in an accompanying explanation or commentary, then such a Thing is quite worthy of becoming an exhibit in the lyrical museum. The purpose of this museum is to expose the endlessly diverse and profound significance of Things in human life, their rich figurative and conceptual meaning which is not at all reducible to the utilitarian function.

Human life is largely constituted by Things and also deposited in Things as in the peculiar geological layers that let us observe the changes in age, taste, attachments, and passions. A child's toys—a ball, a doll, a scoop . . . An eraser, a pen, a pencil case, a school bag . . . A backpack, skies, tennis rackets . . . A desk lamp, a book, a notebook . . . A handbag, a purse, a mirror, a paper fan . . . A wallet, a cigarette case, keys, various documents . . . Scissors, knitting needles . . . A shovel, pliers, a hammer . . . A compass, a watch, a thermometer, a magnifying glass . . . Cups, plates, a familiar chair by the window . . . A simple pebble, once brought back from the sea—the eyes are accustomed to fixing on it . . . Each Thing is included in the whole magnetic field of human life and charged with this life's meaning, directed toward its center. Each Thing has a connection to a particular memory, experience, habit, a loss or a purchase, a broadened horizon of life. The triviality of Things is a proof of their significance, which lacks in "unusual" Things, a proof of their ability to enter the habitude, to entwine with peoples' character and to become a stable and meaningful form of human existence. The world is articulated, "uttered" through Things: it is not accidental that the word *vesch* is etymologically related to *vesti* and originally meant "said, uttered" (compare to the Latin word with the same stem *vox*—voice). To hear the voice, contained in Things and prophesying from within their depth, is to understand them and oneself. The juxtaposition "thing-like"–"human-like" can be established only conditionally, in the framework of a *"human-thing"* affiliation which in its essence is as indissoluble as body from mind. The Thingness is the *man* in a hu*man*, it is his body. Each Thing constitutes a human coming out of himself: into nature or art, into space or thought, into movement or rest, into contemplation or creation. All the major components of human life find correspondence in Things, as in the letters of language that are combined to form fully meaningful actions, situations, relationships. There is not a Thing—from a car to a button, from a book to a candy wrapper—that does not occupy a special place in culture and bring culture within human reach. In doing this it demands from its owner a reciprocate attention and understanding. His own position in the world, the meaning of his existence, is determined by the totality of surrounding Things. A Thing fallen out of signification creates a break in the network of connections with others and with oneself.

Right here, around the Things we encounter at every turn, a field is forming which still awaits an investigation and even demands the creation of a new sphere of knowledge—we could call it *realogy* (from the Latin *res*—thing).[1] So far our ears have not been accustomed to the terms *realogy* or the *science of Things,* but sooner or later they will have to appear. An enormous number of Things that surround us every day fit neither into the framework of museum practice nor the theoretical disciplines concerned with Things such as industrial technology, technical aesthetics, or art history. Of course, before getting into the hands of owners, Things usually go through a factory shop and a distribution system, often they also pass through a designer's office, and sometimes through an artist's studio. But the object of the science of Things is an essence not reducible to the technical characteristics of a *product,* to the economic characteristics of a *commodity,* or to the aesthetic qualities of an *art work.* The Thing possesses a distinct essence that expands precisely at the time when its technical novelty, retail value, and aesthetic attraction diminish. This essence, capable of assimilation and intimacy with people, is revealed more

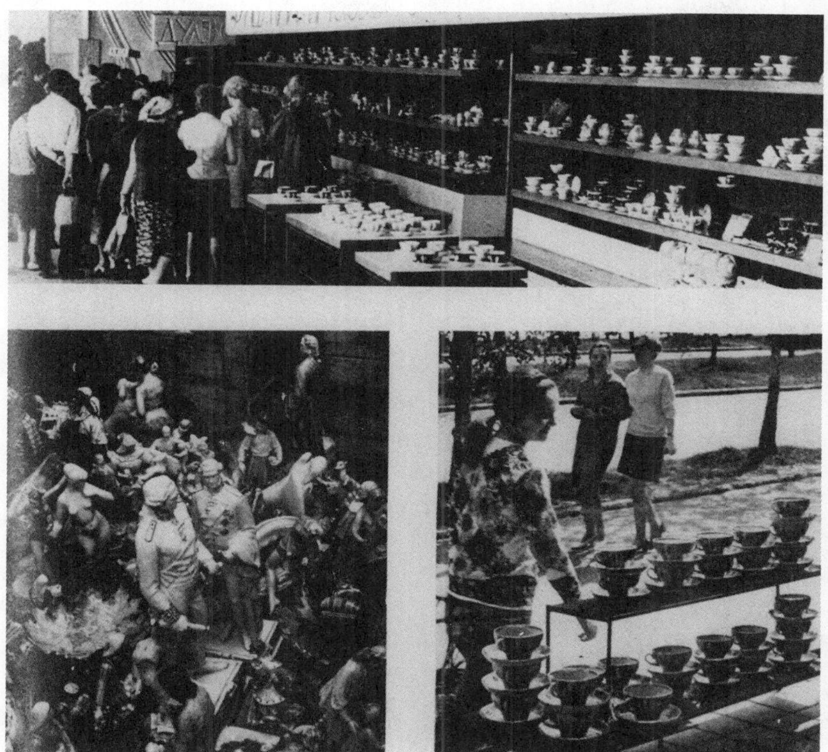

Ensemble of photographs by S. Onanov from Leningrad glass and porcelain factories, in *Dekorativnoe Iskusstvo* 8 (1971).

and more as the other characteristics of the Thing recede in the background, age, and become devalued. The only property of the Thing that expands in the process of assimilation is the Thing's saturation with individuality, its existence as a *property* of man. Each Thing is significant if only because it exists; but it is up to men to unveil its essence through their experience and attention and to turn its absolute self-value into a value for themselves.

The task of realogy as a theoretical discipline and of the lyrical museum as its *experimental basis,* as the *practical science of Things,* is to comprehend the particular, nonfunctional meaning of Things independent of retail value, utilitarian purpose, or even aesthetic worth.

I would like to offer a preliminary terminological distinction between "object" and "Thing," the words found in entirely different types of contextual combinations.[2] "Object" requires an inanimate noun as the direct object of a sentence while "Thing" requires an animate one. We say "an object of what?"—of manufacturing, consumption, export, investigation, discussion, or scrutiny, but "whose thing?"—a fathers', a son's, a wife's, a friend's, or a neighbor's. The language never lies, and in this case it demonstrates, better than any theoretical exposition, the difference between objects and Things, between the affiliation of one and the same phenomenon with the world of objects and the world of subjects. The point is that the Thing in its nature is not an object; it does not function as an object of influence but rather as something belonging to a subject, as someone's "own." "Articles," "commodities," or "antiques" are essentially the types of objects—the objects of manufacturing and consumption, sale and purchase, collection and contemplation. The correlation between an object and a Thing is somewhat like the correlation between individuality and personality, the former being a possibility or a "substratum" of the latter. An object turns into a Thing in the process of spiritual assimilation, just like an individual turns into a person in the process of self-recognition, self-realization, and intense self-development. Another comparison: "He created a good object"—"He did a good thing." The first means to produce something by hands, the second to accomplish an act. The word "thing" in the old Russian originally meant a "spiritual act," a "deed," a "verb," and *theory* must continue to illuminate this meaning still present in our contemporary *intuition* of a Thing.[3] In each object there lies something of a Thing, a trace, or a possibility of human achievement . . .

A lyrical museum is the experience of "de-objectifying" the Things dear to us—not those removed into a historical past, attributed to a distant natural or cultural environment, or belonging to someone else, but personal and "own"—and the test of their true assimilation. Do we really understand what these Things mean to us? Entering into our most intimate world, how do they usher in the broad, all-encompassing meanings and link us with the total system of culture, its traditions and potentials? How are they crossed by the lines of individual destiny and the perspective of personal formation? All of it can be represented subjectively to the extent to which the lyrical "I" of the exhibitor determines the mode of its own expression in the exhibit.[4] What matters is possibility of representation, the presence of a lyrical source in the depths of Things, their proximity to and affinity with the human "I" and its realization in the world.

It is typical for a traditional museum to create a certain epic distance between the Thing and the reality from which it is extracted and which it represents from afar, as if keeping aloof. Such distance is essential in order to establish an objective meaningfulness of Things, to subject them to the tests of time and popular recognition, and to scientifically investigate their authenticity and prototypicality. Yet another kind of museum work is just as necessary—not the epics but the lyrics of Things, which are not just disclosed from outside by a knowledgeable expert but from within the spiritual and cultural situation where these Things function and live inseparably from the lives of their owners. To exhibit and to comment on a personal Thing—this is the opportunity offered to everyone by the lyrical museum. Here the meaning of Things is revealed from the point of view of their realization in life, as being present here and now, on the horizon of consciousness that makes use of them and is embodied in them.

Perhaps these Things are not as significant as those displayed in historical and art museums. Usually a lyrical work is also written not about grandiose events such as the fall of Troy or the Moscow Fire but about a "magic moment," a passing smile, a gentle breeze, or a speckle of dust "on the blade of a pocket knife" (Alexander Block). Here the Thing functions metaphorically or metonymically and expresses ideal through material or whole through part. A lyrical exhibit is like a poetic trope, its literal meaning coincides with the Thing's material existence and utilitarian function while its figurative meaning embraces the totality of emotions and ideas expressed by the Thing.

The lyrical museum has a historical urgency since the personal essence of Things it attempts to capture is coming to the fore only now, at the time of their increasing depersonification.

2. Between the Warehouse and the Dump

The problem of materialistic mentality is one of the most urgent for the twentieth century. The words themselves—"things, thing-like"—are perceived as suspicious, as presenting a danger to spirituality.[5] But Things are not responsible for "materialistic mentality" which is a property of man who descends to Things, and not of Things that always have potential for ascending to man, for being spiritualized by him. It is not necessary to return to manual production as suggested by the discussions of such different thinkers as Morris, Gandhi, and Heidegger. A Thing can be domesticated by man even if it came from the most sophisticated and standardized production line. Eventually it ends up in a home where man accommodates it to his intimate living, endows it with a multitude of meanings—particular and general, conscious and unconscious. The use of Things, be it sitting in a chair, watching television, wearing glasses or reading a book, paradoxically turns into consumption only when a Thing is not fully consumed, not assimilated by the whole being. A typical example is the "consumption" of only the pretty color of a book's cover or at best the plot outline. Consumerism arises when a Thing, after coming home to its owner, remains alienated and unconsumed, as if it were still displayed in a shop window or a shelf.

Twentieth century created two great symbols of the alienation of Things from man: the warehouse and the dump. The first absorbs the Things that have not reached man, that do not need him, that flaunt haughtily their perfect surfaces and bright labels. The second—the Things abandoned, without attention and care, dusty, filthy, rotting and rusting before their time; accumulation and negligence are the opposite yet related phenomena that share one cause—the undevelopment of Things to which man does not give enough of his soul. If a Thing does not enter completely into human life, still retains the sense of a warehouse or a shop window, then its uncollected core is condemned to desolation, meaningless dilapidation, and decay. In essence there is no difference between a warehouse and a dump as one can turn into the other never having reached the sphere of human assimilation—from riches to rags.

The image of spiritless Things has appeared frequently in twentieth-century art. Just recall Pop Art's piling up the heaps of real or realistically reproduced Things, looking brand new and loud, seemingly *still* untouched by human hands. On the other hand, in certain types of avant-garde art, and especially in conceptualism, significance was given to ruined, faded, lonely, and abandoned Things that would *never again* be touched by human hands, perhaps only when dumping them out in the garbage. Yellowed papers, aged documents, broken pencils, scraps of books and newspapers, rickety invalid chairs—such is the grotesque and ironic, sometimes also elegiac, aura of a number of conceptual works, in which words oust things because of their shabbiness and uselessness.

To be sure, in twentieth-century art the experiments with the "ready-made" are not limited by these two extreme views. However, if we look at other orientations of the "ready-made," most of which have appeared in different guises as early as the end of the 1910s and still remain popular in hybrid combinations, we will discover a preference for the faceless, object-like aspects of Things. Constructivism was interested primarily in the techniques and pragmatics of Things, Dadaism in the absurd logic and metaphysics, Surrealism in fantastic transformations, Suprematism in the symbolic coding and deciphering of visual elements. The Thing was perceived and displayed as an attribute of the manufacturing or domestic process, or as an enigmatic object positioned in the boundless emptiness of space, or as a sign of the invisible activity of supernatural forces, or as a fleeting dream whose shapes are changing as it is being contemplated, or as a predatory trap ready to snap its credulous observer. All of this had a lot of poetry but no lyrics whatsoever. The connection of the displayed Thing with the life of its owner, its inclusion in the sphere of real concerns and attachments, the submerged meaning concealed in its singularity—none of this was developed in relation to actual Things to the degree that it was developed in the literary and painterly images of Things, for instance, in the lyrics of Rilke and the still lives of Van Gogh.

Words and paints are more incorporeal than a Thing, and that is why they are well suited to express its spiritual essence—yet the price is the displacement of the Thing itself from the surface of a book or a canvas. The "lyrics of Things" constantly turn out to be on the edge of demarcation in art: the lyrical is stripped of materiality, the material is depersonalized—such are the diverging extremes which are not easily realized or fused. The lyrical meaning of an authentic and singular Thing remains undiscovered. This meaning is transferred into words, paints, photographic and cinematic images, and breaks away from the Thing itself with its full, certain, and irreplaceable presence. Or the Thing is taken for itself, with the richness and diversity of its plastic possibilities, decorative forms, visual symbolism, but in the process it is separated from its inner history and from the meanings accumulated in its previous existence, "before the show," in its interaction with man. For an artist of the "ready-made," who decided to place, for instance, a chair in his installation, it is not important where the chair came from, who sat on it, who talked from it and about what, how it was moved so that the partner in conversation could be seen better—only the construction and the texture of the chair are important.

To join the individual significance and the existential presence of a Thing, to demonstrate their interjacency as much as possible—this is the task of a lyrical museum. Here the spiritual life of a lyrical "I" is not separated from the actual Things, among which it flowed, around which it concentrated, in which it became embodied; here it is not dissolved in literary or painterly images. Neither are the Things separated from their singular fates, from the participation in the lives and experiences of those people among whom they acquired character; Things are not frozen in pure objectness, not turned into material for plastic constructions. The words of a lyrical personage and his Things come together, replenishing each other's insufficiencies and forming a total composition—*vescheslov* ("verbject")—as a new genre of spiritual-material culture.

It is well known that in twentieth-century history a lot of effort was put into tearing meaning apart from the Thing and into setting man's surroundings against him. The twentieth-century art has reflected this alienation in the images of intimidation and pity, in the gloss of Things sanctified as idols, and in the decay of Things untouchable as pariahs. But the shop window and the dump are only the extreme points between which the Thing circulates; although significant as the peaks of alienation, they do not exhaust the essence of the mobile, shifting, and wandering Thing. The Thing's route passes through the human hands and traverses numerous meaningful contacts with human lives. If we take the shop window as a starting point and the dump as an end point, the middle point, which is the heart of the Thing, is still in a *home*, broadly defined as a lived-in world. Here the Thing loses its cool glitter, yet does not fade into oblivion because the same fingers, whose touch dulls the Thing's luster, clear the dust off it. The Thing consists entirely of touches that invisibly sculpt its essence. Not the separation from, the opposition to man, but the proximity to him is essential in Things. Each one is meant to be touched, lifted, moved; some even have knobs and handles that seem to be extended toward the human hands. These are the Things to be displayed in a lyrical museum as the works of *everyday spiritual creation*. Their form may be machine made, but their essence is shaped by the hands whose warmth it exudes.

Our culture is faced with the task of lifting the spell off the Thing and rescuing it from banishment and oblivion; in the process, *domesticity* is unfolded as an immensely important social and cultural category which refers to the Thing's involvement in human life and its complete assimilation to the mind and the body. Certainly a home can be turned into a warehouse or a dump (or perhaps both), but then it ceases to be a home, a place where all Beings and Things relate to each other. In this sense, a lyrical museum is an experiment in self-realization of *domestic culture* which deserves to be represented in a broad context, taken out of the boundaries of individual life and into the larger world, in order that this world could become more and more domesticated and find in a home its origin and its microcosm.

3. The New Memoriality

Currently, the value of a Thing is determined according to the standard which presupposes a commodity status, considers it as a "novelty" attractive to consumers. The shop window figures prominently in the system of material culture as the starting point from which the Thing, blessed by advertisements, enters into life. The system of commercial signs strives to elevate the status of the new Thing by emphasizing its practical advantages, convenience, stylishness, benefits, and reliability. Booklets, brochures, instructions, guarantees, manuals, labels, and other means of describing and certifying new Things are perfected to the smallest details.

But what is lacking completely is any interpretation of the Things that had already served their time—the "anti-shop-window" of a kind where used Things would find shelter and where they would be accompanied by the corresponding certificates and descriptions of a lyrical, memoir-like, meditative nature rather than by advertisements and recommendations. Here the significance would be given not to the price but to the living worth of the Thing, to the meaning it acquired in the service to men. If so many words of praise and approval are found for an unused Thing, why cannot we find words of understanding and sympathy for the tried and true, old Thing that has expanded its utilitarian properties and grown intimate with its owners?

Surely such "anti-shop-windows" would not be set up behind sparkling glass or along busy streets, yet a place could be found for them inside the homes where the Things have spent their lives. Before sending the obsolete Thing to an attic or a dump, where it will end up mixed in with dusty junk or dissolved in a filthy mash, should we not keep it in a special, memorial space at home, in a corner or on a wall, preserving the Thing as a part of life which had become embodied in it and now recedes into the past? If in a shop window each advertised product stands by itself, then a worn-out Thing, singled out because of its special fate among the multitude of similar objects, is definitely worthy of such treatment: now it represents itself rather than a model or a type of product. Perhaps it would be worthwhile to just leave the most precious and "well-deserved" Things hanging on the walls to add depth to a room, a sense of "eternity" where the past shares space with the present and the future.

I will describe my impressions from the lyrical museum already attempted once in the apartment of this author's friends. Things hung on the walls appeared to be beyond life and death, as if they froze in the endless waiting or unearthly devotion. Although departed from the lived-in space of the room where sometime ago they were useful, the Things had not yet moved behind the wall where they would pile up with other junk in a dark corner or, even further, outside the house where they would completely disintegrate into garbage. The wall is a blank, impenetrable curtain between the two worlds from which the Things gaze into *here* before departing for *there*. They had already lost their integral form, but the angular sunken faces are still protruding from the wall like a memorial bas-relief. These newly sculpted masks gaze into the space of the room and into their living counterparts as though they want to remind us of something solemn: a bottle into bottle, a pan into pan, eyeglasses into eyeglasses. The wall—a spatial analog of death—cleaves each Thing into two distinguishable parts, "this" and "that," and bares a core in the form of a descriptive label: the "thing in itself" is now revealed and appears as words on the surface of the magic scission.

Of course, the museum-on-the-wall cumbers the room like any container or a case which adds completeness and sacredness to a man-made object. We put mirrors in rooms in the attempt to enclose the living space, to turn its "eyes inward, toward the soul," but the shining surface reflects and adds weight only to the empirical existence of Things—the fractional, the changeable, the fleeting. The decaying utensils hanging on the walls could become the "eidetic" mirror of meanings, reflecting the fixed and lasting essence of Things; looking into its depth the room would behold its origins, shifting with time, and simultaneously freeze the growing part of its own immortality. Such *wall museums* or *mirrors of memory* in every home could promote a more responsible and unselfish attitude toward the world of Things and deliver us from consumerism which values only the new.

The category of "memoriality" itself must be considered now in view of the changed status of *Things* in the era of the mass production of consumer *objects*.

The traditional memorial museum presupposes that the Thing lives longer than the man and functions to keep his memory. Such correlation was prevalent in the previous epochs: one and the same Thing—a cabinet, a trunk, a set of china, a book—was used by several generations. In our time the correlation is reversed: several generations of Things give place to one another during a single human lifetime. In the prime of his life the owner buries the fulminant Things in the dump, replacing them with Things more fashionable and convenient. Here lies the difficulty often experienced by the founders of contemporary memorial museums: there are no Things left that could illuminate their owner's life or serve as his representatives.

These new social and historical circumstances (the Thing does not change owners, but the owner changes Things) demand a reconsideration of the traditional notion of memoriality. Who remembers whom, who bears the responsibility of a witness? By shortening the useful life of Things, man partly relieved them of the burden of memory but at the same time took this burden upon himself.

Things are assigned an increasingly episodic, "transitory" role in the cultural system of transient and permanent values. If previously the material world, upon which man left the traces of his momentary existence, appeared to be the most stable and "immovable," now human consciousness is becoming more long-lasting and succeeds in absorbing the multitude of changing material worlds. An owner's consciousness is inherited from one Thing to another and acts as the mechanism of succession between them. As Things get lighter, shedding the burden of meaning and the legacy accumulated by several generations, individual memory has to take up the difficult task of endowing them with meaning and cultural status.

A contemporary memorial museum, in contrast to a traditional one, can be imagined this way: Things do not tell about man whom they have outlived, but, in contrast, man tells about Things he has outlived himself, about those ephemeral Things that are close and dear to him, and thus he saves them from falling into oblivion. The permanent takes care of the transient so that, having once entered the cultural sphere, it could remain there for a long time or perhaps forever. Along with the memorials where Things traditionally immortalize the memory of people, there also must be the memorials where people immortalize the memory of Things through lyrical testimonies and with a full sense of responsibility to the culture. Hence another name for a lyrical museum to clarify its intention—*a memorial to Things*. In such a memorial the individual memory becomes an important factor in museum practice and takes up the space to display the Things it preserves.

It is not a question of reconstructing the former, "ancient," good-natured, and welcoming attitude to Things, which was reinforced by the firm belief in their meaningful involvement in everyday life. Our ancestors would hardly have thought of trying intensely to understand surrounding Things or of creating a memorial for them because the homes they lived in were such "memorials."[6] The Thing was meaningful from the start when it was inherited from ancestors, and meaningful at the end when it was passed on to offspring. There was an epical, calm, and appeasing concord with the meaning of Things which did not demand the outbursts of lyricism.

Now these beginnings and ends are split off; a sales display occupies the ancestor's place, and a rubbish heap replaces the offspring. But ever more important becomes the role of the center, of that short distance where man must piece together the *complete* life of a Thing through his *particular* experience, to fill in its past and future from the present. The meaning is no longer received and passed on but created here and now. The lyrical replaces the epical. The epical culture of Things has disintegrated and can hardly be restored, but it is being replaced by the new lyrical culture whose psychological and aesthetic possibilities are different. Our attempts to assimilate the Thing often fail after stumbling against its mechanical facelessness because the Thing is not ours from the beginning. Here the lyrical "daring" must rush into the break formed in the epical connections among Things; it must risk bringing together the disjointed beginnings and ends and create the new, more flexible, and "uncertain" meanings at the borders now surrounded by the meaninglessness and forgetfulness of objects which have no roots or offshoots. The accumulation of Things at the outer limits of consciousness, in the form of enormous piles of goods and cemeteries of rubbish, must necessarily activate a compensatory cultural mechanism and become supplemented by a purposeful preservation of Things in the mind and for the mind . . .

4. The Significance of Singularity

This accumulation has its own, far-reaching economy and even its own "parsimony," wonderfully called "the parsimony of empathy" by Andrei Platonov. Here is a typical quote from Platonov to help clarify the goal of our project:

> Voschev picked up the dried up leaf and hid it in a secret section of his sack, where he kept all sorts of objects in misfortune and obscurity. "Your life had no meaning, thought Voschev with parsimonious empathy,—stay here, I will find out what you lived and died for. Since nobody needs you just lying about here in the middle of nowhere, then I will keep and remember you."

This sack, used by the character to collect Things which do not yet have meaning in order to remember and understand them, is the model for our lyrical museum. We begin to realize that it is essential for man to examine the meaning of even the smallest, most trivial Thing; without this his mind cannot be at ease. In raising critical questions about the meaning of "obscure and rootless" Things, contemporary life brings up the problem that has troubled men for generations—the problem of justifying existence, or *kosmoditseya*. Can the world survive if even one speckle of dust is displaced, if it turns out to be superfluous and unnecessary? Or can a single antimeaning, like antimatter, explode the entire rational order of the universe? The world can be fully justified to man only if everything in it does not turn out to be random and vain. It would seem to make no difference whether the withered leaf exists or not in the world, yet here lies the critical test for human reason which verifies the sensibility or senselessness of the great Whole through such insignificant Things and decides whether to accept or to reject it. Of course, it is impossible to "crack" the Thing with the mind alone—one must pick it up like Platonov's character, to carry it around in a sack, to pass it through one's life in order to become at least a little intimate with it, but in return an object of "misery and obscurity," cured thanks to care and sympathy, can become the herald of the deepest meaningfulness of everything existing.

The memorial of Things is one of the possible experiments in *kosmoditseya,* the justification of the world in its tiniest components. The fact that the modest Things belonging to unknown people are collected here does not diminish but, on the contrary, increases the value of their interpretation. In order to comprehend the nature of a substance, a physicist does not turn to the voluminous rocks but to the smallest particles. Similarly, the order of meaning requires for its comprehension a scrupulous, detailed look, a microscopic penetration into such depth where global meanings disappear and the most minute ones are revealed. Not in the famous cocked hat of Napoleon, not in Stradivarius's violin, but in a piece of thread, a leaf, a pebble, or a match the whole elemental meaning of Things is unveiled. The smallest comprehended Thing contains the greatest justification of the world.

This meaning acquired by Things is gratefully returned to man, confirming anew his own nonincidental nature: *kosmoditseya* becomes the prologue to *antropoditseya.* Another passage from Platonov: "Sometimes Voschev would bend down and pick up a pebble or some caked dust and put it in his pants to keep. He was excited and worried by the almost eternal existence of the pebble in the mud, in the midst of darkness: there must be a reason for its being here, then more reason for man to live." Platonov's character is one of those perceptive eccentrics who find justification for their own indispensability to the world in a zealous and serious fraternity with the "lowest" forms of life. A pebble lifted from the ground and having a certain "reason" becomes the foundation for man's hope—to become fully justified in the world of justified entities.

In this way a converging movement and an increasing meaningfulness is initiated between man and Things. Perhaps most important, besides developing a new feeling of intimacy with his material environment, the visitor to the lyrical museum would leave with a new level of self-confidence, a certain metaphysical vitality, reassured of the non-useless-ness of his own existence.

The author knows through his own experience that it is very difficult to interpret an individual Thing—individuality slips away from being defined in thoughts and words, which are intended for the comprehension of the general. It is easier to comprehend the significance of an entire class or type of objects rather than their single representative—"foliage" or "stoneness" rather than a single leaf or a pebble. Focusing on the singular, asking of it the nonutilitarian, philosophical question: "What do you live for?" one feels indeed how this question rests against the mystery of the entire universe: the singular can give an answer only together with the universe or instead of it.

It is known that abstract thought has evolved into concrete thought in the process of historical development. Perhaps *thought through singularities* is the highest level of this trajectory. The general categories at the basis of all theoretical thinking are not abolished then but tested in the movement to the more and more complete, comprehensive, and holistic representation of the Thing as the synthesis of the infinite multitude of abstract attributes. Logical abstractions, which in the historical development elevated human mind over the empirics of simple sensations, return once again to the starting point, to the singular Thing in order to discover in it the condensed richness of all human culture and the meaning of the universe. The singular, "this," is directly related to the common, "all," similar to how the consistency of material universe is discovered in the elementary particles (and not in mountains or whales). From here stems the hope that *realogy* will not interpret reality only through generalized concepts, or even through representations, which are more concrete, but will find in singular Things the methods for the best description and comprehension of the infinite "this-ness" which surrounds us and leads directly to the foundations of existence.

So far we are convinced that the singular exists and that it is existentially meaningful. To think of it is difficult, to comprehend it completely perhaps impossible; the thought wanders off onto the general and the abstract, onto something that bypasses "this" and extends to the whole class, type, or kind. But just approaching the singular Thing with its nontransient as well as inimitable meaning gives us the important and reassuring knowledge that nothing, even the smallest and the most trivial, is destined to disappear without a trace.[7]

5. Experiments in Thing-scription

Let us imagine what a lyrical museum might look like. The space is divided into a number of partly enclosed cells, separated by nontransparent or slightly transparent walls, as if forming the rooms of a multiroom house.[8] In every such "room" an exhibition participant arranges his display and hangs the posters with commentaries—this is his "personal" space. The displayed Things are authentic, taken from "real life," and each is accompanied with a lyrical description-meditation. All these compartments, into which the entire museum space is divided (not just a house, but also a labyrinth where one can and even ought to get a little lost), are devised to accommodate only one visitor at each particular moment. The specificity of the lyrical space does not allow the exhibition to open vastly, to attract attention of all the visitors at once—on the contrary, it demands concentration and extends the individual contact of the viewer with the displayed materials, fixes his gaze on them. The encounter with Things takes place privately, in the spirit of "singularity" imprinted in our ideational as well as spatial approach to Things which are deep and narrow, absorbing us inside, into the pith.

It is not at all necessary, and is perhaps impossible, for the visitor to view all the displays and the accompanying commentaries in one visit. It is more important for him to feel the vastness of the surrounding polymorphic and nonuniform space. The lyrical museum does not display the works of art made to be specifically *viewed;* it recreates the actual reality of Things which always escapes the bounds of possible perception. All Things fit into a single field of view at once only at a dump or a warehouse—the overgrown and "degenerated" remains of the bygone epical panorama of the world. In a home the single point of view can embrace just a minute part of the surroundings, and that is why it has to shift about without a predetermined path. One can wander for a long time in this home labyrinth, at each turn running into unfamiliar exhibits or seeing the familiar ones from an unexpected angle. The inner world of every individual is open but only from one point, closing off all the others. Thus the museum creates an image of the endlessly wide and voluminous world, where a single common entrance does not exist but there is a multitude of doors, and where nobody meets all at once but everyone meets everyone.

The displays can be either the different variations on the general lyrical theme or its conscious violations, "antilyricism," allowing to experience the museum's presence. There can be detailed commentaries to nonexistent or for some reason absent objects. A display can be "provocative," designed for some type of action as a result of which it would come into existence as a display. A description can be practical or philosophical, serious or humorous, literally corresponding to the Thing displayed or emphatically and grotesquely discrepant with it. In principle it is desirable that individuals of different occupations, ages, and interests participated in the museum so that the world of Things, in which we live and which lives for us, would be represented as fully as possible.

Here the author offers a commentary to the display of his own—the experiment of actual Thing-scription.[9] I would like to simply give the readers a glimpse into the space of an imaginary museum—as far as it is possible in a text and without any really displayed objects. Of course, this commentary, having been brought into the article from another, "lyrical-museum genre," must be interpreted according to the rules of that genre. As a preface let us quote the words of Montaigne, worthy of becoming an epigram to the entire lyrical museum: "My opinion about Things is not a measure of the Things themselves; it can only explain the measure of my view of Things."

A Candy Wrapper

What to say about this candy wrapper with the sonorous name "Bylina" (epic) that got lost on my desk by chance among the much more wordy and significant books and papers intended to be read? Who will hear this word, shouted in haste and quickly broken in embarrassment? A tiny, ragged remnant of consumption-in-a-moment, not even a minute—and a thousand-year-old memory, "an epic!"

Things have their own career ladder that ascends to man, and a candy wrapper is almost at the bottom of it. Sorry is the fate of Things serving yet other Things, all sorts of wrappers, packages, and boxes, that do not have a value of their own but just clothe the more important Things worthy of preservation. Yet even on this secondary level a candy wrapper is in the rear ranks. Perhaps a box or a package can still be reused, but a scanty candy wrapper, opened and emptied, becomes completely useless to anyone or anything.

Yet there is something attractive about it, recognizable as a small but important part of a man's life. Before us there are two pieces of paper, a white one and a colored one, like underclothes and outer garments, the "chemise" and the "shirt" of a candy. The law of all multilayered coverings is in effect here, whatever their "content" may be: the inner layer is plain and colorless, meant to maintain cleanness, the outer layer is bright and colorful, meant to attract the eye. (A middle layer is also possible, the most dense and protective; in human garments it is the armour, in the candy garments it is the foil.) The two purposes appear to be opposing: to hide and to attract, but together they form the essence of a wrapper, through which a Thing at once folds inward and opens outward, exists inside and outside the self. The double- and even triple-layered luxurious vestments give the candy the air of mystery and enticement, appeal and inaccessibility, which is the essence of sweetness. The very layering of the wrapper points to the presence of something tempting and concealed, and turns the process of unwrapping into a prolonged and sweet anticipation of something that otherwise one would partake of only coarsely and briefly. A candy wrapper is the sweetness inside sweetness, the casing of its physical content but the kernel of its psychic content. Here the sweet is moved from the ranks of simple taste sensations into the sphere of psychic state, anticipation, a kind of languor. Apparently children feel it better than adults, keeping candy wrappers not only for their ornateness but also because they represent a certain extract of sweetness that exists besides and beyond language . . .

At the same time this "pure," nonphysiological sweetness finds expression in language, on the packaging label. The wrapper is not only a candy's garment but also its name; and if the paper is the material veil of sweetness, then the label is the expression of its "ideal" meaning. This one is called "Bylina," but here are some other names: "Masque," "Muse," "Sorceress," "Kara-Kum," "Lake Ritza," "Southern Night," "Evening Bells," "Flight," "Firebird," "Golden Rooster." They are unusually beautiful and fairy-tale-like, beckoning to faraway places, stirring imagination. As though the candy's sweetness is not of this world and dwells in the back of beyond, in the land of fantasy. The title on the wrapper corresponds precisely to its mysterious and alluring essence, encloses its enticing secret. It is not accidental that *fantik* (wrapper) sounds like "fantasy," "phantom": only one word is written on the tiny piece of paper, but almost always this word belongs to the realm of imagination. The candy wrapper is a minimal page of fantasy, and the candy is a double fairy-tale, told by the dreamer-tongue to the sweet-toothed tongue, a dream of the embodied language.[10] "Sweet" fantasy descends into the immediate material reality of the tongue whose capacity to idealize is signified by the word on the candy wrapper.

So the two properties of the language-tongue that have drifted apart into the far-reaching corners of culture and nature come together again as two faces of a leaf, recognizing their forgotten kinship in a candy wrapper, this miniature bilingual dictionary that translates from the speaking tongue to the tasting tongue. A candy wrapper is the language-tongue addressing itself, its bodily face addressing the signifying face. It is the dialogue with oneself and a means of reconstructing the unity of one's faculties. This candy wrapper is not such a small thing after all: in it the most abstract dream and the most tangible reality come into contact with each other, nature instills itself into culture and teaches us how to cultivate the beautiful on the tips of our tongues.

NOTES

1. The project of such a discipline is described by the author in the article "Realogiya—nauka o veschakh," *Dekorativnoe iskusstvo SSSR* 6 (1985): 21–22, 44. In the same journal see interesting materials from the discussion around the project and the problem of "the science of Things" in general: V. Aronov, "Vesch v aspekte iskusstvoznaniya," vol. 11 (1985); L. Annenkova, "Realogiya' i smysl veschi," vol. 10 (1986); N. Voronov, "Na poroge 'veshevedeniya,'" vol. 10 (1986).

2. *Slovar' sochetaemosti slov russkogo yazyka* (Moscow: Russkiy Yazyk, 1983), 53, 423.

3. V. V. Kolesov, "Drevnerusskaya vesch," in *Kulturnoe nasledie Drevnei Rusi* (Leningrad: Nauka, 1976), 260–64.

4. An exhibitor is not only the author but also the exposition's lyrical personage whose image is developed through the totality of exhibits.

5. Antimaterialistic attitudes appear almost simultaneously with materialist mentality (the mass production and the consumerist fetishization of Things) and suffer from a similar narrow-mindedness. One of the earliest and most vivid examples of this problem is found in Mayakovsky's tragedy *Vladimir Mayakovsky* (1913)." *Old man with cats:* In the lands of the cities the soulless Things became masters, thrusting themselves on us . . . You see! Things must be cut down! Not without reason I foresaw an enemy in their caresses! *Man with elongated face:* But may be Things should be loved? May be Things have different souls?" This is essential: not to reject Things, lamenting their soullessness but rather to start with a premise that they have a different, separate soul that needs a keen response and is understood through love. Antimaterialism receives the baton from materialism and throws the already alienated Things even further, into a zone of damnation and nonexistence (fixes ethically the results of commodity fetishism), whereas the goal is to bring them closer, assimilate them even when they are originally alienated. The more casual, cold, or "industrial" a commodity is, the more it requires human care in order to become a Thing, an ontological fact; this orphanhood of the majority of contemporary Things should not impel us to indifference but to compassion and kinship in compensation for original rootlessness.

6. Perhaps R.-M. Rilke felt earlier and deeper than anyone that in this crisis of traditional "involvement of Things" and "succession of Things" new creative demands were put forward to men: "For our grandfathers there still were 'a home,' 'a well,' a familiar tower, and simply their own dress or a coat; almost everything was a vessel from which they were drawing something human and into which they laid aside something human. Spiritual and participating things, which are parts of our lives, disappear and cannot be replaced. *Perhaps we are the last ones to know such things.* We have a responsibility not only for keeping their memory (this would be too little and unreliable) and their human and divine (as in domestic divinities) worth . . . Our goal is to take in this transient perishable earth with such depth, such passion, and such suffering that its essence would be 'invisibly' resurrected in us once again." R.-M. Rilke, "Letter to V. von Gulevich, 13.XI.1925," *Vorspvede: Auguste Rodin, Letters, Poems* (Moscow: Iskusstvo, 1971), 305.

7. In founding realogy as a discipline it is useful to appeal to Rikkert's ideas on the creation of "individualizing" sciences which (in contrast to the "generalizing" sciences) are concerned with the meaning of singular phenomena (G. Rikkert, *Filosofiya istorii* [St. Petersburg, 1908], 19). Such sciences include not only history, which investigates the meaning of singular events on the axis of time, but also a discipline x which would investigate unique formations of meaning on the axes of space. What we tentatively call realogy is a science of Things as the formatory units of space, as the limits of meaningful decomposition, through which its saturation with value and culturally significant metric system are revealed (similarly to how history reveals time's saturation with value in the events as units of meaning). According to contemporary views in humanities, Things impart textual properties to space. ". . . Things illuminate in space a special *paradigm* and their own order—*syntagm,* i.e. a *text* . . . According to this concept, space, realized (actualized through Things) must be understood as text proper" (V. N. Toporov, "Prostranstvo i tekst," in *Tekst: semantika i struktura* [Moscow, 1983], 279–80). Thus realogy is a science of realized space, i.e. decomposed and filled with Things, of its textual properties which are translated into linguistic texts through the *verbject* genre. Lyrical museum is a space of two languages simultaneously—the language of Things and the language of words—which because of this proximity discover the possibilities and limitations of their translatability.

8. The general idea of this design belongs to the linguist A. V. Mikheev. The concrete and practically realizable project of a lyrical display was developed by the artist Francisco Infante. Described below is a conceptual literary project.

9. Compare to the experiments of other authors-participants in the proposed exhibition: V. V. Aristov, A. V. Mikheev, "Texts with Descriptions of Thing-Displays of the 'Lyrical Museum,'" *Vesch v Iskusstve,* 1984 Conference Proceedings (Moscow: Sovetskiy khudozhnik, 1986), 324–31.

10. In Russian "language" and "tongue" (anatomical) are expressed by the same work *yazyk.*—Eds. note.

The *Ropes* of Ilya Kabakov:
An Experiment in Interpretation
of a Conceptual Installation

1. Description

In the Spring of 1985, Ilya Kabakov invited me to visit his studio to see his new work, *Ropes,* which I am tempted to call a "painting" because of certain considerations elaborated in what follows, although many will certainly disagree with this definition. In fact, this work has little resemblance to what we are used to calling a "painting." There is no canvas, no frame. It is neither painted nor drawn, it does not hang on the wall, etc.[1]

This is what it looks like.

In the studio sixteen ropes, six and a half meters long, are strung parallel to each other, approximately a meter and a half apart and the same distance above the floor, that is, at eye level. Various small objects and labels are tied to these ropes at eight-inch intervals. Each object is suspended from a short thread at the rope level or slightly lower, and a strip of white paper with an inscription written in black ink is hung below it on a two-inch string. Although the objects and inscriptions are connected to each other by strings, most of the time there is no connection in meaning.

What are these objects, these things? It is hard even to call them "things" because they are knick-knacks—small splinters and frag-ments of some rubbish or trash that would be thrown out into the

Alexander Rappaport, " 'Veryevki' Ilyi Kabakova: Opyt interpretatsii kont-septualistskogo assamblyazha" ("The Ropes" of Ilya Kabakov: An experiment in interpretation of a conceptual installation), *Sovetskoe Iskusstvoznanie* 26 (1990): 33–61.

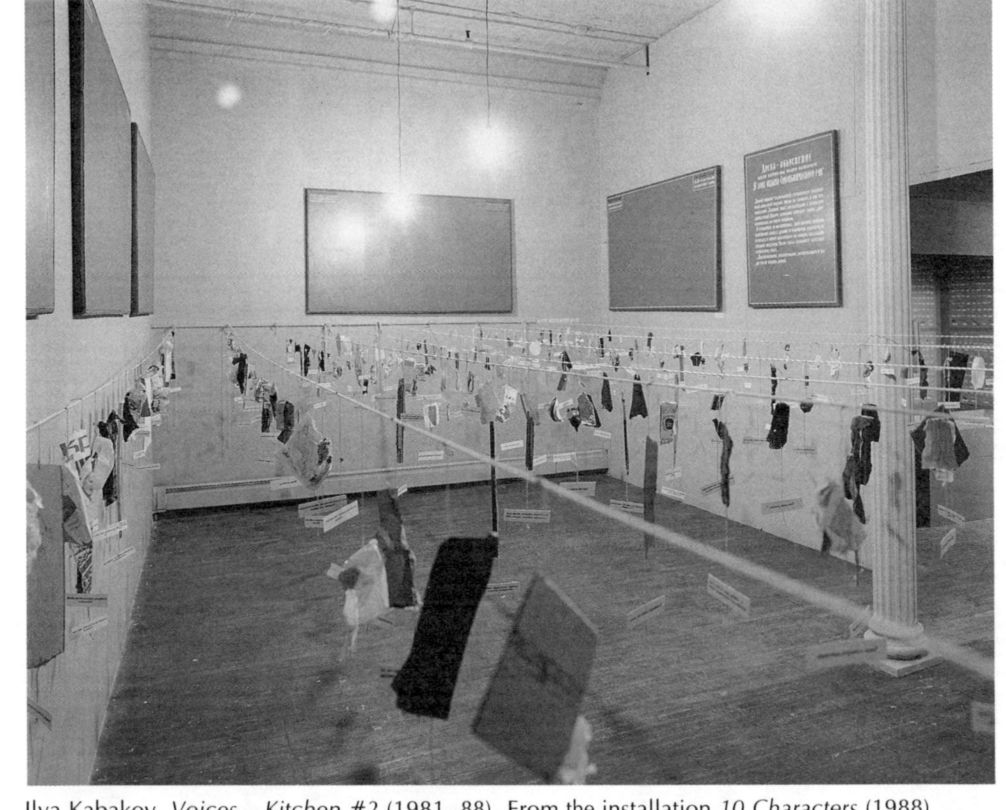

Ilya Kabakov, *Voices—Kitchen #2* (1981–88). From the installation *10 Characters* (1988). Courtesy Ronald Feldman Fine Arts, New York. Photograph by D. James Dee.

nearest garbage can: candy wrappers, cigarette butts, pencil stumps, scraps of paper, receipts and bus tickets, beer bottle corks, bits, shreds, rags, etc.[2]

All in all, an enormous number of pieces and scraps of material environment (perhaps around 500) are suspended from these sixteen ropes like rubbish that had been hung outside to dry or, more precisely, to be publicly displayed. The fact that none of the displayed objects has a marked value or meaning supports the idea that this is really nothing but "refuse": you would look here in vain for a museum of relics, memorable trophies, or significant reminders. This is the most common rubbish, taken out of a garbage can and arranged in a strict order. The second part of the exhibition convinces us further: there is a huge plywood box on the floor filled with similar objects, but here they appear as true "refuse," that is, in a pile.

The inscriptions under the objects can also be called refuse, only of a verbal kind. They, too, are pieces and scraps, although not of objects but of speech or sentences uttered some time ago. What this speech was and who composed the sentences is unknown as much as it is unknown from which bottle of what brand of beer came the stopper hanging from the rope, whose pencil stump this is, or what route the bus ticket came from. They are scraps of speech like "bye now" or "and I thought he would call before leaving." Such verbal litter is encountered on the streets and in crowds just as often as scraps of paper, candy wrappers, and cigarette butts at train stations, and usually we tend to ignore both. The latter, according to the laws of urban propriety, must be collected and swept up by janitors, but we just turn a deaf ear to speech, since air cannot be cleansed of the communal verbal refuse. But here all of it is collected with the zealousness of a museum archive and presented in a way most convenient for observation and reading.

Obscenities, blurted out with or without reason, constitute a large portion of the verbal refuse. There is no sense in quoting these fleeting cusses as their character is as familiar to everyone as the sight of a cigarette butt.

Such is Kabakov's painting in a brief description. I should especially point out its laboriousness. The author collected and arranged this material and verbal rubbish over a period of several months with the thoroughness and scrupulosity of an entomologist and has put a lot of effort into the painting.

I should add to this description that according to the author's intention the painting was meant to be placed in a museum rather than stay in the studio where it was made. I think that Kabakov envisioned the Pushkin Museum in Moscow where it would have been installed in the central space of the Grand Ball Room, but another museum interior also would have sufficed. In this way, the unimportance of content—rubbish and litter—should have created a contrast with the sparkling interior. According to the author, this refuse must be placed in the "cathedral of art" alongside the eternal treasures of human culture, and in such context the unimportance of content would find its conceptual meaning and monumental significance.

Further, I will discuss some possible interpretations of this work and give my own reading of its specific features.

2. Interpretations

Kabakov's work may seem puzzling to a viewer accustomed to traditional painting. It may seem either a joke that has nothing to do with art, or a silly prank unworthy of a real artist. Certainly, the obscenities elegantly inscribed on the labels are most offensive. The naive viewer begins by examining them, but having encountered the foul words a number of times, he tends to stop this examination in disgust unless he is confused by the modest phrases among the inscriptions such as "Have you taken the temperature?" or something just as innocent. Then he begins to suspect that the artist did not really intend to insult the viewer. The object part of the installation also bores one quickly since all these stumps and butts are of no interest in themselves, although one's dignity can be offended here, too, since the viewer is forced to stare at garbage.

There are no special aesthetic qualities or great ideas in this painting. On the contrary, it suggests complete and final degeneration of contemporary art. Instead of a painting there is filth and rubbish, so that even if you call this "garbage" the insult would be ineffective: it is real garbage, and, moreover, it tries shamelessly to get into a museum. The critical argument usually advanced against Modernism—"Anyone can do this"—is easier to apply to this work than to any other. And it is true: anyone can get a cigarette butt and hang it from a thread. It does not, however, occur to everyone to collect all this and arrange it in a museum, but this is not usually discussed. There is a certain truth to such perception. The existence of this painting suggests that something is happening to the art world and its aesthetic ideals. It's hard to say whether we are dealing with a single incident of assault against the great cultural treasures, with the evidence that something in the world of high art forces the artists to stoop low, or with a phenomenon, which is not art at all. But if this phenomenon is not art, the question arises—"What is it?" It does not belong to science or technology. Perhaps we can think of it as information. This speculation can lead to the interpretation of Kabakov's work as a slanderous parody of a world where the artist can see nothing but rubbish and obscenities. But after pondering this for a minute you understand that the work is apolitical: material and verbal refuse exists in all countries and under all social systems.

Of course, it is possible to see an act of vandalism or mischief in the work. But again, thinking it through, we will have to question this view. The criminal act is constituted, first of all, by the fact that it is "not drawn." If the rubbish were painted in oils or watercolors, drawn with pastels or made into an etching, it would have been possible to admire the artist's skill. Rubbish in itself is not in conflict with art ("if you only knew from what litter the poems grow and know no shame . . . ").[3] Yet rubbish (whether material or verbal) is found unacceptable in the nontraditional type of art, provoking the talk about vandalism and other similar subjects which have been brought up in relation to Modernist works for a long time. Indeed, Kabakov's painting is a Modernist phenomenon in the tradition of Surrealism and Pop Art which originated with the famous *Fountain* of Marcel Duchamp.

The same device is used here—a clearly nonartistic object is placed provocatively in the context of an art work; an object from the world of refuse, water closets, and related manifestations of "material, bodily lowliness" is opposed to spiritual and elevated symbols of human culture. An element of Duchamp's *épatage* is present here along with the related symbolic oppositions such as "high—low," "material—spiritual," and "significant—insignificant." In Kabakov's painting, however, these devices are interpreted and transformed in ways that deserve close consideration. If avant-garde stands for something greater than a trick or a prank, then it is necessary to analyze the works of avant-garde art in detail, without throwing all of them into one general category. This is how traditional paintings are analyzed, and nobody would think that it is unnecessary to analyze them in detail because they represent once again something painted with oils on a canvas and because this has already been done before.

A work of art can have many meanings, like any other fact of life, and the multiplicity of interpretations is a legitimate context of its existence. The goal is not to counterargue but to multiply points of view, not to cut short but to enrich its interpretations.

The expansion of interpretations carries an element of artistic and theoretical fantasy and play. Among interpretations we can find the kind whose existence is justified only by the fact that they are sensible and noncontradictory—critical tricks of a sort. Those who call such interpretations the "twists" are right in their own way. They can be justified only if we realize that the accepted system of values, which seems normal to us, may itself turn out to be a "twist" from a historical perspective.

A sensible "twist" is nothing but an investigation of the field of interpretive possibilities, the field which has no "twists" in itself, just like the realm of chemical elements knows neither poison nor sweetness: it is the realm of fundamental reality, on the canvas of which a situation creates its norms and its "twists."

Let us try to divide the interpretation of Kabakov's painting according to the categories of form and content, and show how this partition fuses into a coherent conceptual construction.

3. Thematic Content

Refuse and attributes of "bodily lowliness," which in this case appear as inscriptions and objects, clearly continue the "genre" tradition of representing the life of lower classes in art. Originating with comedies of antiquity and having been transformed in recent times, the "genre" is present in Critical Realism as well as in Naturalism and Hyperrealism. The images of social ills, moral filth, the underworld, and scum are not new to world art. The representation of this filth and dirt can take the form of undistinguished behavior or objects. Speech, imitation of dialects, and verbal commonplaces can also serve to represent it. All such phenomena are usually presented in either apparent or indirect opposition to high art, noble topics, and elevated moral ideals and values. Sometimes we find the combination of high and low, as, for instance, in the life styles of the Cynics in Ancient Greece, the wise men of Taos, fools, or jesters. As a rule, the representation of filth and bodily lowliness corresponds to democratic attitudes which oppose themselves to aristocratic culture. After the French Revolution, the representation of bodily lowliness and filth turned a new shade, which cannot be quite described as democratic, although it has not yet been fully understood. The images of the poor in Gorky and the descriptions of the underworld in Dickens and Dostoyevsky are charged with yet additional meaning. Along with the direct opposition to all sorts of elevated ideals another orientation is being produced in the heart of the new democratic culture—the orientation toward representing the everyday life which is opposed to the extremes of both the high and the low, and represents the middle between the aristocratic life and the criminal underworld.

If in the low, filthy, bodily, and beastly manifestations of licentious flesh we can still see a life energy and an instinct of the reproduction of species, they no longer exist in the grayness of the everyday and the ordinary. It becomes a lifeless mold of the violations of law and order.

In some of Kabakov's works, litter appears precisely in such decent form: a schedule for taking out the garbage in a communal apartment symbolizes that aspect of social life in which the vital functions of democratic citizenry are primarily concerned with the necessary, but absurd in its pedantry, order of performing common everyday duties.

In other works by Kabakov, as well as the writers and artists of his circle, we also see a resurrection of the sentimental democratic attitudes toward the insignificant facts of life. Such is the Museum of Things proposed by Mikhail Epshtein: the touching essays devoted to burnt matches, cigarette butts, and candy wrappers.[4] Besides recreating the attention paid to the common object as the symbol of common man, this work also introduces a new formal and ontological orientation: a kind of magnifying glass that scrutinizes reality on a new scale.

This new scale of description of people and objects has a significant peculiarity: the atomization of life and behavior points to empty spaces in the interpretations of reality. If classical absurd pointed to the emptiness with a tragic or satirical intonation, here we are presented with objects that are not even worth contemplating. The ontological and ethical meaning of this strategy is connected to the new tendencies in the worldview, poetics and ontology, where a shift in values and a revision of object hierarchies are taking place. The concept of pollution in the context of the ecological crisis foregrounds the value of cleansing and leads to a reconsideration of the nature of filth and everything related to it: the refuse of urban environments, speech, behavior, and thought. The problematization of the categories of filth and cleanness turns out to be important to the rethinking of the contemporary standards of life and democratic consciousness. Until now we have evaluated the material environment with criteria inherited from the times of aristocracy. Today the process of understanding its previously ignored components is only beginning. These include common speech, now the object of attention in linguistics, and all sorts of anomalies and deviations, previously attributed to the categories of perversion and amorality, as well as many others.

Along with the sarcastically absurd or sentimentally elevated descriptions of all this refuse, or the hygienically designed plans to remove it, the attempts to interpret it without falling into extremes are also being proposed. This point of view has attracted Kabakov for some time since he sees refuse as a kind of mystery of our living world. We can attribute to the realm of such attempts his endless "garbage novel" where he has collected the bits and pieces of some insignificant objects, his interest in the character of Plyushkin,[5] who Kabakov jokingly calls the "father of contemporary museum planning," and also the "garbage can" theme in Kabakov's series of white background paintings.

The common leitmotiv in these explorations is the insight into the special artistic and vital qualities of an insignificant layer of existence. This is why the "genre" aspect of Kabakov's painting cannot be interpreted only in social, cultural, psychological, and political terms. It is rather a problematization of a layer of material life than the passing of judgment, although we cannot brush aside the fact that a certain degree of evaluation is also present. The categories of "filth" and "refuse" themselves refer to a system of values, and Kabakov does not at all ignore the "filthiness" of filth. He accepts filth for what it is, without ennobling or elevating it.

However, we would not be able to properly understand the meaning of this filth without undertaking a formal analysis of Kabakov's painting. Such analysis, as the second half of a cipher, contains another important aspect of his intuition, and only by putting the two parts together can we hope to gain a complete understanding of this work, although compositional forms certainly cannot be understood in isolation from thematic content.

We can easily imagine valuable things hanging on the threads instead of litter and garbage: candies, pens, or coins, while words of wisdom and aphorisms would be inscribed on the labels instead of empty phrases and obscenities. The compositional meaning of the painting would not be changed by such thematic transformation, but the mode of contemplation would still be left unclear since the painting is dramatically different from familiar easel painting or monumental sculpture as well as from other conceptual works by Kabakov himself. This is why it is necessary to analyze the formal organization of the painting and the ontological categories on which it relies.

4. Formal Analysis

Certain peculiarities of the painting's organization will not appear new to those who are familiar with the work of Kabakov and other avant-garde conceptualists. These peculiarities are typical for the constant compositional and formal explorations of this group of artists.

First of all, this is a struggle against representation and representability proper. In a number of Kabakov's paintings we see an inscription or an object itself instead of a representation. Some works present a description of the missing representation (the painting *Soccer Match*), others contain a representation which turns out to be a copy of a representation, that is, "a representation of a representation."

Another theme characteristic of the conceptualist avant-garde is the attempt to directly correlate the plastic, narrative, and spatial components of a painting with words. In the case of *Ropes* the numerous inscriptions continue the texts of albums, tables, and lists previously created by Kabakov.

The third theme has its origins in "expo-art" or art that is intended to be displayed in a particular way, turning exhibition design into a language. *The Fly with Wings* and the screens and windows made in 1984 belonged to this genre. The current painting is conceived similarly. Moreover, *The Fly with Wings* was also meant for the interiors of the Pushkin Museum, although the principle of its spatial arrangement was different. However, the idea of creating a contrast between an art work and a museum context has been preserved.

As already mentioned, all these themes of formal and compositional explorations appear to have nothing in common either with the narrative and thematic content of the painting or the issues of the democratic world of objects and environmental ontology, as described earlier. However, since the ontological and poetic meaning of reality depends on its material substance as well as on the spatiotemporal conditions of its perception and composition, we can argue that the material layer is ontologically related to the spatiotemporal structure. The experience of structural analysis, accumulated by art theory and literary studies during the past decades, attests to the fact that the thematic-figurative and the formal-compositional planes are closely connected in the final analysis, and a critic's task is to outline the ways to understand these connections. To do so it will be necessary to discuss certain formal and compositional categories and problems important to the understanding of avant-garde experiments and their relationship to classical easel painting.

The categories and problems of "frame" and "fragment" are particularly important here. The category of frame and the category of fragment are closely related because framing is a method of carving out a fragment of reality. The fragment in its turn can be interpreted as a "whole" (the world), as in the case, for instance, of icons or classical Renaissance paintings, or as another fragment, which frequently occurs in "genre" paintings, landscapes, and photojournalism.[6]

Another category we must turn to in order to make sense of Kabakov's painting (which is far from obvious) is the category of light or atmosphere. The theme of light and atmosphere attained a metaphysical significance for avant-garde.[7]

The metaphysical white background is directly evoked in Kabakov's white background paintings, primarily produced after 1984, as well as in his albums where paper plays the role of the white background, and even in his manuscripts such as *The Ant* exhibited for contemplation rather than for reading.

At a first sight, there cannot be any "background," "atmosphere," or "light" in the *Ropes* since there is no surface for them: objects and inscriptions are hung in the air, and although the inscriptions are written on small strips of paper, I don't want to take this disjoined background into account yet, even though it is quite important, as we will see later.

The themes of background, light, and frame converge in the uniquely constructed link between word and image, sign and object, where the relations of iconic and phonetic signs are played out. According to Charles Pierce, these two types of signs are essential to human culture. However, semiotics turned its attention to the study of iconic signs only recently, having been preoccupied with symbolic, or verbal-phonetic, signs. In this respect, little research has been done on the relations of iconic and verbal signs since the areas where these relations are topical just recently have become the objects of analysis.[8] These areas include the display screens, upon which the verbal and iconic signs (drawings) appear; the field of illustration, poster and advertising design where more research has been done in this direction than anywhere else; and finally the philosophy of form, which usually upholds the traditional methods of verbal-conceptual approaches, or simply ignores the word and image relationship.[9]

In Kabakov's painting we see objects and words while representations are practically absent. But the things that are arranged on the ropes and constitute the painting's narrative stratum should be seen not as real objects but rather as the iconic, plastic signs of these objects. In fact, the replicas of the objects could have played the same role in this case. On the one hand, they are real objects: pencils, tickets, bottle caps, etc.—but since they are taken out of circulation and out of their material contexts and exhibited for contemplation— they are transformed into their own, so to speak, autonomous signs.

Thus, in terms of reference, the signs are autonomous, signifying themselves while in terms of form they are iconic, being the three-dimensional plastic copies of objects. Their three-dimensionality is important only from a compositional point of view, as a fact that they hang on strings in three-dimensional space, that they can rotate in this space, etc. However, this means little from the point of view of perception. It makes no sense to examine the objects carefully from all sides, as one would a sculpture or an architectural construction: aspects and viewpoints add nothing to their meaning. Each object is grasped at once, in a moment, like a sign. Therefore, although strictly speaking there are no images here, we can still talk about the use of iconic signs.[10]

In Kabakov's painting the labels, attached to objects, are not the names of objects or their descriptions. Yet we cannot see the forced disparity that René Magritte relied on in his time. The aggravation of paradoxical, absurd incongruity between a drawing and a title was important for Magritte. But here there is no such aggravation: any object and any accompanying inscription can be easily exchanged for another from the rubbish pile nearby. Magritte represented objects. Kabakov represents or assembles their fragments, thereby destroying the entire semantic basis of composition; the semantics, the meaning of objects is already destroyed by fragmentation; the meaning of words in these bits of phrases is similarly deprived of any symbolic load: all of this is rubbish. Nevertheless, as we have seen earlier, this is rubbish "problematized" as a category, rubbish that inspires a question regarding its ontological status in the world surrounding us.

The act performed by Kabakov in the problematization of refuse is the opposite of Magritte's intentions. He does not really juxtapose the verbal sign (word) to the iconic sign (object) but likens them or at least brings them closer in a certain semantic space that is still tentative. In Kabakov's composition, the words and the objects are intentionally impoverished, forced into a single category—"rubbish"—which levels and likens them rather than juxtaposes and isolates. The words and the scraps still maintain their individual meanings, but this is the last moment before they are finally ground into sounds and matter, this is the last phase in the existence of words and objects before they turn into dust and ashes.

Nevertheless, the rapprochement of wasted objects and wasted words maintains their hierarchical distinction: they occupy strictly separate levels of composition, never being confused.

This fact points to the device most frequently used by Kabakov to juxtapose words and images. He juxtaposes words and images in a space where both lose their specificity, a space neutral to the syntactic rules of phrases and images—a space of charts or tables. Table, as a type of representational space, has been used by Magritte and the conceptualists. The tabular form proved to be at once monumental, transparent, convenient, and capacious. Although table is related to the concept of framing, its formal possibilities for visual compositions have been investigated relatively little. Certain varieties of tables were realized in the idea of multiple screen in film and video, in the design of exhibitions, and in all kinds of scientific illustrations—educational and audiovisual aids, manuals, textbooks, as well as in such entertainment graphics as charades, rebuses, and crossword puzzles. Yet I don't know of any serious analysis of the table as a type of representational space, as an ontological universal. But in the case of *Ropes* we encounter just this kind of ontological claim to translate the universal ontological form of the picture frame into the tabular format.[11]

I will try to outline briefly the fundamental characteristics of a table that differentiate it from a picture frame and from a page of text because these very characteristics make it so appealing to the work of conceptualists. But first we must turn once again to the simple semiotic structure of a framed painting that lies at the basis of all avant-garde attempts to overcome it.

The symbolic conventionality of a painting as a surface fragment (most often a flat surface) is frequently emphasized. This surface is limited by a frame (most often rectangular), the sides of which are parallel to the principal vectors of the world, that is, the horizontal and vertical lines. A painting is a symbolic object referring to the "world-at-large," that is, to an autonomous and whole entity, the events of which (objects, figures, and other signs) become meaningful due to their own configurations and also due to the place they come to occupy in the representational field formed by the frame.

In speaking about the "space" of a painting, the emphasis is usually placed on its multiformity, the symbolic significance of which is similar to the multiformity of the "quarters of the world." Notwithstanding the differences, such multiformity is common to many visual language systems: Egyptian reliefs, icons, and the realist paintings of antiquity and modernity. This is what distinguishes the space of a painting from the space of a page or another writing surface, which contains no other meaningful units except for the orientation of lines (vertical or horizontal, depending on the system of writing). Indeed, the meaning of a word does not change depending on whether it is placed above or below, although certain connotative connections to painting are responsible for the usual placing of titles at the top rather than at the bottom of a page.

It is rarely noticed, however, that inside a painting delimited by a frame we encounter another important phenomenon which is a direct result of the semiotic construction of a painting—the atmosphere or the substance of the painterly space. The space of a painting does not only have the compositional and geometrical characteristics: it is also endowed with the substance-like qualities. It forms a kind of "matter" which can be transformed into various actual embodiments: the golden background of icons, the transparent depth of a Renaissance painting, the dark background of modern portraiture—but in each case it is not a purely geometrical surface with different signification of points, it is also a substance-like, natural world where light, darkness, and their tangible materiality are very important. We could say that the filling of the painterly space with the substance of light and darkness, the golden glow, or a special atmospheric transparency is not just a concession to human perceptual sensitivity which craves to see in a make-belief world the real attributes of the real world; it is also a special symbolic sign of the world beyond the painting—not just a delimited part of a surface. That world lives a life of its own, but it needs light and air to be truly a life, and these make-belief yet real light and air materialize within the framed space of a painting. Such light and air do not exist in a textual space of writing, although to a certain extent there is also light here (the glow of a white page, e.g., especially important to images on paper—drawings, etchings, and engravings). Especially since the development of printing a number of common characteristics link paintings to pages or sheets of paper, that is, the rectangular format, the rigid distinction between horizontal and vertical lines, the brightness, and even a certain hierarchy between center and periphery. Their most fundamental difference, however, lies perhaps in the absence of the substantiality of background, the absence of atmosphere and light that are inherent in a painting but are unnecessary to a page of written text. A page of text resembles a painting to the extent that it also delimits a space from the outside world creating room for its own content: margins, type, lines are all necessary conditions for the demarcation as well as for the creation of text. Beyond this, the life and meaning of a text are formed according to the laws and principles peculiar to verbal signs, so that the margins, format, color of the paper, and other features of a page cease to draw attention and no longer play a part in the production of meaning. Although a book as a designed object brings back these considerations, the contemplation of a book or a page is completely different from the process of reading and comprehension of a written text, and in the latter these characteristics of a page matter little. It is not so in a painting where we can neither separate the meaning of representation from its spatial position nor the space itself—with its visible, physical, palpable qualities—from the meaning and content of the represented.

If we now turn to the space of a table or to the relatively similar space of a window display, we will see something intermediate between the painterly and the textual spaces. The tabular space has its own frame which demarcates, sets apart, and contains the display, be it an object or its representation. The peculiarities of hierarchical division between the upper and the lower parts, the surface uniformity, etc., are maintained here as well. But in contrast with the painterly space, there is no atmospheric background or special make-belief substantiality. This space is empty in two ways: semantically, that is, it is not meaningful in itself, and materially, that is, it is just an empty space meant to contain something else such as a display.

Speaking about the space of tables and window displays, it is hard not to mention the space of theater, stage, and film screen. There is no room here for a detailed analysis of these spaces, but it is worth mentioning that their very existence provides opportunities for the culture and the arts to experiment with all kinds of analogies and juxtapositions, substitutions and replacements, which free up the originality of compositions and ideas, and allow the manipulation of the composition situated between the extremes of a painting and a written page. The most important feature of the space of a theater or an exhibit is the relation to the viewer's space; its conventionality is semiotic rather than physical. This is what makes possible the playful attempts at erasing the border between the space of the viewer and the space of the image or the stage. Cinema, on the contrary, prohibits the physical interaction between the image and the viewer; as the "effect of presence" intensifies, so does the effect of "absence" of the viewer from any real space with the exception of the hypnotic space of imagination. However, we must note that the effect of hypnotic fixation is not connected so much with the illusory power of the screen image but rather with the moment of discord between the essentially heterogeneous spaces. Therefore, a museum space, a tabular space, and a textual space also can produce rather strong intoxicating or hypnotic effects when exhibited in special circumstances. The reason for this is the clash of the unconnectable, unfusable, and unmatchable spaces. In fact, the clashing of textual and representational spaces almost always contains a shade of intoxication exploited consciously or unconsciously by Kabakov and the entire avant-garde.

The significance of the atmospheric naturalism of painterly space is extremely important for the very origins of representation and consequently for visual culture in general. The transition from the hieroglyphic to the phonetic system of writing permitted setting apart the material painterly space and propelled the development of the entire post-Egyptian visual culture. This has been pointed out already by Marshall McLuhan.[12]

The fusing of the tabular and painterly types of framing began with the Byzantine and Russian icon painting, but the book and the printing press really spurred the process. Frequently, a book illustration is just a groundless picture or drawing—half-sign, half-image, perhaps under the influence of decorative arts such as coinage, and all sorts of decorative images on porcelain and in architecture. One way or another, the tabular frame becomes closely interconnected with the painterly frame. Imagination has to fill in the perceptual conditions created by the background of a painting but absent from these images. For instance, the white background in a watercolor portrait can be easily perceived as a quality of air and light. The conditions of perception change somewhat when an inscription is moved from the outside to the inside of a frame. Then the image and the inscription appear on the common background, which as a result becomes ambiguous, acquires two meanings: the atmospheric background of an image, and the textual background of a written page. A frontispiece or a book page become these kinds of objects in an ambiguous relationship to the frame and the background; there is no actual frame, but its function is performed by the margins and the edge.

Several methods of playfully combining images with the textual background can be considered as examples of these types of compositional condensations. A rebus is one. Here the representations of objects are subordinated to the laws of textual space while not spatially connected to each other. Magritte gives us another example when he places in an atmospherically charged landscape not objects but words which play the role of objects and are perceived almost like objects despite the obvious paradox. The third, intermediate example is the display case where instead of an object we find a written document, or the stage of a Shakespearean theater where instead of a backdrop with the depiction of a forest the inscription "forest" could be found.

Let us turn to another important aspect of the possible juxtapositions of words and images, this one concerning the degree of specificity of the represented object. A truly specific and individual object cannot be described by a concept. At best it can be signified with a proper name, although even such naming presents us with the specific appearance of the object. Visual representation is capable of communicating this specific appearance, but it is not always intended for such a purpose. The majority of images lack specificity and represent not the specific forest or the apple but an apple, a forest, or a pond in general. Thus such images function more like hieroglyphs than representations as such. As paradoxical as it may seem, this concerns not only the means of representation but the intention as well. Photographs may also refer to a forest in general and not to the particular forest, a human being in general and not the particular woman, etc.

We can see that the relationship of words and images is multidimensional, and such conditions as the degree of specificity and the natural quality of space play an important role. This opens the way to new juxtapositions, combinations, and experimentations.

The device of framing has yet another specificity which receives a new meaning in tabular structures—the ability to fragment the image of reality. This ability is realized most clearly in photographic and cinematic search for the "frame," but it had been utilized by painting and drawing long before photography appeared. Landscape paintings representing all sorts of "nooks and corners," such as a corner of an interior or a separate scene, are the examples of landscape fragmentation. Fragmentation of the world as a poetic device, being closely related to the ontological problem of the integrity of the world, is also encountered in formal constructions of a framing type. In this case, the functions of the frame and its symbolic meaning are inverted, taking on a new significance. When a cinematic or a photographic frame delimits a fragment, the frame no longer symbolizes the integrity but rather the partiality of representation. However, the atmospheric, material affinity of the represented fragment with some integral reality gains an even greater significance.

Textual space, as opposed to painterly space, is not connected with the idea of integrity of a text's content, but in tables we see an intermediate stage of the relationship between a fragment and a whole. Each cell of a table is a fragment of the larger whole which is comprehensible only at the level of the entire table. Moreover, a table cell is a fragment of meaning and not at all a spatial fragment of reality seen as if it were through a grid. The cells of tables, which we find in the paintings of Magritte or Kabakov, have little in common with Dürer's drawing apparatus. Rather they originate from a different source, from the realm of logical constructions and at the same time from the realm of vending displays, reminiscent of the market stalls—this multistage theater where objects and acts are not connected to each other.

While analyzing the ground of a table cell, we realize that its character is complex and hybrid: it is a real microspace for a display or an object; it is also a textual space where words or symbols can be placed as well as a logically organized "subspace" of a certain whole.

This whole, however, is no longer that of a mythological integral world symbolized by the Cosmic Tree or frame of a painting but that of a logically arranged completeness of a table. Right now it is difficult to say anything more precise about the character of the integrity and partiality in terms of space. It has not been investigated enough yet, but we must emphasize its intermediate character in relation to text and image and insist on the primary logical system of relations among cells in this type of table.

It is true that in *Ropes* such cells do not exist, but to a certain extent their function is performed by threads of that canvas or foundation from which the bits of objects and the inscriptions hang. Taking into consideration what we have said about frames and space, let us attempt to scrutinize in more detail the meaning of these pieces of things and words. Let us recall that the phrase fragments and the pieces of things are in correspondence with each other and form a kind of fragmentary unity which is composed not of things, objects, phrases, thoughts, or names but of events and situations.

The bits of these events cannot be fragmented from the outside, with the help of a frame, and there is hardly any reference here to any outer frame which would segment the real life events and objects like a grater or a sieve. Here the frames perform a clearly organizational, or indeed a tabular, function.

The means of producing this medley do not belong to the painting. They are on the outside and perhaps belong to life itself, although it is not easy to understand the nature of the grinder which produces this forcemeat of words and objects. Yet maybe in some secret corners of consciousness clues to the nature of the grinder play a role in the production of meaning.

5. Interpretation

Having made these preliminary remarks, we can try now to understand the interpretive effect produced by Kabakov's painting. Its point is the ontological problematization of the categories of "filth" and "refuse" which is achieved through the play of symbols and visual signs. The space of this painting combines the spaces of display, image, and text with a vague admixture of the tabular space. It is a medley of grounds where an atmospheric materiality is tossed up with the logical aura of a textual ground. The bits of speech on the labels, taken out of context with their new form contradicting their content, create an effect of a sonorous or noisy background. In a painting filled with images or text, the surrounding space becomes the "nothingness" beyond the frame, the absence, the null space. Similarly, the speech resounding from the labels is surrounded by the silence of space. The best background for this verbal litter as well as the most contrasting background for the fragments of object-world would have been indeed provided by a temple-like museum interior. The point is not the physical silence, which may not be there, but the fundamental dichotomy of sounds and meanings taken on contrasting scales and registers.

Museum context becomes here a frame of sorts, where the classical decor functions as the frame's traditional attributes, but inside the boundaries of the frame we see something intermediate between a text, a painting, and a table. The iconic hieroglyphic quality of the fragments of objects and text endows the ground of the painting with a special semimaterial, semisymbolic-textual glow, which is required by the entire structure of the text and which is perceived subconsciously yet quite graphically. This is characteristic of expo-art aesthetic. However, here it is presented in a new key since there is no exposition as such: to read and to examine what is arranged on the ropes is meaningless.

The absence of expositional meaning constitutes the major difficulty in the perception of the painting, and the solution to this difficulty, it seems to me, lies precisely in the fact that the emptiness of content does not obscure but, on the contrary, illuminates and foregrounds the ontological, formal basis of the work, its semiotic kernel, in other words the fundamental conditions for the existence of these fragments—the kinds of grounds and atmosphere that maintain their characteristics achieved through the ages of developing techniques for constructing paintings, texts, and tables.

Formal aspects of Kabakov's composition point to these grounds and conditions of existence of texts and images rather than unfold the meaning of the fragments themselves. This gives rise to a curious contamination of logical relations. The condition of these objects' existence in the structure of the painting and the conditions of their existence in real life are fused into a common problematic. The categorical and ontological status of these objects within the painting's poetics and their categorical and ontological status in life are drawn near and come into a single focus. After all, "filth" and "dirt" must have their place among the categories, and we begin to guess that filth and dirt are those things that are left outside a certain system of categorical, ontological, and material relations.

There is no filth or dirt in nature because nature's system is self-enclosed and absorbs everything into its sphere. Filth and dirt are the creations of civilization and exist only inside the special spaces defended from enemies and from nature—the spaces of homes, cities, inside borders, on the territories of which the norms and conventions of behavior are established. If culture could have ecological ideals, then the criterion of a culture's achievement could be the absence of dirt and filth. There is no filth in an ideal city because it is removed; there can be no filth in an ideal society because, as in nature, every object always, at each stage of its being, can attain a dignified place in its system.

Such is one possible interpretation of the painting deduced from the intersection of its formal and thematic aspects. However, I would like to draw a few more analogies between this painting and other works of visual art in order to justify the chosen term "painting."

We already made it clear that three types of frames, three types of space with their specific substance characteristics, are fused in Kabakov's new work. First of all this is the space of tables or display windows where we can see a peculiar white emptiness of space into which we can walk and where we can move and look around. This expositional space is evoked by the intention to place the painting into the strict surroundings of a museum, by the isolation of each object, and by the label-like quality of the inscriptions. Although this is more reminiscent of an exhibition in a science museum than an art show, the point remains the same: the expositional space retains the peculiar light of a showcase, the peculiar ample showcase spatiality, and the peculiar showcase emptiness.

Second, this is the space of a text because its elements are not at all drawings or sculptures but signs even if they are of a hieroglyphic kind. In their totality, these signs vaguely form a text, perhaps it is an absurd or nonsensical text, like *zaum* or a calligram, or a playful and decorative text. Still, because of this fundamental textuality, it evokes the glow typical of a white sheet of paper or a book page. The label inscriptions are not so important here, although the ease with which they merge in the structure of the work speaks to the essential consanguinity of things and words in the textual whole.

Third, this is the space of a painting and the special atmospheric substance of a painting. I believe that it is this space and atmosphere that are crucial in the final analysis, although I was not convinced of it right away. Several times I saw the work under electric light, and the associations with a painting did not arise. But when one time I saw it during the day, in the sunlight, its painterly quality became obvious. The more I thought about it, the more certain I was that the painterliness is cardinal here. Of course, it would be risky to reduce the meaning of the work's formal organization to a painting. The viewer himself can discover and choose these different spaces, and accordingly find this or that subject matter and this or that light in the painting since the freedom of viewers' choice is one of the greatest virtues of Kabakov's artistic effort, expressed in this work with the most sincerity and clarity. Nevertheless, it is the painterliness that creates the sense of rest, completion, and resolution which can be confirmed by the work's actual likeness to a painting and the fact that it inspires contemplation.

Kabakov's painting absorbs the formal and thematic traditions of European avant-garde displayed clearly in Pointillism, abstraction, and Cubism. Although Kabakov's painting has a certain representational structure, it is organized around noniconic signs. This is a painting created on textual material—a verbal-textual painting or, if you will, a painterly text. The hybridization of mediums and compositional devices should not obscure the well-known classical analogies but, on the contrary, must broaden our knowledge of the compositional possibilities of modern art.

The affinity with Pointillism is very direct: the elemental parts of the painting are the points that almost lose their meaning as objects and merge into a flowing reality reminiscent of the atmospheric substance of Impressionism yet different—it is the substance of the flow of human behavior in the object-world and in speech.

The affinity with abstraction is also quite straightforward: the meaning of things and objects proper as well as the symbolism of words and phrase fragments are erased. What comes to mind is Mondrian's tabular structure of canvas which retains the atmospheric effects of classical painting but loses its spatial organization. Of course, other examples of abstract art are relevant here, especially those with dispersed and regular surface texture.

The affinity with Cubism is simpler yet—the technique of collage, quotations, and the combination of real object textures.

There is no sense in overstating the role of these affinities. They were just suggestions to support the idea about the painterliness of Kabakov's work. There is also a fundamental difference: Kabakov's painting, as opposed to a traditional painting, is "accessible" to viewers; one can walk inside of it and exist in its space. Here, it seems, the analogies with painting should end and new analogies should arise—with art forms that elicit viewers' participation such as architecture, performance art, happenings, etc. In reality, though, the viewers' participation in Kabakov's painting is of a contemplative character. One is not expected to rearrange the objects, kick them or cut them off, as happens at the shows of performance art or happenings. Not because it is prohibited or improper with regard to the artist's work but because it is simply meaningless. To place the painting in a museum is only to emphasize this limitation. The painting is meant for contemplation even though it seems that there is nothing there to contemplate, nothing to look at, nothing even to imagine: in front of us is a laconic and empty structure of similar, although multiplied, scraps of material and verbal litter. Down on the floor they are piled up; up here, at eye level, they are sublimated and accurately hung out in some metaphysical space of a reality with characteristics similar to those of the spaces assimilated by us: the textual and the painterly, the tabular and the museum, yet it does not correspond to any of them. You look down and see the filth and the litter in their "natural" this-worldly appearance; you look up and see all these garbage objects in some type of other-worldly cleanliness and light, as if cleaned of the usual contempt to which they have been accustomed. They soar like spirits or angels without justifying their new status by a new use, or a new symbolic function. Indeed, they have soared up from their ordinary state to another state which has no name but which is very closely connected to the fundamental sources of human culture. In other words, they are withdrawn from the real social world and exist in the world of culture as such (and not any particular culture) where they are arranged in the most pure environment—the environment of visual categories— order, regularity, light, orthogonal lines and axes, the combination of many types of frames and atmospheric media which make this environment of categories breathe and live.

This abstract painting or abstract conceptualism purifies contemplation itself. This is a kind of "Favorsky's light" of culture purified with an ascetic prudence of all the material and conceptual temptations for the mind, by means of mere rubbish and scum.

If this is true, then the artist's idea was properly fulfilled and the placement of other, more valuable objects, and other, more thoughtful speech into this space would have overshadowed the pure light, the celestial sphere, or the horizon of this culture in its fundamental principles. Accordingly, no matter how close we get to the painting, even if we walk into it, even if we touch, handle, smell, or taste the objects on display, or if we read aloud the words and laugh at their silliness, still we cannot erase the distance which the artist created between us and the pure spaces of cultural ontologies. In our physical, bodily, social, and cultural reality, we are unable to enter the space of this painting, and this is why it really is a painting since every painting is painfully inaccessible to the body and exists for contemplation only. The contemplation of the hodgepodge of objects, behind which the ground of conceptual categories shines through, giving sense and meaning to everything, makes the perception of this painting different from theater and cinema: here our physical presence is not detracting in any way. But that is only the physical presence whereas the metaphysical presence depends on the degree of our perfection. Perhaps angels are capable of taking for granted a half-burnt match or swimming in the pure light of the universe, but the force of gravity pulls us toward the heinous earth, the idea of Being is too abstract for us to live it through. Only that which has been freed from the practical function, which has served its time and which has died can attain this. And if death is in some sense the continuation of life, although within its other ontological horizons, and if culture in its fundamental categories knows no death as nature does not know it, then these minute objects give us a unique opportunity to observe the ascension to eternity in a graphic form yet without the conventional anthropomorphic idealization of religious images. The social or sociological meaning of the painting is overshadowed by its metaphysical, spiritual pathos shining through the insignificance of the foreground—the litter and garbage hung from simple black threads.

6. Ontological Postscript

Yet even if the above interpretation of Kabakov's painting is acceptable, the question remains open: Why did he choose this form? Would it not be easier to create a traditional painting, without having to turn to such complicated and elaborated formal structure? After all, this work is highly inconvenient for the artist as well as for the viewers. It is impossible to reproduce, it cannot be transported, it is bulky. Can such a structure become typical? Is it possible to assume that other subjects and themes be realized in the same form? There is no certainty, and it appears that the form created in this particular case runs the risk of remaining to be the only example of its kind.

All the more strange is the fact that the artist, being perfectly aware of the inconvenience of this form, spent so much time and energy to create it. We begin to suspect that the artist's caprice is not the only point here and that behind this form lay some other substantial circumstances that have to do with the life of forms in visual arts. This suspicion is, of course, relevant to the entire avant-garde and not to Kabakov's painting alone. Nevertheless, it is useful to consider the appropriate motives and circumstances in relation to this particular painting rather than in general terms.

If we accept that a form has content and meaning, then the problem of the choice of form—be it traditional or avant-garde—ceases to be "formal."

It would be incorrect to say that classical forms of art have died, grew obsolete, or degenerated. On the contrary, the art of the past grows in popularity year after year. Books are published, exhibitions of icons, painting, and other forms of traditional art are put together. There is not a period in the history of civilization that has lost value and that steadily attracts less interest. The actuality of traditional forms is not decreasing overall, and we cannot claim, as did the theorists of the avant-garde, that traditional forms are dead and obsolete. They live in their own ways.

Nevertheless, we must consider the fact that masterpieces belong to the formal systems of particular eras. We can accept the traditional forms of monumental painting or sculpture, but it would be vain to hope to create through them something approximating Vélazquez or Phidias in greatness. It appears that forms are not symmetrical for creation and contemplation: satisfying the requirements of contemplation, they cannot satisfy the requirements of creation. A closer analysis, however, is capable of discerning a fundamental difference in the modes of contemplation of traditional and contemporary forms. This difference has to do with the ways of including the viewer in the meaning of a work. In order to clarify this, we must return to the category of intoxication or hypnotism of perception.

Contemplation of traditional art forms, which are being assimilated more and more today, is characterized by a broad and pluralist appeal and evokes a certain nostalgic intoxication or hypnotism. Immersing ourselves into the meaning of paintings of other epochs and experiencing their perfection, we slip out of the space and time of our own life and enter another life—bygone and devoid of fears and problems, like a dream about the past where no one is dying any longer. In this contemplative aestheticism and escapism we are able to enjoy even the scenes of torture and battles. The fears and pain are lulled by the traditional art form as this very form along with its real content is already extracted from reality and lifted into eternity. It is so sweet to exist in this eternity which preserves for us the mesmerizing aroma of life, yet renders it harmless. The hypnotic power of such contemplation makes it an opium for eyes and ears. The spectacle of historical art forms is a true spectacle where the viewer and the object are separated by a transparent yet impassable divide of a historical rupture.

If we try to create in a traditional form, then purposefully or involuntarily we begin to exploit this specificity of traditional form, representing the actual thematic content of our time in the forms of distant historical reality or even in the forms of eternity. The resulting fusion of present and eternity can be used, for instance, to give a portrait of a contemporary an air of something illuminated by history or associated with eternity. It is flattering to be represented in the style of the old masters precisely because the image imparts on the subject even before death the dignity of a historical personality which has not yet been deserved. This fusion of time and eternity has a hypnotic and intoxicating power, which in turn is capable of demobilizing. It does not awake but lulls to sleep. Other modes of combining the formal qualities of space and time in a painting can have an opposite effect and function as "alarms" waking the viewer from blissful inactivity. Interestingly, these forms can also be constructed on the basis of contemplative relations. The early twentieth-century avant-garde refused categorically the very idea of contemplation along with the traditional art forms related to it. One of the main goals of art was the mobilization of viewers, as it is well known from the history of the avant-garde: all possible frames and boundaries between art and life were marked for destruction and overcoming. As the experiments of Productivists later demonstrated, the unforeseen result of this type of mobilization was the destruction of art itself that can exist only under the conditions of a certain distancing from reality.

The overcoming of framing and contemplation must be relative; some formal and ontological conventions of traditional historical forms must be overcome, yet at the same time the fundamental conventions of art as such must be maintained. Only by meeting these demands will art be able to attain urgency once again, to become stimulating rather than tranquilizing, and still remain art with all its aesthetic characteristics without becoming an object of religious cult or an industrial product.

The role of avant-garde art and art theory under these circumstances gains an importance greater than the elucidation of purely artistic values, since through them the way leads to the elucidation of general ontological phenomena of contemporary life. Marshall McLuhan once wrote that artistic experiments in contemporary art strive to elucidate the real conditions of changing life, which are veiled by the traditional, conventional categories of understanding and perception of life.[13]

The relationship between "content" and "form" in contemporary art is to a certain extent the relationship between traditional ontological content and new ontological reality or new ontological phenomenology of life. Works of art turn out to be hypnotic when both the content and the form are immersed in the traditional, that is, partial and past, categorical conditions of existence, when they are bracketed out of actual relations that quilt contemporary life. That is why they are so sweet and so intoxicating. Such are kitsch and folkart as well as the academic Retro style and the routine forms of artistic practice, which, besides their educational value, belong to the sphere of leisure, entertainment, and pleasure. Avant-garde belongs to this sphere of hedonism and intoxication to a lesser degree, and that is why, more often than not, it evokes irritation as a disturber of peace and quiet sought by people exhausted from life.

Let us add that to evaluate the success or failure of the construction of such ontological and poetic forms by the avant-garde right after they appear is as difficult as to describe their true anthropological meaning. The new form remains ambiguous until historical distance allows us to see its social, cultural, and human meaning, until it allows us to move this form into the category of "content" and to consider it verbally, that is, by the means of concepts and terms with their stable meanings.

That is why a painting such as this presents a puzzle for an art critic and philosopher as well as for the artist himself. It is impossible to demand from the artist and the critic an exhaustive explanation because the relationship between the conditions of contemporary life and the contemporary means of communication and cognition is still in flux. Life runs ahead of our means to understand it, although an artist can create on the borderline of this understanding. The mystery that dwells on this borderline is one of the most fundamental mysteries of life—the mystery of the historical development of new forms. Perhaps there is a profound truth in the fact that it is organically connected with the mystery of the meaning of life, which is essentially ahistorical: Kabakov's painting, privy to both the historical and the eternal conditions of the existence of art and culture, also becomes privy to both mysteries which are not devalued by the attempts of a philosophical mastering of their meaning. The multiplicity of inner dialectical contradictions, expressed by the content and the formal construction of Kabakov's painting by virtue of participation in these two fundamental mysteries, makes the painting a living work of art, a work that reveals its meaning to the extent that a viewer would want to undertake the labor and the risk of comprehending it.

NOTES

1. According to accepted terminology, similar spatial constructions are called installations. This term, however, seems less convenient to me because it expresses only the technical aspect of the matter and does not get across all the semantic richness of the concept "painting."

2. If the painting were close at hand, I would have given a more precise description. But unfortunately I saw it a long time ago and can remember the concrete details with difficulty. Since then *The Ropes* has been sold in the United States and is hardly accessible. I hope that this description from memory will still be sufficient to convey the main points of my interpretation.

3. A quote from a poem by Marina Tzvetaeva.—Eds. note.

4. Mikhail Epshtein, "Vesch i slovo: K proektu 'liricheskogo muzeya' ili 'memoriala veschey'"; V. V. Aristov, A. V. Mikheev, "Teksty s opisaniem veschey-eksponatov 'liricheskogo museya,'" *Vesch v iskusstve: Materialy nauchnoy konferentsii* (Moscow, 1986), 302–31. (The revised version of Epshtein's essay is included in this volume.)

5. A character from Gogol's novel *Dead Souls*.—Eds. note.

6. The problem of fragmentation and framing is developed in the work of

Moscow artist Ilya Chuikov, who uses such devices as quadrangular frames, painting on frames, frame in linear perspective, etc.

7. Boris Groys once was going to write a paper on the topic "Malevich's White Background." A number of ideas from this lecture, which never took place, were developed in his other presentations, for instance, in a presentation at the seminar on theory and history of design at the National Research Institute for Technical Aesthetics (VNIITE) in 1982. See *Tekhnicheskaya Estetika* (Moscow, 1982).

8. N. A. Dmitrieva, *Izobrazhenie i slovo* (Moscow, 1962); V. A. Alfonsov, *Slova i kraski* (Moscow, 1966).

9. In the realm of computers the problem of dynamic sign turned out to be more urgent, while for animation and conceptual painting the problems of content came to the foreground. Thus the problems of formal analysis, so well established by Marshall McLuhan, remained without the much-deserved attention.

10. The marshaling of turning a "painting" into a "picture," i.e., into a hieroglyphic sign rather than an image, is ascribed to the Primitivists.

11. Tabular frames are encountered in Egyptian art and in icon painting. But in Egyptian art the matter is complicated by the fact that the writing itself is iconic, whereas in icon painting the table had not yet received the logical meaning developed in the nineteenth century.

12. Marshall McLuhan related this ontological search to the development of mass communications, in particular radio and television. See Marshall McLuhan, *Understanding Media: The Extensions of Man* (New York: New American Library, 1964).

13. Marshall McLuhan with Harley Parker, *Through the Vanishing Point: Space in Poetry and Painting* (New York, 1968).

Mass Celebrations in a Totalitarian System

One of the most impressive and mysterious phenomena of the Stalin era are the mass celebrations of the 1930s and 1940s. It seems remarkable that the prewar period of deprivation and Stalinist repressions also witnessed the unprecedented number of balls, carnivals, and other celebrations. During the years between 1939 and 1941, 111 mass celebrations were conducted at Leningrad's Central Party Committee Club. Every year in Moscow more than thirty theatrical rallies were organized (not counting the state and local club events), gathering together up to a million Muscovites. According to observers, "The crowd was alive, it felt free, uninhibited." On weekends in Neskuchny Park one could see young women dressed up in Russian native costumes dancing the gypsy dance with great enthusiasm. Not far, under the multicolored lights suspended from trees, others were dancing the fox-trot. An invisible brass orchestra was playing the swift Rio-Rita. Couples were strolling along the alleys, playing guitars, singing songs about "the brave Captain" and the "Black Baby."[1] A 1930s poem by Osip Mandelstam expresses the sweeping breadth of outdoor festivities, when it seemed that "all Moscow was swimming in skiffs."

How to connect these facts with the repulsive image of Stalinism created today by the press? Is it possible to talk about a genuine com-

Alexander Zakharov, "Massovye prazdniki v sisteme totalitarizma" (Mass celebrations in the totalitarian system), in *Totalitarizm kak istoricheskiy phenomen* (Totalitarianism as a historical phenomenon) (Moscow: Association of Soviet Philosophers, 1989), 284–301.

munal enthusiasm, or was it a paradoxical, unhealthy process ("the dream of reason"), subordinated to a system of psychological brain-washing of the masses? In contemporary fiction, events of that time are frequently depicted in a parallel coexistence of the two worlds—the world of light and the world of darkness, which practically never came into contact with one another. In the first world industrial records were set, balloons were launched into the stratosphere, young pioneers were marching, while in another . . .[2] It is necessary to clarify to what extent this image corresponds to the actual worldview of the prewar years rather than having been influenced by the later experience of, say, the 1960s–70s.

It is noteworthy that the idea of a two-world culture, the official and the popular, was already being developed by Mikhail Bakhtin during the 1930s–40s. In Bakhtin's book devoted to François Rabelais the two worlds came together or, more precisely, thronged in the chaos of the Medieval celebration—the carnival.[3] It is logical to suppose that in a certain period the tendency toward indoctrination and the spontaneous popular activity could fuse, together forming some intermediate phenomenon—the mass state (totalitarian?) culture. Although this synthesis had a relatively superficial, unstable character and did not affect world history in a substantial way, it must be granted that some works of Socialist Realism are quite charming. Let us only compare the things that deserve comparison and, in particular, mass Soviet celebrations with the already mentioned Western European carnival or American popular culture. In this fascinating borderline area between art and life we can discover a number of peculiarities in ideas, language, and the means of self-expression that are marked by the lives of entire generations and, perhaps, to a certain extent anticipate contemporary conflicts.

The concept of totalitarianism is specific to the twentieth century and characterizes a type of interaction between masses and a charismatic leader. Recently a lot has been said and written about charisma. We are interested in the masses: how they emerge and grow, how the direction of their action is formed, how unified communal emotions are produced, etc. The patterns of this phenomenon have not been sufficiently investigated. I would like to think that the following notes about mass celebrations will contribute to the clarification of this very important set of questions.

"Revolution Is the Celebration of the Oppressed and Exploited"

It is appropriate to start the excursion into the history of celebrations with May of 1918, when under the direct influence of the Revolution there was a spontaneous surge of mass theatrical initiatives. This year in Petrograd, Moscow, and other large cities multitudinous performances were organized where demonstrations and street battles had recently taken place. According to their organizers, they were intended to emphasize the epoch-making significance of the October Revolution, to demonstrate the depth of the break with the past, and to realize in artistic and figurative form the peoples' hopes for socialism. Thus, on the Marshall Field in Petrograd, the solemn funerals of the Revolution victims were accompanied by leaders' speeches, marches, burning the symbols of the "old regime," and singing the Marseillaise. Later on, at the time of military communism, agitational performances were staged outdoors despite the severe material scarcity, for instance, *The Mystery-Play of the Liberated Labor* at the Stock Exchange Building on the Neva River or the dramatization of *The Taking of the Winter Palace*. Thousands of Red Army soldiers, young workers, students, and professional and amateur actors participated in them.

Piotrovskiy, one of the first directors of mass spectacles, noted the following tendencies in the evolution of the early Soviet celebrations: (1) the mass chorus as the principal force, moving the action; (2) temporal continuity with the overall episodic structure; (3) the introduction of real objects and actions: an army parade, a rally, a battle; (4) and especially the treatment of space as a topographic "reality."[4] The worldview, created by these celebrations, was essentially utopian and mythological. They represented the act of creation of the ideal New World—with the final triumph of equality, universal fraternity, and eternal justice. Revolution was experienced as a mystery and a mystification, as magical leap from the "kingdom of injustice" to the "kingdom of freedom." Differences between the opposite categories of existence—the desired and the possible, the present and the future, holiday and everyday—were erased. Real time was hardly experienced, as in one and a half or two hours of performance the entire history of mankind passed by, from the revolt of Spartacus to the

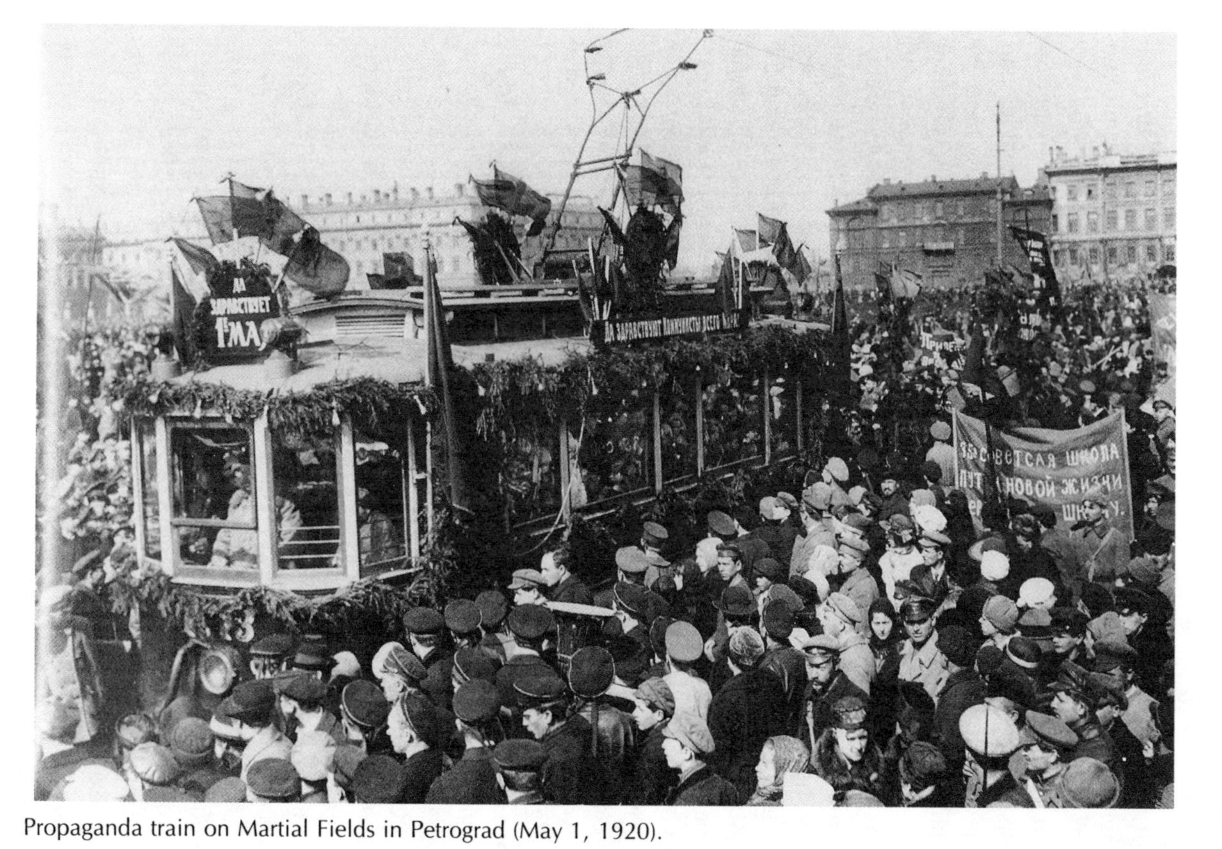

Propaganda train on Martial Fields in Petrograd (May 1, 1920).

recent shot of *Aurora*. Space was also perceived in an unusual way, as though the action was moving from the theater stage to the city, to the country, to the whole planet. Although this did not really happen, the expansion of space was always implied in the concept of the celebration, in its script. The character of the recent social upheaval disposed to "collective, vibrant, and public openness, which involved everybody and everything . . . In literary and intellectual realms people were searching for an America, wanted to discover antipodes, rushed to look at the Western half of the Earth, and asked 'what is beneath us?'"[5]

It is interesting to see what place was allocated to the individual in this refracted, fantastic world of celebrations. The subjects of dramatizations were usually simple: "workers accomplishing Revolution," "Red Army soldiers in battle," "Antanta advancing," and so on. In one production the organizers came up with the idea to block the way to the stage area with extras dressed up as Tsarist gendarmes; people had to use force to get through the "lines." The significance of everyday, individual details was minimized and reduced to the function of social sign markers, separating "now" from "before," "ours" from "theirs." Piotrovskiy emphasized: "At the foundation . . . lies the same constantly modified device: *not simply to dress up, but to be transformed*. Moscow workers turn into world heroes, and recruits into victorious soldiers of Revolution."[6] This sentiment could not be limited to the times of celebration; to some extent it was carried over to the everyday mentality, to the image of an inner "I" inseparable from the collective "we." The signs of an early, heroic stage of such transformation can be seen in the painting *Bolshevik* by Boris Kustodiev (1920) depicting the giant figure of a worker carrying a red flag, in the poem *Twelve* by Aleksander Block, and in many other works of the period. On the whole, celebrations gave to the common folk the feeling of enthusiasm and liberation from the centuries-long humility and oppression; they also tended to evoke the feeling of self-superiority.

Scholars point out a number of contradictions in the early Soviet celebrations.[7] Despite their democratic, truly national character, the participating masses were on the whole passive. The abundance of movement and impressions was strangely combined with the static character of inner experience, which was as if holding still on the same pathetic note. Already in this period the elements of a ritual, which after dozens of years would be experienced as the symbols of "stagnation," were established: demonstrators marking time before rostrums; long, wearisome meetings; reports; empty salutations, etc. These celebrations were pleasant to look at from the outside, but to participate in them was rather tiresome and boring.

The desire of artists and directors to somehow enliven the celebrations, to make them more spontaneous, clashed with the narrow cultural tradition and low level of the workers' aesthetic education. Perhaps this is why Mayakovsky's *Misteriya-Buffo* failed on the opening night, and the decorative work of the artists of the World of Art movement and the experiments of Mark Chagall and Kasemir Malevich in Vitebsk were bashed by critics. The leadership of the Theatre Department of the People's Committee on Education was suspicious of the concept of "new *sobornost* (communality)," proposed by Vyacheslav Ivanov and Aleksander Skryabin. Some elements of folklore and street theater were introduced into the celebrations: round dances, rhymes and chastooshkas, farce, and mummers. But on the whole the culture of the past was rejected. Thus, during one of the Christmas celebrations, the workers of Proletarka Factory in the city of Tver threw out from their apartments and hostels 1,200 icons and burned them in the presence of 3,000 spectators. This symbolic act was preceded by the demonstration of the workers' children. There were 870 icons burned at the Yenakiev Mine.[8] For a long time mass celebrations had the gloomy character of a "storming" of the central respectable neighborhoods by the inhabitants of city outskirts.

The productions of the first years after the October Revolution strongly resembled the celebrations of the French Revolution of 1789–93. They shared such common aspects as immense scale, the desire to create monumental "live pictures," the graphic aggression, the military pathos, which became especially strong in France after Napoleon came to power, and the attempts to substitute the institution of Church with something like an unofficial atheistic religion (in one case the cult of Reason, "Supreme Being," in another the belief in World Commune).[9] Incidentally, this resemblance was emphasized consciously by revolutionaries of the new formation, who considered it their duty to learn from the Jacobins.[10] At this time, following the instructions of Lunacharsky, the book *Songs and Celebrations of the French Revolution* was translated from the French, and the diaries and the letters of David, the main artist-director of the celebrations of the

Republic, were published. In Petrograd at the Academy of Sciences a sociological laboratory for the study of world celebrations (obviously, revolutionary) was established. Due to a number of circumstances, not the least being the internationalist claims of the party ideology and its general strategy for the modernization of the country, Communist reformers were inclined to choose the way already taken by the Russian princes who accepted Byzantine ways, and subsequently by Peter the Great.

"Workers and Peasants Deserve More Than Spectacles"

During the 1920s–30s Western cultures witnessed a phenomenon that corresponded to some extent to the spirit of the Soviet experiments and tendencies. In many countries, primarily the industrial ones, mass celebrations and performances were taking place: in England the open air Shakespeare productions, which attracted up to 100,000 spectators; in the United States Hollywood shows and pageants, dramatized parades with floats; in Germany religious and historical plays, the performances of folk theaters; in Switzerland and Italy carnivals; in Spain bullfights; and so on. In the short time between the two wars the spirit of carnival was in the air, capturing not only the common people but many intellectuals as well. Among them were Romain Rolland, Thomas Mann, Herman Hesse, Jose Ortega, and Ernest Hemingway. The most sensitive and astute of them connected the celebrational boom with the cleft formed in classical European rationalism from which the new twentieth-century social mythology was emerging. A transition to the mass industrial society was being prepared together with the corresponding changes in the structure of everyday practices, types of sensibility, and collective and individual consciousness. These could not be readily adopted from science or high art but required a specific mass "enlightenment." Lunacharsky wrote: "In order to be able to experience themselves, masses have to express themselves *in action,* and this is *possible* only *when . . . they become the spectacle for themselves.*"[11]

Celebrations, gathering huge crowds, had occurred in world history before. But then masses acted as socially and culturally heterogeneous. They were divided into estates, guilds, or communes. These were not celebrations of the Organization but celebrations of organizations, in which separate social groups preserved their special character. In the twentieth century, for the first time, the mass appeared as a monolith, as a unified body. If in the past, for instance, in the communities of antiquity or the Middle Ages, the mass formed episodically and accidentally, now the formation of masses, the *massification,* became a goal in itself. Consequently, traditional concepts such as "democracy" and "people" experienced a deep crisis, the striking illustration of which are Fascism and Stalinism.

It is important to note that in this particular historical moment we are dealing with the early stages of the process—the formation of masses fundamentally specific to the new era. Gathered into supranational enclaves, millions of people still functioned as raw material with unpredictable reactions; this material had to crystallize into something more defined. Apparently, celebrations played an important role in this process. Before the spread of radio and television, they fulfilled the function of mass communication in a direct and personal manner, facilitating self-identification, self-knowledge, and also, in a certain sense, the development of the capabilities of a mass individual.[12]

In this context, the borrowing of aesthetic forms of spectacles was widespread, especially with respect to the organization of stage space, the methods of "montage" of separate scenes, and the musical and artistic arrangements. In 1927 a Soviet author wrote that "during the last few years mass productions in Germany were becoming extremely similar to ours."[13] Later, totalitarian regimes in both countries imparted certain specific expressive features to their celebrations; for instance, in Germany—the organization and coordination reaching pedantry, militant nationalism, the notorious "animal" symbolism in the decoration of processions and parades, the abundance of all kinds of technology, a more open erotism, etc. In the beginning these distinctions were not so noticeable. It is as though the celebrations had a common root, and the two sides saw no reason to conceal this.

The Soviet-German cultural relations of the 1920s–30s is a very complicated and delicate problem, which deserves a special analysis. It is possible that the way in which National Socialism had been perceived was influenced by the fact that in the early period it pronounced itself a part of the German workers' movement, which Russian Marxists always highly respected. If, for a number of reasons in the realm of high culture, contacts were difficult, in the realm of so-called popular (mass) art—theater, cinema, design—they were much more intense. In the 1920s, political theater—Red Cabaret—was transplanted from Germany to the Soviet Union. On the other hand,

Bertold Brecht spent some time in the USSR, and then attempted to apply his experience with mass performances back in Germany. Soviet Blue Blouse went on tours to German workers' theaters.

German expressionists shared with Soviet avant-garde movements the striving toward objectivist (concrete) art, the firm ideological content, and the erosion of borders between viewers and performers. The common final goal of these explorations was envisioned as the creation of a new type of popular spectacle, combining entertainment with serious educational work. It was proposed that the theatrical conventions and attributes such as footlights, curtain, and stage are abolished, so that working masses would not perform the plays of professional writers but freely express their thoughts and feelings through the script they would create themselves.[14] As it turned out, the genre of political carnival was best suited for these ideas—a variety of agitational celebrations intended mainly for the marginal strata of city inhabitants.

The middle of the 1920s can be considered the heyday of the Soviet art of mass celebrations, when it was grounded in amateur productions of workers' clubs, drama clubs, and the emerging social organizations such as professional, sport, women's, and youth unions. The coexistence of various artistic movements, not yet brought under a single state control, was allowed. Among them were the so-called fellow-travelers: Futurists, Constructivists, Imaginists, and others. Moscow and Leningrad witnessed the brilliance of productions by Meyerhold, Tairov, Radlov, and Evreinov. Artistic discoveries were immediately transferred from theatrical stage to festival squares, and from there, enriched by popular experience, back into theater. Undoubtedly, Vladimir Mayakovsky, whose influence was boundless, dominated the scene. It seemed that he alone contained all of the mass celebrations.

On the streets, satirical laughter was heard everywhere, biting, frank, and without mercy for "them" or "us." The leaders were not spared either. A new kind of celebration—the industrial carnival—became the favorite kind of spectacle in the late 1920s. During the processions, along with the familiar puppets of the White Army Officer or the Factory Owner, the figures of the Slacker and the Lousy Worker emerged, inevitably being beaten up by the muscular Front-Rank Worker. Spades and axes were forged in the mobile shops before the eyes of the passersby, the presses were printing festival proclamations, and confectioneries baked "on the go" were being sold. Grotesque and pantomime were popular. Because of the mixture of industrial and political-agitational motives, amusing three-dimensional caricatures appeared, for instance, a nine-feet-long boot of Skorokhod (a Russian folktale character) with a bourgeois writhing under its heal, or Atlanta placed in a huge galosh with the mark of the Red Triangle Factory. In the carnival even the "Lenin's Electric Bulb" was not an abstract metaphor—above the Leader's head a real electric light was shining, like the nimbus of a saint.

However, even at that time the main idea—to turn celebrations into the art "for the people"—began to appear problematic. Their unnatural and mechanical character as well as emotional scantiness were felt, and this irritated many, especially the intelligentsia. Popular celebration, torn apart from its intrinsic national spiritual traditions, often turned into a meaningless commotion and hubbub. Moreover, the apathy of the people, forcefully driven into the cities by the genius of Stalin's industrialization, grew stronger. The workers were less willing to go outside during holidays, and if they did, their mood did not always fit the model of optimism. In these conditions, the sociocultural type of the revolutionary celebrations experienced a crisis, lost the quality of a spontaneous volunteering, and for the first time organizers were faced with the task of stimulating popular activities "from above."

During these years the country witnessed the institutionalization of a pseudoprofessional type of activity, which can be called *massovodstvo* (mass-direction), that is, the "pure" art of manipulating masses. There appeared a great number of people who were neither artists nor actors nor writers, but who showed up everywhere and tried to command everybody. *Massovik-zateinik* (mostly frequently a local union activist) did not take under his control celebrations only. At the higher level of government the principles of mass organization were being worked out for industry, transportation, construction, and even education. Hundreds of journals and brochures with titles such as *Massovik* (Mass-Organizer) and *Massovaya kulturno-prosvetitelnaya rabota* (Mass Cultural-Educational Work) were published. At the same time, certain general principles of the mass-directional techniques were worked out most effectively at celebrations.

The description of one of the festivals, prepared by the methodological group Massovoe Deistevie (Mass Action) tells us how this was done. (The group's work was considered to be a preparation for the opening of the international Red Stadium, the place where holiday celebrations of the world proletariat were to take place.)

On August 12, 1928 on Lenin Hills in Moscow games and swings are set up; a boy is tossed up on a tarpaulin, somebody cuts off prizes; others are breaking up with sticks a clay head of Chamberlain. Lots of amusements. Young people with red arm bands are standing nearby.

"Are you the director?"

"No, I am one of the administrators."

"What is the difference?"

"I don't direct anything, but only preserve order, help to direct."

"What then is the educational role of all these amusements?"

"None. These things play a supplementary role—they gather disorganized people into dense groups; once you gather the masses, it is easy to take them."[15]

As a commentary we should note that here *massovod* (mass-director) in a clever and simple way solves the problem which preoccupied Confucius and Plato: how to make power pleasant and joyous for the people. Under normal circumstances, there are at least some "sparks" of common sense to prevent manipulations of this kind. The sight of a nicely dressed crowd attracts attention, but psychologically it can also repel and even induce fear, especially if the crowd is in a state of excitement. To get over this barrier, it is necessary to tear people away from everyday routine, to submerge them in an unusual, extreme situation, or, at least, to distract them with games. Let us see what happens next.

. . . A horn signal sounds. The tarpaulin and the attractions disappear in a moment, and next to the suddenly disoriented people appear the administrators, running around with red flags and megaphones.

"All comrades line up in order!"

Surprise and—organization! Within three minutes the crowd of many thousands, taken unaware, is arranged into a column of two ranks. Those who had not yet lined up run closer, trying to find out what is going on and . . . remain in the ranks.

The voice from the megaphone is heard:

"Listen, listen! Here, in Moscow, the capital of the only country that belongs to the workers, we are beginning a game, terrifying for the world bourgeoisie and joyful for all workers."[16]

The sport competitions, merry-go-rounds, workers' festivals, and parties are all forgotten—the world is split in two parts, two "fronts" are standing face-to-face. Shots resound, shells and hand grenades break up, rockets soar up, and smoke screens cover up the "fronts."

The preserved film footage and other documents show that such celebrations were not at all rare. Elderly people, including the workers, were skeptical about them, in a way similar to how today's veterans look at contemporary youth culture and rock-and-roll. But the importance of these celebrations for the training of Komsomol leaders, as well as the entire generation which carried on its shoulders the burden of World War II, is hard to overestimate. N. Makeev, a participant in the war, writes in his letter to a newspaper: "The process of transforming the world on new foundations was so contagious that we were offering our hands and our hearts—just take them! Our great love for the Motherland prepared us for hard ordeals. We valued the Soviet way of life and that is why we were not afraid of death. The world that opened up for us was worth any sacrifices."[17] One cannot ignore such evidence of belief. The "new man" of mass society could have been strong and freedom-loving in his own way, but these qualities had a peculiar characteristic: they showed up only in a two-rank line.

"Life Got Better, Life Got Gayer"

At the end of the 1920s Soviet domestic policy underwent a radical change, which was immediately reflected in the character of celebrations.

In this period attendance at demonstrations became mandatory for all employees. The routes along which the columns of demonstrators moved were fixed and calculated in detail. Standard decoration strategies were approved, and among them the leaders' portraits took up an important place. Amateur posters made by the demonstrators themselves were confiscated and destroyed. Secret brigades of "mass activists" were formed under the observation of Party committees. At proper moments they were instructed to jump onto tribunes and fill the air with screams and wild expressions of emotions following a previously prepared script. Questionnaires disseminated among the *massoviks* included such questions as, "Did the audiences, among which you were working, know who you were?" or "Please report all the conversations you overheard regarding yesterday's celebration."

The conduct of mass celebrations attained the character of an assembly-line production. City and district headquarters for the organi-

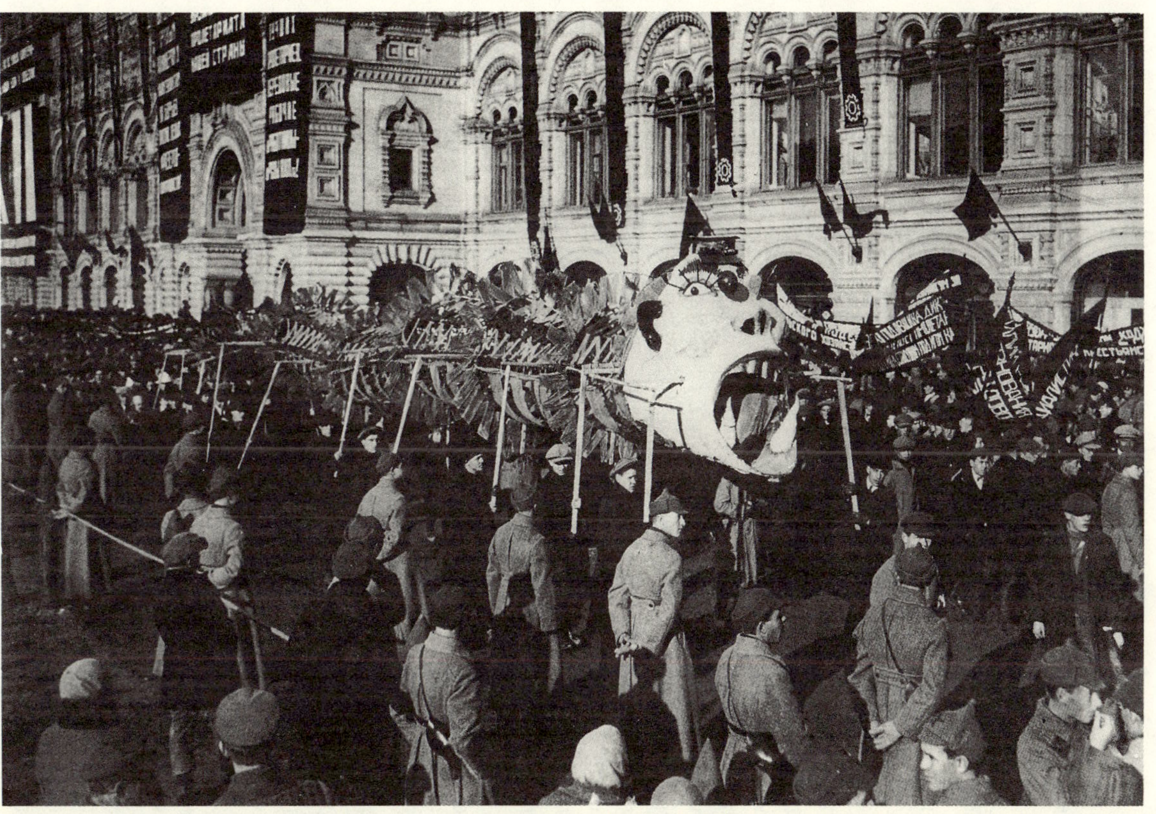

A column of demonstrators on Red Square, Moscow (November 7, 1929).

zation of celebrations were created, working in a military style: an order, a command, an execution, a report. In general, all celebrations, including sports events and children's parties, became military in spirit. Preparations for the inevitable war (obviously, expected to be defensive and victorious) were openly declared an important task of the state, hence the endless reviews at schools, song and military formation competitions, shooting contests, gas-mask training, etc. In 1935, during the Book Day, model maneuvers of the ordinance regiment were organized in Moscow under the slogan "Book is the best weapon!"

The role of violence in the celebrations of the prewar years is striking: the scenes of reprisals of "imperialists," "social traitors," "kulaks." Perhaps all these activities, being playful in spirit, were not experienced by the participants as violence but rather as the demonstration of force, a joke, or a ritual murder. However, this kind of humor will not seem so innocent if we recall that in 1926, during the trials of the Industrial Party, the workers in Moscow were marching with posters depicting a single word: "Death!" This was repeated during the trials of 1937–38. Was this the expression of aggression, characteristic of totalitarianism, or was the true meaning of demonstrations to channel, to lull its own fear?

Studying the 1930s–40s literature about mass celebrations, one involuntarily feels disappointed and repulsed. Obviously, a powerful force was at work, trying to organize everything, to cleanse celebration from everything human and, most important, to deprive it of the healthy taste of freedom, without which real joy is impossible. The rulers only feigned the admiration for the spontaneuty of mass action, and in fact did not trust the people, doing everything to stifle the expressions of nonsanctioned activity from below. Published in 1927, a book by E. Ryumin, a literary critic close to the Proletcult leaders, expressed the official point of view on celebrations. The author admonished: "Spontaneous activity of the masses must be carefully prepared, organized and directed by the nucleus of command and by the groups responsible for work motivation, which should be, if possible, little noticed by the masses themselves. It is necessary to nip in the bud any attempts on the part of some individuals to express their 'self' at the expense of the collective and to the detriment of its creativity."[18]

In fact, these were rather direct instructions for the educators couched in an intellectual form. The script of a celebration had to

(1) foreground the political ideas and slogans of the day; (2) exclude "subtle feelings"; (3) never depress the masses, but on the contrary, "call into a new attack, toward new glorious victories." As an example of a culmination of a May 1 celebration, it was proposed to announce on the radio that the last remaining capitalist state fell and the International Union of Socialist Republics was formed: "Labor is the only ruler on Earth." Athletic exercises were particularly emphasized: "The goal of a sport organization is to produce a clarity of movements, a precision and even flow of action by introducing elements of gymnastics to the movements of masses during the celebration. The mixed, nervously excited, motley crowd of many thousands should turn into a harmonious, grand, monumental, creative collective of participants."[19] In their excited imagination, *massovody* saw the image of flower beds formed from human bodies, regularly moving to the sounds of a chorus and symphonic music, and in apotheosis forming the letters of sacred names. This is the image made familiar from the works of Zamyatin, Huxley, and Orwell, and also . . . from the very recent Soviet celebrations of the 1970s–80s.

Of course, this reactionary aesthetic utopia could not be realized painlessly. Newspaper articles and reviews of the Stalin period were full of complaints that celebrations were not as successful as desired. There were calls to eliminate the "bourgeois" popular celebrations (in the original the word "popular" rather than the word "bourgeois" was put in quotes); the celebrations of the 1920s were criticized for being too mixed and ideologically uneven. Some examples of this political "vigilance" are worth quoting.

One of the Leningrad schools came to a demonstration with a big poster depicting a pioneer with a horn, a pig, and the inscription: "Was a consumer—now a producer." (This did not receive approval.) The employees of Pulkovskaya Observatory carried large air balloons with slogans about advanced work achievements and the fulfillment of the Five-Year Plan. A reviewer criticized the demonstration organizers for the air balloons which resembled soap bubbles and, therefore, referred to "overblown achievements." The workers of Myuntsenberg Factory marched with a row of completely bald green heads. According to the assurances of one of the participants, these were very acute political masks, representing Western capitalists. (This was more or less accepted.) But: "The extremity of stupid bungling in costumes was shown by the trouble-makers of Red Triangle Factory who dressed up as Pierre and Arlekin."[20] The authorities needed stability most of all, and carnival constantly shook it up.

Although they developed according to their own laws, mass celebrations absorbed and reflected the distinctive signs of the time: the successes and failures of the economy, collectivization, the construction of new cities. Naturally, all this was presented in rosy colors, because the real price of the "achievements" was carefully concealed. On the other hand, some safety valves were still left for real feelings. Just before the war, unexpectedly for ideologues, lyrical songs appeared at celebrations—first about the native land or nature, and then about love. This had to be tolerated because it was clear that the "International" was not enough on which to build patriotic propaganda.

Still, the invisible but prolonged and persistent pressure of the bureaucrats started to strangle popular celebrations. Satirical carnival laughter (according to Bakhtin, ambivalent and directed simultaneously at the world and at oneself) gave place to flaccid humor incapable of either denying or asserting anything. A semantic transformation was taking place: the carnival procession turned into a parade, the get-together of friends into a banquet, the symbols into badges and emblems. In other words, the narratives about one's own life celebrations were turning into representations of abstract speculative ideas to be seen by the Others (government officials, world proletariat, external and internal "enemies").

In the end, the mass celebration separated into two component parts already mentioned above. The first part was celebratory, serious, even somber, accompanied by the heavy steps of marching columns, tanks in the back, and the young pioneers up front. All this was moving, greeting Stalin or the local leader, while the leader, the only one standing motionless as if at the center of the Universe, would respond by waving his hand to the masses or saluting them. Here the exaltation, called in Western literature the "love for power," was present with a certain degree of sincerity. The second part of celebrations consisted of popular merrymaking. If celebrations had retained something untamed, live, and spontaneous, it was pushed aside from the squares and into clubs and city parks, then even further—into countryside resorts, tourist centers and, finally, into private apartments.

In general, mass celebrations allow a number of possibilities for the realization of totalitarian tendencies: crowding and the anonymity of

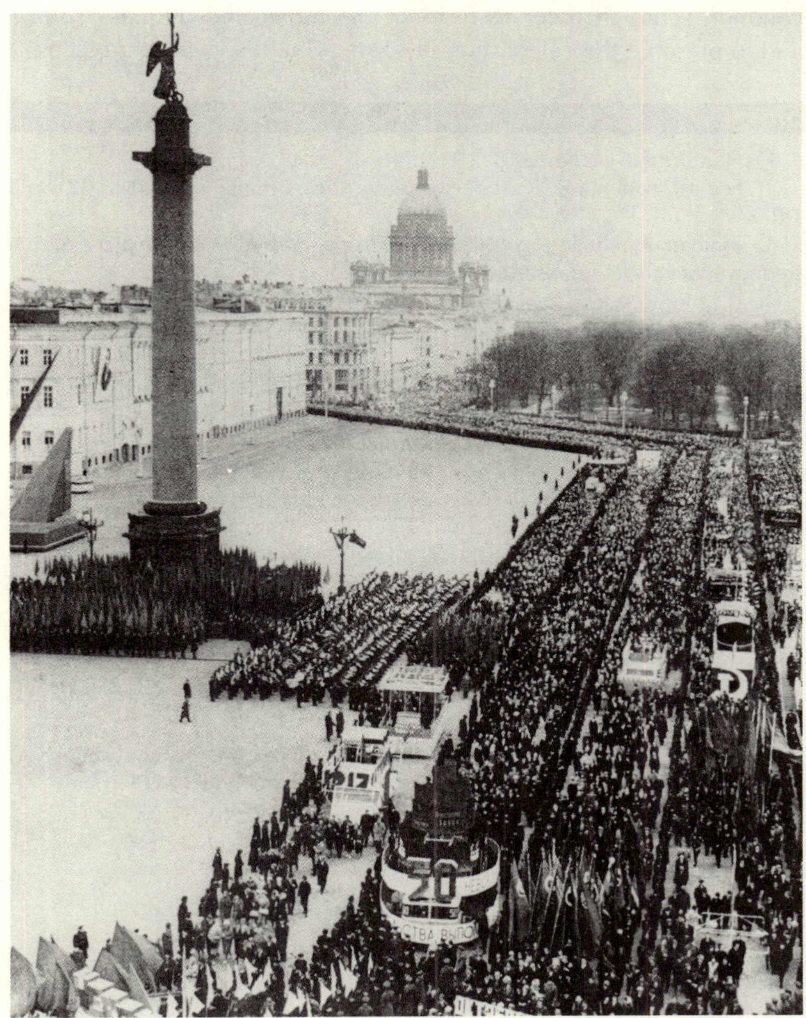

Demonstration in Leningrad (November 7, 1972).

communication; close physical contact, creating the effect of emotional infection; activities exceeding the norms of everyday life; the emergence of a collective euphoria, when the weakening of an individual will is compensated by the involvement in a larger collective symbolized by the figure of a leader, the party, the nation, or the state. Under these psychological conditions, one must have experience and common sense in order to resist being intoxicated by mass culture and to preserve the celebration in spirit, which is its proper place.

NOTES

1. *Narodnoe tvorchestvo* 8 (1937): 48.
2. See for instance R. Rozhdestvenskiy, "Dve Strany," *Izvestiya*, 23 April 1989.
3. Mikhail Bakhtin, *Tvorchestvo Fransua Rable i narodnaya kultura srednevekovya i Renesansa* (Moscow, 1965).
4. A. I. Piotrovskiy, *Za sovetskiy teatr* (Leningrad, 1925), 25.
5. Bakhtin 1965, 295.
6. Piotrovskiy 1925, 26.
7. A. I. Mazaev, *Prazdnik kak sotsialno-khudozhestvennoe yavlenie* (Moscow, 1978), 282–300.
8. *Komsomolskoe rozhdestvo: Sbornik* (Moscow, 1923).
9. M. Ozuf, "Ot termidora do bryumera: Revolyutsia govorit o samoi sebe," *Vek Prosvescheniya* (Moscow-Paris, 1970), 306; *Agitatsionnoe iskusstvo pervych let Oktyabrya* (Moscow, 1971).
10. Following the law of historical "echo," the call-over of the two revolutions continues. At the celebrations devoted to the 200-year anniversary of the French Revolution, the Kremlin chimes sounded their famous bells at Champs Elysée while the ensemble Berezka and the dancers of the Leningrad ballet pranced.
11. A. B. Lunacharsky, "O narodnykh prazdnestvakh," *Vestnik teatra* 62 (1926): 4.
12. O. N. Yanitskiy, "Sotsialno-informatsionnye protsessy v obschestve i urbanizatsiya" in *Urbanizatsia, nauchno-tekhnicheskaya revolutsiya i rabochiy klass* (Moscow, 1972), 52.
13. E. Ryumin, *Massovye prazdniki* (Moscow-Leningrad, 1927), 18.
14. P. M. Kerzhentsev, *Tvorcheskiy teatr* (Petrograd, 1920).
15. *Massovoe deistvo: Stsenicheskie igry* (Moscow, 1929), 9.
16. Ibid., 9–11.
17. N. Makeev, letter to newspaper, *Sovetskaya Rossiya*, 31 March 1987.
18. Ryumin 1927, 45.
19. Ibid., 44–45.
20. *Opyt organizatsii massovogo prazdnika* (Moscow-Leningrad, 1931), 101.

Paper Architecture in the Age of the French Revolution

Theory always leaves a mark on the work of the avant-garde. While theory arises out of the formulation of a problem, the avant-garde represents, so to speak, the space of the problem. Rather than addressing the kinds of problems faced by a theoretician in the process of mastering the mental field between Vitruvius and Le Corbusier, I would like to turn to a problem faced by the avant-garde without the theoretician's help.

I have in mind the problem of architectural meaning. The significance of this problem for the avant-garde is beyond doubt. The moment of the avant-garde's birth was accompanied by the question "What does it mean?" The question is crucial because of its urgency and apparently is still unresolved. Indeed, the contemporary view of architecture as an abstract art, incapable of communicating concrete meanings, was absolutely impossible, for instance, in the nineteenth century; it emerged in architectural theory precisely beginning with the avant-garde.

Let us take a theoretical digression before continuing. We begin with the basic model of architectural language which is rarely used. The existence of two methods for analysis of architecture as art—a stylistic and an iconographic one—implies that the very object of investigation has two distinct semantic structures. Their difference is based on the aspects responsible for carrying meaning.

Attempts to adopt the semiotic model of language to architecture

Gennady Revzin, "Bumazhnaya arkhitektura v epokhu Frantsuzskoy Revolutsii" (Paper architecture in the age of the French Revolution), *Arkhitectura SSSR* (Moscow) 3 (May–June 1990): 108–13.

ran into the impossibility of finding an architectural element, analogous to a word in natural language, which would carry autonomous meaning. These attempts were concerned with the stylistic language of architecture. Indeed, the semantics of style does not emerge from the sum of meanings produced by separate elements but rather as a result of prescribing meaning to stylistic categories and establishing their connections with general cultural categories. For instance, Wöllflin's "openness" of artistic form turns out to be the formal analog of the striving toward infinity, which is equally characteristic of the architecture of Borromini and the differential calculus of Leibnitz, that is, baroque mathematics; it represents the semantics of baroque style. To look in baroque architecture for one distinct element signifying "infinity" would be meaningless.

Everything is radically different in iconographic language. A distinct element—a motif, a stable compositional scheme—carries meaning that is defined and quite autonomous. For instance, a temple cupola usually signifies a heavenly dome, regardless of period or style.

Certainly, the cupola example is unique to architecture, which is essentially nonrepresentational. Such meanings are infinitely more rare in architecture than stable compositional schemes. What do these schemes signify? Let us take order as an example. Its meaning is well known—order means Classicism, that is, classical order signifies Rome in the Renaissance, Rome and Greece in Classicism, and Renaissance in neo-Renaissance. In other words, an architectural scheme receives meaning from its original architectural tradition and signifies this very tradition. When using order, an architect evokes the already developed signification, which is quite independent from the meaning of his future work. Here we are dealing with semiotic processes or, more precisely, with symbols, if by a symbol we understand a sign which preserves the memory of its past use.

This short discussion should be sufficient to understand the role played by iconography in architectural language. An architect borrows from it "ready-made" meanings and a "common language." With its help he expresses his views on the established system of conventions. For example, when Giulio Romano in Palazzo del Te moves metopes down from frieze, he neither relies on traditional iconography nor transforms it. By transgressing the clear and logical scheme, he tells about the crisis of the classical ideal of harmony and rationality. This crisis accounts for the deep tragical meaning of Mannerism.[1]

Put differently, iconography is the conscious employment of tradition. And this is what architectural avant-garde negates, thus having to deal with an extremely complicated problem of the loss of iconographic language, which must be substituted by something else. The problem of this substitution is the central subject of this article.

The architecture of Boullée, Ledoux, and their followers will serve as material for the discussion. Considering them in the context of architectural avant-garde is well justified. Many ideas of the French paper architects were "actualized" by twentieth-century avant-garde. Theoretical study of their work was initiated against the background of Constructivism: perhaps the first serious work on this topic was the book *Von Ledoux bis Le Corbusier* by Emil Kaufmann.[2] We can even say that the architecture of the French Revolution was the first rehearsal for the avant-garde architecture, similar to how the French culture around 1789 was the rehearsal for the events of 1917.

Before turning to the analysis of architectural language of paper architects, let us try to understand the nature of their pathos—what they were trying to express with this language.

Perhaps the central work of paper architecture is the Eye drawn by Ledoux, which reflects the theater in Besançon reconstructed by him. Realistically rendered, this Eye attracts the attention of scholars by exerting a certain magical effect (Magritte, who repeated this composition almost exactly, took advantage of this). D. E. Arkin, scrutinizing this work, or rather being scrutinized by it, came to the conclusion that in the drawing Ledoux was verifying the results of his reform of theatrical interiors (Ledoux was the first to place seats in the pit, which at the time functioned as a gallery for the lower-class public), that is, it was as though Ledoux was carefully considering the results of his reform from the viewers' point of view—hence the Eye.[3]

It should be noted, however, that Ledoux was hardly inspired by democratic ideas. "This will rid us of the heckling rabble," he said with the precision of a real architect in reference to this reform, apparently thinking that it is easier to seat the lower-class public (who previously had to watch performances standing up) than to bear their disorganized behavior.[4]

If Ledoux were really verifying here the consequences of his reforms, then the Eye should have reflected the stage and not the interior of the theater, that is, it should have looked from the auditorium and not from the stage. But even from the stage the Eye "gazes"

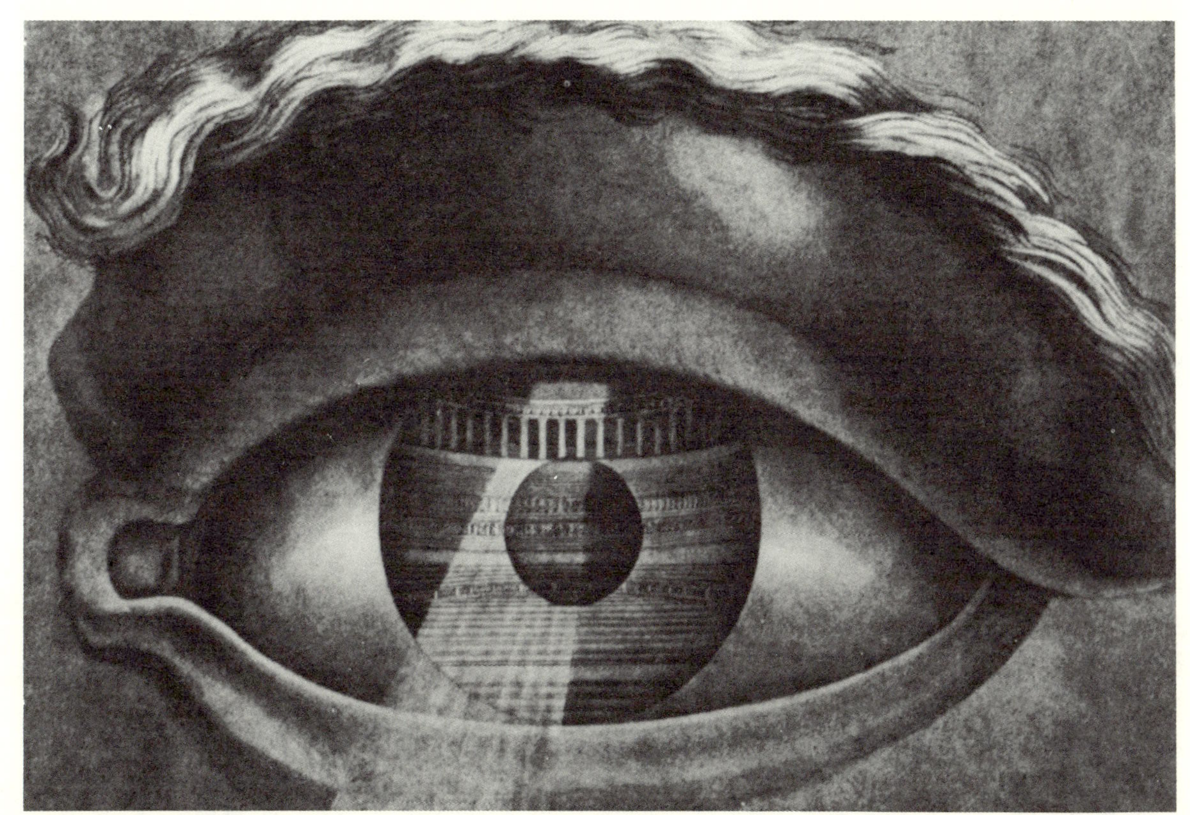

Cl. N. Ledoux's view of the interior of the Théâtre de Besançon.
Bibliothèque Nationale, Paris.

in a strange way. It looks at us from the geometric center of the stage space—the point from which nobody could have seen the theater except for a Zephyr or an Eros lowered from winches. In other words, this eye does not belong to anybody, no person could look through it.

The Enlightenment was in love with capital letters such as Education or Virtue. Before us is the Eye with the capital "E," or more precisely the idea of an Eye. It is possible that Ledoux, who was a Mason, consciously programmed the associations with the All-Seeing Eye. His theater appears here before the idea of Vision, Vision as a law of Nature. It is as though Ledoux fixes the moment when Reason looks upon his theater to verify whether it corresponds to its laws.

This gaze of Reason is constantly felt in the projects of the paper architects. They seem to open up the abysses discovered by the Enlightenment in the universal rationality of the world. The presence of this heavenly eye gives the projects an almost cosmic proportion. In this respect, *Vision Inspired by the Cemetery at Chaux* by Ledoux is typical. He creates a cosmic view of the planetary spheres floating through the Universe and represented as analogs of the sphere in which the cemetery at Chaux is situated.

The universal and cosmic character of the projects imparts them with a somewhat mystical character. Cemeteries and cenotaphs, which comprise a good half of the projects, became the favorite subjects. Architecture strives to express something for which living people become obstacles. The world turns into a city of the dead, where everything that could be changed has been changed and where eternal peace has set in.

Newton's Cenotaph was as important for Boullée as the Eye was for Ledoux. The Enlightenment Utopia of total rationality is expressed here perhaps most completely. It is particularly indicative that Newton became the conceptual center of the work. For the Age of Reason, Newton was living proof of the general applicability of the laws of the Universe and the possibility of knowledge. His influence was not limited to physical sciences but spread into all areas of culture. For instance, Newton's ideas influenced the creators of the American Constitution, who tried to come up with laws which would take into account all situations in life and regulate them in a manner similar to the law of gravity. Metternich's famous balance of powers, which startled the contemporaries, was thought of exactly like Newton's balance.[5]

The preceding discussion is sufficient to argue that paper architecture represents the architectural analog to the Enlightenment theory of total rationality. Let us return to the question, asked in the beginning: In what way was this idea expressed, what was the structure of the language of paper architecture?

The question is even more appropriate given that paper architecture of the period of the French revolution is also called "the speaking architecture." And here we come across a certain contradiction. V. L. Glazychev laconically expressed the current view of the phenomenon of speaking architecture, calling it the "direct realization of metaphor."[6] Thus, in this view speaking architecture is associated with such projects as the Woodcutter's House in the form of a pyramid of stacked wood by Ledoux, or the bridge with piers in the form of boats by Boullée. In the final analysis, it is the matter of representational motifs.

It does not even matter that such phenomena have only an indirect connection to the principal works of paper architecture, which consist of experiments with simple geometric forms. The ideas we discussed above cannot be expressed with the help of such metaphoric language in principle. Indeed: here, Universal pathos of Reason; there, games with metaphors. Here, cosmic abysses; there, stacks of wood.

Finally, and most important for our discussion—here, style; there, iconography. Representational motifs constitute the type of elements of architectural language, which are autonomous and independent from the overall meaning; in semiotic terminology they are iconic signs. The Utopia of Reason will not be found in such motifs; it lies somewhere else—in the emphasized regularity of graphics, in the sparsity of representational means, in striving toward simple geometric figures, or in the colossal scale, that is, in the totality of features which comprise an architectural style as a formal category.

Yet, Ledoux called his works "symbolic poems." If we assume that the principal meanings in the works of paper architects are conveyed by style, then what about these symbols? A paradoxical situation emerges: having interpreted the work of paper architects, having related them to ideas of the age, we did not get any closer to an understanding of the structure of their architectural language.

Spheres, pyramids, and cubes, continuously repeated in the projects of Boullée and Ledoux, make us think that these are the very symbols. The total vagueness of these symbols shrouds the architects' work in mystery. Paper architecture fatally turns into a cryptogram of a rather morbid character, considering the obtrusive interest in cemeteries. Therefore, "the key to a number of conventional forms has to lie in the symbolic ciphers of Freemasonry."[7]

These words were said in the context of the 150-year anniversary of the French Revolution. We lived through the 200-year anniversary, yet the search of masonic ciphers has not produced any results. Perhaps, the hypothesis itself is incorrect. If we have a ciphered message, we should apply to it the elementary principles of deciphering. From this point of view the task becomes as elementary as a school exercise.

Let us apply the deciphering methodology to the sphere. We will analyze the meaning of the sphere in a number of concrete cases and then attempt to arrive at its general meaning.

1. Boullée. *Newton's Cenotaph*. The cenotaph genre produces two meanings: invariability in time (eternity), and sacredness. The monument celebrates Newton, who discovered the generally applicable laws of the Universe, that is, the perfection of Reason.
2. Ledoux. *Cemetery of the city of Chaux*. Signifies eternity and sacredness.
3. Ledoux. *Vision Inspired by the Cemetery at Chaux*. The drawings connect the Chaux cemetery with the mysticism of Cosmos. Sacredness, universal scale.
4. Ledoux. *House of Ploughman*. In the philosophical context of Enlightenment, the work of ploughman is the perfect occupation. Meaning: perfection.
5. Lequeu. *Temple of the Earth*. Here the idea of Earth signifies sacredness. The sphere represents a planet, which gives it a universal scale.
6. Lequeu. *Temple of Equality*. Sacredness, universality, perfection.
7. Sobre. *Temple of Immortality*. Invariability, sacredness.

As we can see, the meanings are repeated although the subjects are substantially different. In general, we can define the meaning of a sphere as "universal rational perfection, invariable in space (universal scale) and time (eternity), and representing sacredness." Thus, we have a new "word" of architectural language. Let us now try to understand its specificity.

First of all, what we have is a kind of modification of the meaning

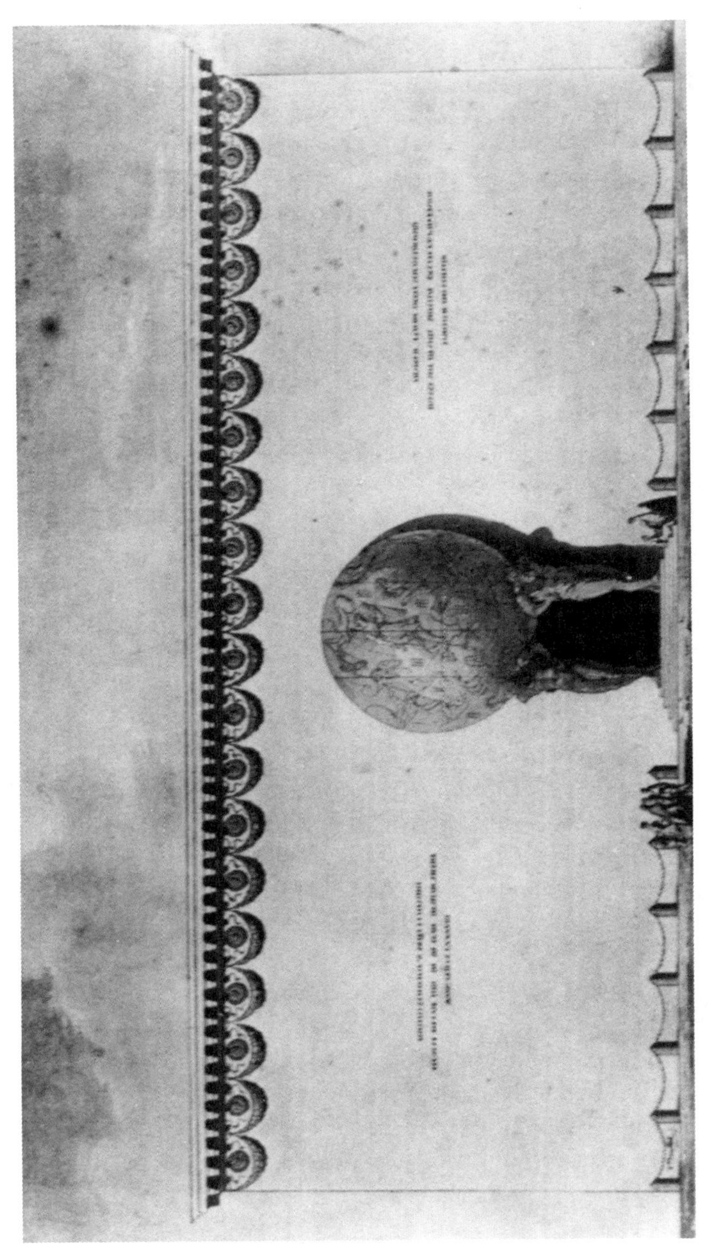

L. Boulée, *Library*. Bibliothèque Nationale, Paris.

of cupola. Indeed, cupola, as the metaphor of heavenly dome, used to signify perfection, constancy, universality, sacredness, and other attributes of the sky. The genesis of the meaning of sphere from the meaning of cupola is supported by an indirect consideration. Boullée's plan for the Library contains figures of Atlases supporting a sphere, which is covered with the constallations of stars. This popular allegorical motif originates from the myth about Atlas, who upheld the celestial dome, that is, the sphere here represents the sky.

However, sphere as the word of the new architectural language is essentially different from cupola. Already in Newton's Cenotaph it does not signify the sky in its perfection but rather "perfection" itself, becoming the sign of an abstract idea.

Here we see a radical transformation of the structure of architectural language. Indeed, such meanings as "perfection," "rationality," "harmony," that is, abstract ideas, had never been communicated with the help of stable iconographic schemes; they were expressed through style. In this case we witness an emergence of an architectural sign with the meaning "perfection," that is, before us is a stylistic meaning communicated through iconographic language.

Having negated traditional iconography, architects found a new way, a new language. Let us examine this experiment from a theoretical point of view or, in other words, evaluate the extent of its generality.

Students of the early 1920s Russian avant-garde have pointed out, largely in passing, that the architecture of the French Revolution was among the influences on the new architecture. Gradually, this statement attained the status of a historical fact. Among recent publications of this kind, I will mention an article by a recognized historian of architecture, William Curtis, devoted to French utopian planning, its traditions and influence on world architecture. The article includes a comparison of the works by Boullée and Leonidov.[8] Indeed, in Leonidov's well-known project for the Lenin Institute we find a "reference" to Boullée. The detail is remarkable because here the sphere can be related to the art of French paper architects not only formally but also semantically as it signifies perfection and the truth of reason. This is not an isolated coincidence. For instance, similar kinds of references can be found in the competition projects for the Christopher Columbus monument, which ranged from most innovative to most traditional.

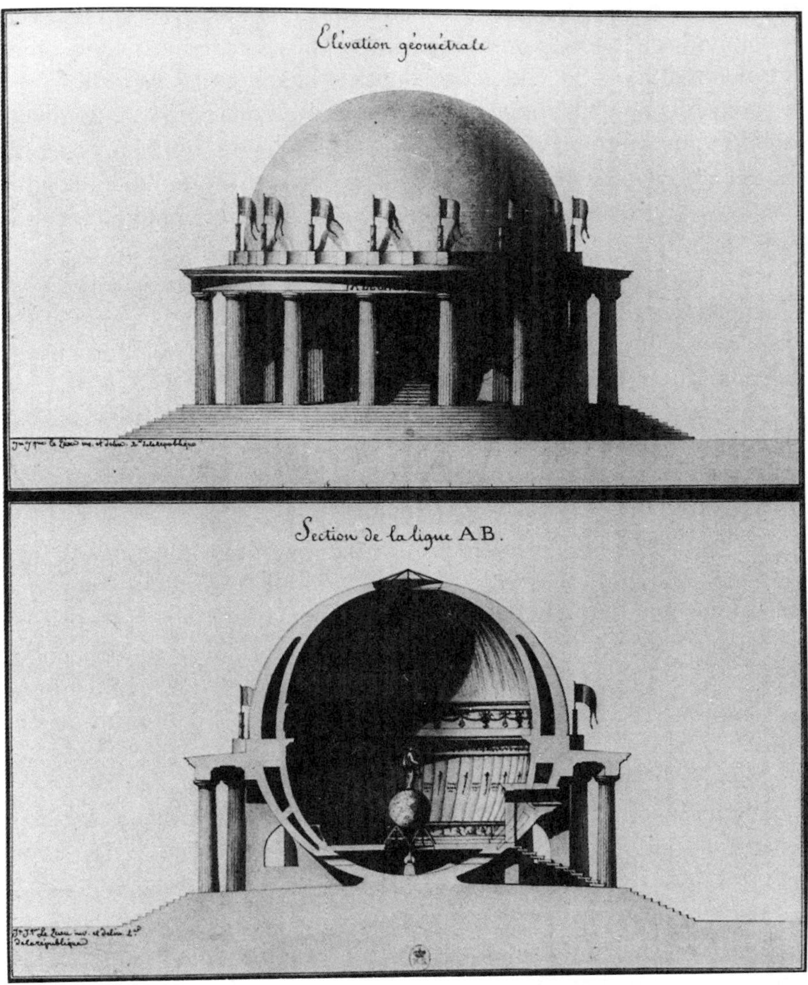

J.-J. Lequeu, *Temple of Equality*. Bibliothèque Nationale, Paris.

What makes this connection even more remarkable is that we do not have any basis to claim that the projects of French paper architects were known to the Russian architects. On the contrary, it is more probable that they were not known to them. Therefore, we are not faced with the insignificant and trivial fact of borrowing. The coincidences are independent of each other; the very logic of artistic conception has led to similar results, which proves the generality of this development.

Let us try to understand this logic. Experiments with simple geometric forms were characteristic of the 1920s avant-garde since its inception, and even since the preceding stage when attempts were made to adopt avant-garde painting and sculpture to architecture. In connection with this, we may recall the *Spacial Constructions* by Alexander Rodchenko, constructed by repeating simple geometric forms such as a circle, an ellipses, a triangle, and a square; or the *Prouns* of El Lissitsky. The reasons for their emergence are correctly interpreted as the desire to find primary elements of architectural form. "The point was to discover certain primary elements of artistic expressiveness, in themselves without signification and understood as an alphabet of artistic-compositional system."[9]

Yet although these elements lack meanings analogous to those we found in a sphere, it would be a mistake to think that the problem of signification of primary elements was of no interest to the avant-garde artists. They were concerned with finding a different kind of signification, one that was psychological. Each of the primary elements was thought to provoke a relatively defined set of emotions. An INKhUK questionnaire, compiled by Kandinsky, is suggestive in this respect: "How do you see a triangle—do you feel that it is moving, where, do you see it as more witty than a square; is the sensation from a square similar to the sensation from a lemon; what is a canary's song more like—a triangle or a square."[10] Thus, the emotion provoked by a primary element was understood as its meaning.

We saw that in the work of French paper architects there was an attempt to communicate stylistic meanings with the help of iconographic language. At first sight we are dealing with something principally different in the work of the Russian avant-garde. The following circumstance, however, should be taken into consideration: the beginning of the twentieth century is the period when formalism appears, that is, the theory of style is born. Most important, style was understood to be the expression of psychological substance. Theoreticians of formalism, including Russian avant-garde artists, saw stylistic formations as the result of particular psychological types. From this idea emerged Wörringer's Oriental and Gothic man, or Wöllflin's "German and Italian feelings of form."

In this context, the search for primary elements with defined psychological significations can be interpreted precisely as the transformation of stylistic meanings. These elements became the "formulas of form." Notably, they were used to characterize historical styles as well. Thus, in an essay about Tatlin's *Tower,* Nikolai Punin writes: "The spirit of our time is best expressed by the spiral, similar to how the Renaissance is best expressed by the equilibrium of the parts of a triangle."[11]

Thus, we see the same development: the transformation of a stylistic language into an iconographic one. Let us now turn to the central question of this article: What does this transformation mean?

Let us return to Boullée. The desire for perfection and rationality is the common project of the Enlightenment. However expressed stylistically, this desire is always marked by an author's personal experience. Recall Buffon's definition: "Style is the expression of man." But if the meaning "perfection" is assigned to a distinct element, it becomes a part of common language. Iconographic language is specific because it does not belong to one architect but functions as common property. "Perfection" is no longer dependent on individual desires but becomes objective. In the process, iconography, that is, common language, ceases to depend on the past. This is not the language of inherited conventions but the language of strict philosophical truths.

The same can be said about the iconographic language of the early twentieth-century architectural avant-garde. The desire to find psychological laws governing perception of simple geometrical forms, to find a system in which every element signifies unconditionally the emotion it provokes, is the desire to get away from subjectivity and to make architectural language objective.

Iconography becomes the expression of objective signification. This is why we see the strong alliance between the architectural avant-garde and science—the eighteenth-century philosophy and the twentieth-century psychology. It is impossible to underestimate the importance of this transformation of iconographic language.

It is well known that avant-garde art is life-asserting and inspired by the desire to reconstruct the world. In order to be imbued with the idea of such reconstruction, one must believe in possessing the objective truth. By refusing the established conventions of architectural language, by accepting the objective, "scientific" signification, the avant-garde gains confidence in its own veracity and, as a result, the belief in its ability to accomplish revolutions.

1. In more detail about this proposed structure of architectural language see G. H. Revzin, "Semiotika v arkhitekturovedenii: problemy vzaimootnosheniya s drugimi nauchnymi paradigmami," in *Teoriya architektury: sbornik nauchnykh trudov* (Moscow, 1988).

2. Emil Kaufmann, *Von Ledoux bis Le Corbusier; Ursprung und Entwicklung der Autonomen Architektur* (Vienna: R. Passer, 1933).

3. D. E. Arkin, *Arkhitektura epokhi frantsuzskoi revolutsii* (Moscow, 1940), 32–33.

4. Jean-Claude Lemagny, *Visionary Architects. Boullée, Ledoux, Lequeu* (New Jersey, 1963), 105.

5. A. Toffler, "Foreword: Science and Change," in Ilya Prigogine and Isabelle Stengers, *Order Out of Chaos: Man's New Dialog with Nature* (New York: Random House, 1984), xiii.

6. V. L. Glazychev, *Evolyutsia tvorchestva v arkhitekture* (Moscow, 1986), 359.

7. Arkin 1940, 32.

8. William Curtis, "Paris Grand Projet," *Techniques et Architecture* 385 (1989): 118–19.

9. S. O. Khan-Magomedov, "INKhUK: vozniknovenie, formirovanie i pervyi period raboty, 1920," *Sovetskoe iskusstvoznanie* (Moscow) 80 (1981): 343.

10. Ibid., 346.

11. Quoted from P. Ya. Khiger, *Puti arkhitekturnoy mysli* (Moscow, 1929), 20.